ASSESSMENT AND ESL

Barbara Law
Mary Eckes

- -

ASSESSMENT AND ESL:

On the Yellow Big Road
to the Withered of Oz

Peguis Publishers
Winnipeg Manitoba Canada

Printed and bound in Canada on recycled paper ✪

03   04   05   7   6   5

Canadian Cataloguing in Publication Data

Law, Barbara, 1950

    Assessment and ESL: on the yellow big road to the Withered of Oz

    Includes bibliographical references and index
    ISBN 1-895411-77-7

1. English language – Study and teaching as a second language – Evaluation.* I. Eckes, Mary, 1954–
II. Title.

PE1128.A2L38 1995   428.'007   C95-920119-X

Editor: Annalee Greenberg
Book design: Laura Ayers
Cover design: in house

The publishers acknowledge with thanks that copyright material, page 274, was used with permission of the North York Board of Education, for this publication only.

Peguis Publishers Limited
100–318 McDermot Avenue
Winnipeg, Manitoba
Canada R3A 0A2
1-800-667-9673

CONTENTS

PREFACE

"Mom, can I have a snack?" asked Barb's seven-year-old one night.

"You can have an apple."

"I can't eat apples."

"Why not?"

"I don't have any front teeth, remember?"

"Ummmm." Long pause. "What have you been doing with all the apples I've been putting in your lunch?"

"Giving them to my friends."

Barb was stunned, not to mention outraged, over the thought of all those apples she had been buying and dutifully packing during the last three months that had been slipping, unbeknownst to her, into the hands and tummies of Kate's friends.

We have come to the conclusion that education and assessment are much like packing school lunches for your children. You put in everything that you think your child needs, all the necessary food groups, making it attractive and palatable. Then you send it off, hoping it will get eaten. The lunch box comes back empty, but you can't assume that the child has actually eaten what you packed. He may have traded those cookies for a candy bar, taken one bite of the apple and thrown it away, or chucked the entire contents of the box in the trash. There are three main ways for you to check to see if your child has actually eaten the lunch: ask him (monitoring closely for truth); see if he's ravenous when he comes home, if he's growing (or getting seriously skinny); or simply volunteer for lunch duty and watch him eat. The first one is only partially revealing of what happens: he may tell you, he may not. The second method is far removed from the actual fact: by the time you see your child losing weight, the lack of lunches has gone on for quite some time. The third—if not entirely feasible or practical—is of course the most effective. You can intervene when necessary, negotiate, and change the menu if it's not meeting the child's tastes and needs (or number of teeth).

The comparison to assessment is easy. Standardized testing, like weighing and measuring a child against the bathroom door every New Year's Eve, is a natural and logical part of quantifying growth. Parents want to know whether their child is growing, learning and achieving at a rate that is considered normal for his age. But it often occurs after the fact. It's the day-to-day watching of your child growing, of listening to what he says, of monitoring his eating habits, who he plays with and how much television he watches that tells you who your child is and what he's all about. This kind of assessment is ongoing. It is the observation of development as it happens, rather than the final product. Parents and teachers are masters of this art—it's what they do. Ask any good teacher and she can go on and on about what any one particular student can or can't do.

This fine art, this mastery of the craft of child-watching, has been invalidated in recent years and relegated to a less-than-important status, to be supplanted by impersonal, easy-to-read-and-quantify standardized tests.

The assessment of non-English-speaking students is not clear-cut. The regular standards and criteria that are used to assess English-speaking children cannot be used as reliable yardsticks. When a student does not speak the language of the test, it is difficult to gauge whether he knows the material and just doesn't have the English to display the knowledge, or whether he truly doesn't know the material.

There are many variables that come into play with students who do not speak English as their native language. Many of the things we take for granted with our regular students—an understanding of American culture, a basic background in government, science, math and reading—cannot be assumed with newcomers. We cannot even take it for granted that they understand that print has meaning. Giving a fair grade to a student who can barely read, who has just arrived from a foreign country, is a tangled issue that needs serious thought to resolve.

There are also many wild cards: students who arrive in senior high school with no previous schooling and have to learn such simple things as sitting in a desk; students who do not adhere to the time-line we impose on them, who learn at much slower rates than we consider normal because they have so much to learn in knowledge and concepts, on top of the materials presented in class; students who come to us with moderate to severe disabilities, whose problems are beyond our abilities to understand, diagnose and help correct. How can we assess them, and measure the knowledge they have and the gains they are making?

Those who do not understand these issues (unfortunately, many of our policy makers fall into this category) try to impose time limits to ESL schooling, advocate buying software instead of paying teachers, worse still, relegate students to remedial status, and, worst of all, advocate eliminating services altogether. And, those who do not understand, try to use the same yardsticks on our ESL students without allowing them the time, the attention, and the input they need to achieve on a comparable level with mainstream students.

This is a modest book. We do not pretend to have all the answers to alternative assessment. In the past several years there has been a great deal of interest in and a burgeoning amount of research on this topic. But little attention has been paid to how this can relate to non-English speakers. As with our previous book, *The More-Than-Just-Surviving Handbook*, we have tried to make sense of the literature and the theories and apply them in a clear and usable way for the teacher in the trenches.

We have filled the book with examples drawn from our own experiences and the experiences of others.

We have many people to thank for their help in writing this book. To the teachers who so willingly and generously shared their expertise, their stories, and their students' work: Cathy Tegen, Bong Hee Lis, Dan Jones, Judy Lewis, Mary Miller, Corri Gossen, Heidi Meissner, Mary Delie, Debby Moon, Caitlin Cogburn, Dolores Duncan, John Patterson, Teresa Greer, Mary Marcus, Cherie Mornard, Andrea Davis, Ellen Kallio, Jackie Deeb, Miss Huong. We thank them for their input and their critiques. We'd especially like to thank all the students who have passed through our lives, made us laugh, enriched us, and made the struggle to write this book and fight for the betterment of their lives worth the effort. We'd like to thank our editor Annalee Greenberg for her patience and her careful attention to detail.

And, as always, we thank our loving families for their patience, their tolerance, and their continued support throughout these long years of struggle.

About our title: This book has been through many incarnations and had many titles (*Barb and Mary Have an Adventure; Mary and Barb Screw Up Again; But Officer, We Were Lost!; Why Isn't Chest Plural?*). Finally, the dilemma answered itself. The theme of this book is being able to look *through* the errors to the meaning intended, and so it was natural that we choose a title that incorporates one of the many delightful miscues we have encountered during our careers. Taken from one student's story retelling of the *Wizard of Oz*, it seems to sum up the idea that learning is a continuum, and that assessment must follow the same path. The titles of chapters are the same; each one conveys the theme of the chapter and takes some thought to under-stand the meaning that the writer or speaker intended to convey. Some are self-explanatory, such as "Flying without an Earplan." Some need an explanation. Mary was stumped when two students repeatedly came to her desk and said, "Kiss me, teacher," all the while giggling shyly, to return to their desks when she didn't know how to respond. After much puzzlement and embarrassment, she finally realized they were saying, "Excuse me, teacher." Then she could respond appropriately. We have no clue to the meaning of one title, "Determining the Navel Assigned to the Factor." But it seemed to be a natural for that chapter, since so many people argue for standardized testing and use the results without any idea as to what has been measured and what the results really mean.

Editor's note

One of the dilemmas facing today's editor is that of retaining writing clarity while ensuring gender balance. This relates specifically to the use of the personal pronouns *he/she, him/her, himself/herself,* and so on. Using both forms in all cases makes for particularly awkward reading. In this book, we have chosen to use masculine pronouns in references to students. We assure the reader that no affront is intended.

INTRODUCTION

For the first four months Hiro (affectionately called "Clueless Joe" because he never got jokes) was in the United States, he ordered nothing but hot dogs at the school cafeteria. He didn't know any other words for food, and couldn't read the menu. He just pointed and said, "Hot dog." Now, three years later, he tells his teacher, "I don't eat hot dogs any more."

◆

Jenny was brought to the middle school speaking not a word of English. She was eleven, but her parents insisted on enrolling her in the seventh grade. Their rationale was that the education system in their own country was so far advanced from the U.S. system that she would be losing a year of academic instruction, and when they returned to their country Jenny would be held back a year. Jenny was very shy, but she proved to be an exceptional language learner and within three months was speaking colloquial English without an accent. By year's end she was competing with her peers.

The sixth, seventh, and eighth graders wanted to put on a play. Barb laboriously typed up the script to *Stone Soup*, but they rejected it. So they decided to write their own lines to *Cinderella*. Jenny was Cinderella. The play was a success, and the ESL students, performing for the entire school, received a standing ovation. Jenny and her family never went back to their country. Today Jenny is a successful dentist. Whenever she sees Barb she says, "Remember when we did Cinderella? Wasn't that fun?"

These incidents in the lives of Hiro and Jenny are steps in their ongoing continuum toward competence in English and in school. One of the great joys of working with second-language learners is watching that magical unfolding as each one grows and gains competency in a new language. The challenge is to capture that growth and record it. Because growth is dynamic and ongoing, assessment should be too.

There has been an explosive growth of both interest in and publications on alternative assessment since we started working on this book. However, most of these books are about native-English-speaking students written for mainstream classroom teachers. While many of the ideas, methods and solutions are the same, non-English-proficient students pose a special challenge for the teacher who wants to grade fairly and give credit for work done, concepts mastered, and progress gained. Trying to grade or chart the progress of a student who speaks little or no English, cannot communicate what he knows, does nothing in class, and hands in little or no homework can be a perplexing dilemma.

This book has been written for those of you who are working with English-language learners—elementary and secondary, mainstream and ESL—to help you understand not only new ways to document progress, but also to understand the progress an ESL student makes and the growth that may not always be apparent at first glance.

In this book we have undertaken to

- distill the latest research on alternative assessment, literacy development, and second-language acquisition
- apply this research to the special issues of learning to speak, read, and write in English as a new and additional language
- suggest activities to foster proficiency and competency in both oral and written language

CHAPTER OVERVIEW

In Chapter 1, "Kiss Me Teacher: WHAT TEACHERS NEED TO KNOW," we discuss the information teachers need to have about their non- or limited-English-speaking students to make appropriate decisions concerning placement, curriculum, and educational objectives.

Chapter 2, "What Shape will We Use? Red! TESTING VS. ALTERNATIVE FORMS OF ASSESSMENT," explores the problems traditional standardized testing poses for ESL students. We propose that alternative assessment can lead the way toward fairer and more accurate assessment and showcasing of a student's abilities, as well as proficiency and development in language and academic content.

Chapter 3, "Determining the Navel Assigned to the Factor: INITIAL PLACEMENT," tells how to identify students whose first or home language is not English, the steps to take in assessing proficiency, and factors to consider on how to place students appropriately. We give three scenarios to illustrate what issues to consider during this process.

Chapter 4, "We're Working Hardly: EMERGING LITERACY," discusses the theoretical framework teachers must start with to really understand what it is they're looking at. We provide a base for understanding emerging literacy and proficiency by exploring the research and providing examples of growing competency and mastery in both oral and written expression.

In chapter 5, "Diving for Pearls in their Shelves: HOW AND WHERE TO FIND INFORMATION," we discuss how to find important information about students: observing them working, sampling their work, and using traditional measures. From this, we can determine the strategies they are using, their understanding, attitudes, interest, and degree of control over language forms.

Chapter 6, "The Santa Maria, The Pimpas, and the Ninny: CHECKLISTS, ANECDOTES, AND CONFERENCES," examines these three ways of collecting and documenting important information about student progress.

Chapter 7, "Flying without an Earplan: STORIES FROM THE TRENCHES," presents vignettes of four students whose varying abilities and language needs presented unique challenges for their teachers. Then we show how the teachers responded and the types of educational decisions they made for their students.

Chapter 8, "The Final Nail in the Coffee: GRADES," discusses the thorny problems of grading ESL students and the issues involved, as well as the decisions you have to make when trying to grade fairly.

Chapter 9, "Lunching Several Measures: PRESENTING THE INFORMATION TO STAKEHOLDERS," is about systematizing information about students, presenting the data in usable form, and how to hold conferences with limited-English-speaking parents.

Chapter 10, "Fight to The Spinach! MAKING THE CHANGE," gives suggestions for the process of changing methods of grading and for collaborating with other partners in the educational system to make these changes a reality.

THE FOUR THEMES

In our first book, *The More-Than-Just-Surviving Handbook*, we discussed the process of learning another language effectively around four basic themes:

1. Real language
2. Whole language
3. An enabling environment
4. Learning is a continuum, and errors have a place and a role within that continuum

We can also discuss assessment within the framework of these four themes:

◆ **Real language.** Real means that language has a purpose; it is meaningful, authentic, and relevant. The reasons students have for using language must be more than simply to please the teacher and get a good grade. People use real language for many reasons: to order a hamburger, to ask their mother for an allowance, to convince their teacher to give them an extra day to write their paper, to tell a joke, to make friends, and so on. The language upon which the student is being assessed must also have a purpose. The language and the situations must be the kinds that students encounter in everyday life, rather than the contrived language used to illustrate a phonic principle or what someone has decided is "easy" language.

Research shows that students often perform more poorly on tasks that are dull, uninteresting, meaningless, purposeless, boring, or frustrating than they do on tasks that have a purpose. When the student can't see the point of what he's doing, or if the cost of trying is too high in terms of his expected rate of success, he may not give the task the time, attention, or effort it requires.

Forester and Reinhard (1989) write:

> ...evaluation of children's reading and writing should take place while they are actually reading and writing and not in situations that are supposed to simulate reading and writing. This makes it possible for the teacher to learn about how children use the many resources that are available to them from their classmates and from print material.

Real assessment, then,

- ◆ measures the progress of students engaged in authentic tasks
- ◆ involves tasks that have meaning to students

◆ **Whole language.** For many years we thought that language and literacy skills were the sum of their parts, that teaching the parts would lead to adequate understanding of the whole, and that testing the parts would give us insight into the student's grasp of the whole. We now know this is not true.

Davies (1992) writes: "language is not a set of unrelated bits...it forms a whole...the bits must be integrated and tested in combination with one another." Assessment tools do not fragment language. They don't just measure spelling, or grammar, or word lists, or comma splices; they measure language use as a whole. Shuy (1981) writes: "tests of grammar and phonology are not accurate predictors of effective participation...functional language competence is far more crucial. That is, a child's ability to seek clarification or get a turn seems much more critical than his ability to use past-tense markers."

"Whole" means that there is a context for the language being used. *The Primary Language Record* (Barrs et al. 1989) states: "Reading cannot be examined in total isolation from talking, listening and writing, so it is important to consider each child in the context of her/his language and learning experiences." According to Gumperz (1966): "Context is thought of as the physical setting, the people within the setting, what the people are doing and saying, and where and when they are doing it. Language is embedded in the flow of daily life." In terms of assessment, we mean that language is assessed within the environment, not divorced from it.

"Whole" also means assessment does not isolate one skill from another. Reading is not separated from writing, or from listening and speaking. What a student says about what he writes is important. His comments about what he has read reveal much about what he has understood. The drawings that illustrate what he wrote, and the actions he pantomimes to explain a situation, are all clues to competence.

Wholeness in assessment, then, means

- the context of the situation is as significant as the task itself
- tasks consist of more than just rote memorization
- individual tasks are not isolated from other people or from other skills

- **An enabling environment.** The learning environment must be conducive to learning. An enabling environment means several things. First, it means a positive orientation on the part of the teacher and fellow students that allows a learner to behave naturally, and feel truly capable of expressing himself openly without fear of ridicule or punishment. Second, as we pointed out earlier, the environment, and consequently assessment, should focus on positive achievement rather than negative failure. Too much testing is punitive, focusing on the errors and the failure of students to measure up to a standard. According to Murphy and Pennyquick (1992), emphasis should be on "meaningful and positive descriptions of what pupils know, understand, and can do."

Enabling assessment, then,

- is constructive, not destructive
- recognizes the student's achievements, not his failures
- treats the student as a person worthy of respect, not a number
- gives the student a chance to experience success in a wide variety of contexts at many different levels
- provides a continuous record of tasks and stages that the student has achieved successfully

For instance, In figure I.1 Song Jo meant to say:

What do you do today? How old are you? I'm 9. I'm 9 years old. I had cookies. Peanut butter cookies. Salted.

Although it is easy to be taken aback at the errors and to look at the deficits in this child's language capabilities, it is important to focus on what he *can* do. We ask: what does Song Jo know?

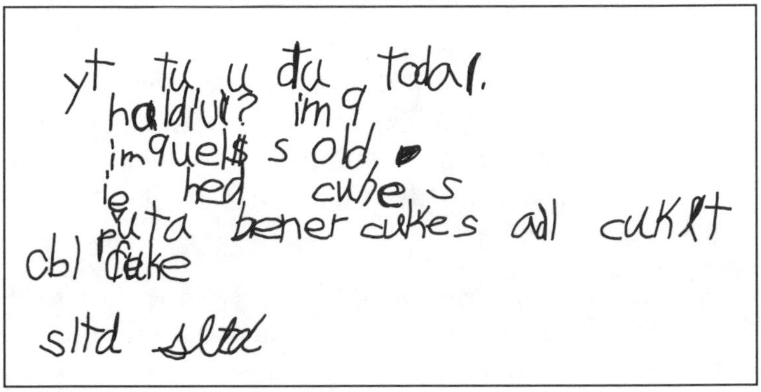

Figure I.1

- ◆ He knows word boundaries.
- ◆ He knows cursive.
- ◆ He knows the correct orthography of several English words: *I'm, today, old.*
- ◆ He has a strong grasp of English phonic principles. (The "words" *yt, tu, u, du* and *cukes* reveal that he understands the concept of sound/letter correspondences and can make reasonably accurate guesses.)
- ◆ He is familiar with English punctuation. He uses a question mark.

◆ **A continuum.** Forester and Reinhard (1989) speak of learning as a journey: it is not enough to note that children are giving correct answers on exercise sheets, in oral reading, when copying down words or spelling words from a list. The question becomes: can they and do they transfer that knowledge readily to new and different situations? Or do they simply know it at the imitation or product level? Observing the children's small steps forward will tell you far more about who has truly internalized knowledge and where individual children are along the learning continuum.

This means that every student travels the road at his own pace. Because Nok and Veapasert arrived at the same time does not mean that we should expect them to be at the same level of proficiency.

And we cannot become impatient and worry because it takes one longer than the other to get there. We cannot judge developing English students according to a preset time line, considering them failures or disabled because they do not achieve competence as fast as we would like.

For example, when Rosa says, "Tengo toys," (I have toys) she is demonstrating progress. She is making the transition from monolingual Spanish to English, a piece at a time.

This also means that errors are not necessarily an indication of a problem. Errors do not denote failure to learn. According to Goodman (1988)

> ...errors, miscues, or misconceptions usually indicate ways in which a child is organizing the world at that moment....Errors also indicate interpretations which may in no way be wrong, but simply show that the child has used inferences about reading or listening which were unexpected...the [observer] who understands the role of unexpected responses will use children's errors or miscues to chart their growth and development and to understand the personal and cultural history of the child.

Often errors signal the onset of leaps in knowledge, as, for instance, the explosion of invented spelling with children just on the verge of putting reading together. In whole-language classrooms teachers encourage approximations and invented spellings with the faith and certainty that, over time and with continued exposure to the desired and ideal forms, children will learn them. Teachers of ESL students also encourage approximations, sentences that contain both languages, and creative grammar, because they know these features indicate the student is moving forward toward proficiency.

Understanding that learning is a continuum means

- all students are given the time they need
- there is a place for errors

CONTEXTUAL ASSESSMENT

It is upon this conceptual framework that we will build our case for assessment, and continue from here to demonstrate how.

The most fundamental premise that underlies all others is that the student does not come to the classroom "alingual" (with no language). He comes with the ability to speak, with varying levels of competence, in one or more languages. Therefore, we must observe him where he is, assess his ability, and use that ability to make decisions about what to do with him next.

To assess accurately, to record, and to use what the student is accomplishing and where he is on the learning continuum, we need to gather as much information as possible before making decisions about a student. But it isn't enough to just gather data for its own sake. It doesn't do any good to have piles of notes, or bursting portfolios that sit on the shelf. That data needs to be catalogued in accessible ways and changed into usable information. Then the information must be used to help the student progress.

These are the major steps that make alternative assessment viable. It's a challenging process, but in the end, it's worth the effort.

Figure I.2

Adapted from Rhodes and Shanklin, *Windows into Literacy*, 1980.

Principles of ESL Assessment

- Assess authentic use of language in reading, writing, speaking, and listening.
- Assess literacy and language in a variety of contexts.
- Assess the environment, the instruction, and the students.
- Assess processes as well as products.
- Analyze patterns of errors in language and literacy.
- Base assessment on normal developmental patterns and behavior in language and literacy acquisition.
- Clarify and use standards when assessing reading, writing, and content knowledge.
- Involve students and parents, as well as other personnel such as the ESL or mainstream teacher, in the assessment process.
- Make assessment an ongoing part of every day.

WHY WE HAVE WRITTEN THIS BOOK

We have written this book so that you, the reader, equipped with tools and knowledge, can document the progress of the second-language learners with confidence, and be able to accept and welcome all learners.

We have included many of our own experiences, as well as the struggles and mistakes made over the years. We have filled the pages with many examples and anecdotes to make the theory real, and to illustrate the sometimes uneven, often difficult and arduous path toward mastery of our language. This book itself has been a struggle, and while we learned a great deal, we also discovered that as teachers we—like all other teachers—already knew the basics of assessment: observing students closely for signs of growth and mastery, and finding joy in that growth.

1

Kiss Me Teacher:
WHAT TEACHERS NEED TO KNOW

In this chapter we discuss

◆ where we are coming from
◆ why we need to assess students
◆ what we want to find out when we assess
◆ what effective assessment is

WHERE WE ARE COMING FROM

Barb's early years

The seed for this book began long ago, from the experiences of Barb's early years as an ESL teacher in a university town in the Midwest. Her first two years she was assigned as an itinerant teacher to the "Gypsy Run," going to seven elementary and two middle schools. All students were mainstreamed, with Barb meeting them whenever and wherever they fit into her busy schedule. If the state had a policy concerning non-English-speaking students, nobody knew what it was. Often decisions about placement were made standing in the hallway outside the office while the parent disappeared out the door. No initial placement tests were given. There was no curriculum, no guidelines to follow. It was difficult, if not impossible, for Barb to schedule time to see the classroom teacher and find out what and how the child was doing.

During Barb's third year in the district, she was given a self-contained classroom of second-language learners, thirty or so children from grades one through five. Among them, they spoke eleven different languages. There were thirty levels of English proficiency and thirty different sets of needs. Barb was instructed to "teach them English" so that sooner or later they could return to the regular classroom.

Out of Barb's nebulous job description arose several questions and certain real and difficult problems:

Who belonged in ESL and who didn't? How could she tell?

Anyone whom the classroom teacher decided needed services was sent to Barb's class. No one provided Barb with criteria to assess whether a student needed her or not. On the first day of school she was given a

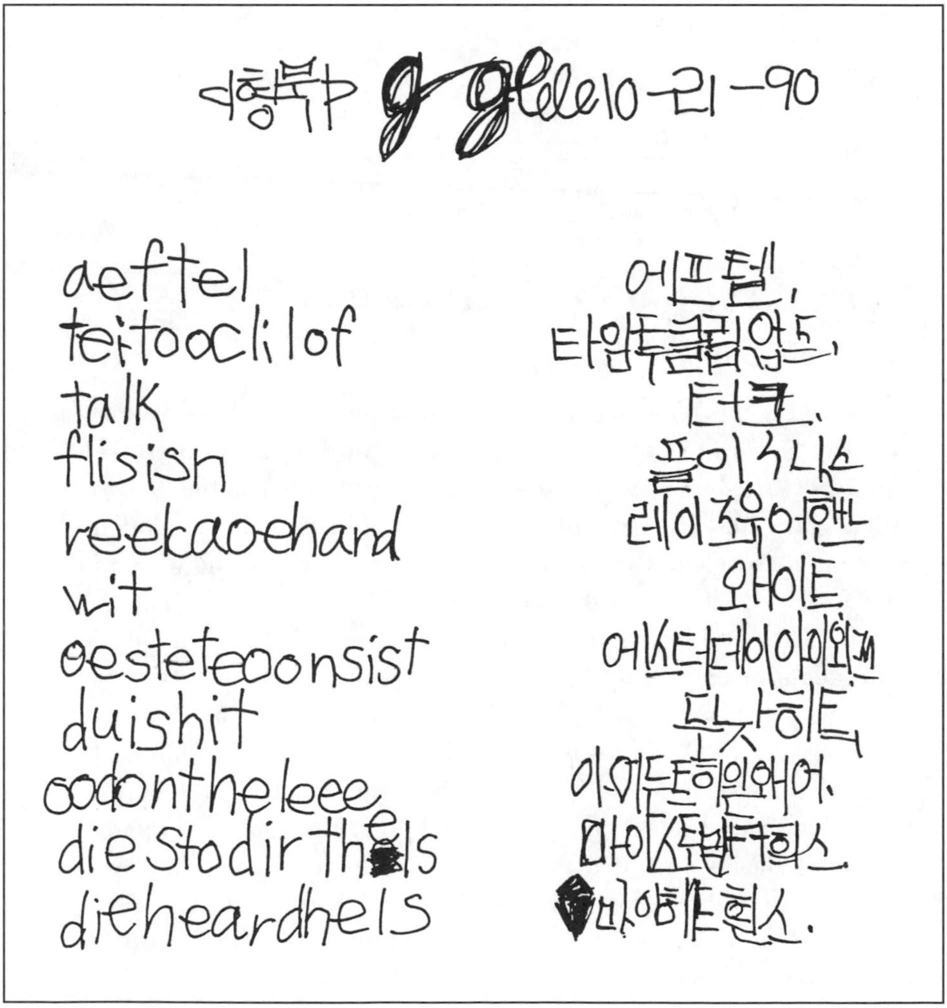

Figure 1.1

list of over sixty children who "needed help"; she had to decide, without benefit of guidelines, who to take and who to leave in the mainstream classroom.

Figure 1.1 (left) illustrates the work one recent arrival, Jung, handed in. Based on the work sample, Barb had to answer: Can he function in the regular class? How much does he know? Am I willing to set him adrift in a classroom when the options are pretty much all or nothing—either my class or alone in the mainstream?

What would she teach them?

There was nothing to tell her what her priorities were and no one to help her decide where to start. The previous ESL teacher had worked on making paper umbrellas, conjugating verb endings, and doing dittos. Barb looked at John and Laban, who could read and write in Chinese but knew no English; at first-grader William who was on the verge of reading in English; at Chatphet, who would be going on to the middle school next year; at Vaji, who didn't seem to be doing much in either Farsi or English. Barb sensed these children didn't need to just learn to speak English; they needed to learn how to read and write in English. Time was passing. A year spent simply learning how to speak correctly was a year lost on learning the content of the curriculum.

Barb answered the logistical problems by grouping the children loosely by age and competency levels. The class read and wrote together. They did Language Experience activities long before Barb had ever heard of the term. They worked on themes such as "cities," "jobs," and "dinosaurs." After a basic lesson, they would break into groups with activities geared to the level of each participant. At the end of the year each worked on units about the countries they came from, with demonstrations given by parents from each individual country. They filled out passports, detailing in their own words what they had seen and learned about their country.

When Barb decided on what to teach, how could she be sure it was relevant and aligned to what the students were doing in the mainstream curriculum?

Barb rarely knew what was going on in the student's regular classroom. With her mornings filled, her afternoons taken up by kindergarten and the "extra-help" children, she had little time to talk to classroom teachers. Communication was "catch-as-catch-can" in hallways and the teachers' lounge. Conversation was often limited to "How's he doing?" "Oh, fine."

How could she be sure the students were learning?

Barb watched. She listened to the children as they worked, studied the writing they did, and observed their behavior throughout the day. She talked to her aides and compared notes on what they had seen. Documenting that progress was another issue altogether, however, and the idea of portfolios in the classroom had not yet been developed. She attempted to put together a "report card" but nobody was happy with it because it didn't show much.

How was she to decide when to send the children back to the mainstream classroom full time?

There was no established procedure or criteria for exiting the students in her class, and it was a struggle to mainstream the children. William, for instance, was a problem. He talked constantly while Barb was trying to lead a lesson, got up and ran around during Rug Time, picked fights with other students, and wouldn't stay on task during group work. He had entered school in the United States in kindergarten, had been in the self-contained classroom since his arrival nearly a year and a half before, could speak English fluently, and was ready to read. It was clear to Barb that he could be successfully mainstreamed. However, when she approached the classroom teacher and broached the idea, Mrs. Smith curtly stated that they would have to meet with the principal. At the meeting, Barb presented her case. But because she really didn't know much about assessment and couldn't document in any concrete way what William was capable of doing, she was unable to convince them. Mrs. Smith accused Barb of trying to get rid of William because he was a behavior problem (which he was); Barb secretly harbored the notion that Mrs. Smith didn't want him back for precisely the same reason. So, over Barb's objections, and what she intuitively knew was the right decision, William stayed in ESL.

Was the self-contained program the right program for the children?

When the self-contained program was set up, Barb was quite vocal in her objections to it. Bad mistake. She was assigned to teach in it. Before she even set foot in the classroom, the principal made it clear that she and the teachers would be happy with the setup; he was not about to change it.

For Barb, with so many children at so many different levels, the logistics were overwhelming. In addition, the children, isolated from their peers for most of the day, made few English-speaking friends. Furthermore, all but a few teachers seemed to relinquish responsibility for them, leaving the entire burden of teaching to Barb. Worst of all was the one-size-fits-all mentality that assumed that since the children all had the same "problem"—not knowing English—one teacher could, in the course of a morning, teach five grade levels of children adequately.

Mary's early years

Mary had a different experience. Her first ESL assignment was at the Language Assessment Center (LAC) in southern California. The center provided intensive ESL instruction for newly located Indo-Chinese refugees. They attended daily classes that were four hours long. These were split into two two-hour shifts shared between two teachers. The students were grouped according to capabilities, and the classes were open entry—students could come in at any time during the semester, and teachers could move them from level to level when they were ready. The students stayed in the program for approximately six to nine months and then moved into other programs or job training. The curriculum at the LAC focused on survival skills the students would need to succeed in their new environment. Teachers had six major themes they were supposed to cover, but the materials they used and how they used them were left to them. They had access to the resources the center provided, or they could create their own. Texts were available, but the director discouraged teachers from using them too frequently as she did not want teachers teaching from manuals. They were encouraged to keep the English meaningful and tangent to the students' experiences.

Teachers met every day to coordinate during the students' twenty-minute break. This gave them time to share materials, ideas, observations, and so on. Once a month the break was extended and a few teachers would be asked to present a successful technique or observation to the entire group of approximately twenty teachers. They were kept abreast of ESL theory by presentations from experts in the field, by publishing companies who wanted feedback from them on new materials, and by interested professors at the nearby universities. They were encouraged to attend ESL workshops and to share what they learned with the rest of the group.

What made this program such an essential part of Mary's growth as a teacher was the constant input and support that was built into it. She never felt she taught in a vacuum. She knew she could get support from her supervisors and peers when she needed it. If she felt stumped, she could bounce ideas off her partner or other teachers for help. She also thrived on the access all teachers had to the theory, methods, and people in the newly developing ESL field. Granted, twenty teachers in the same room trying to discuss the best method for teaching ESL was usually chaotic. But with so many different personalities and backgrounds, the diversity was wonderful, the ideas challenging, and the pace frantic. It was the most exhilarating teaching assignment she had ever had, and the most challenging. By the time she moved to northern California four years later, her teaching abilities had broadened and deepened to prepare her for the less supportive assignments she would encounter later.

Which reality is the real world?

We would like to think Mary's experience, not Barb's, is the norm. But is it? States and provinces have policies; districts have plans. However, with large numbers, working in a vacuum, teaching populations that change year by year, many teachers face the same, if not worse, difficulties than Barb did.

Further, the number of students speaking a language other than English who enroll in schools is rising. In the United States, approximately one in seven students comes from a language-minority background, and in the twenty largest school districts the percentage increases to one in three. In cities such as Los Angeles, Toronto, and Vancouver, the numbers have become truly overwhelming—in some schools 95 percent of the students speak little or no English.

Different schools, districts, states, and provinces have responded differently to the influx of non-English-speaking students. Some districts have well-planned curriculums and programs, with coordinators and placement procedures established. Many others have chosen not to deal with the situation at all—the ESL teachers themselves assume the burden of testing, placing, monitoring, and exiting students from classes or programs—if there are any. Whether you are in a situation where testing/placement is not one of your responsibilities, or whether it all falls to you, the challenge of assessing student progress is still your job.

WHY WE NEED TO ASSESS

Before we answer the question of why we need to assess these students, even more fundamental is: Who cares? Back in the bad old days of Barb's short-lived career in the self-contained classroom, the other teachers seemed to be content to let her go merrily on her way, taking all the children off their hands until they were proficient in English. This "take-'em, fix-'em, don't-send-'em-back-until-they're-ready" attitude rears its ugly head in many places.

But there are stakeholders in the picture who have different needs, different philosophies and issues they are grappling with in the lives of our students. The stakeholders must make different decisions with the information they are given. These stakeholders are

◆ administrators
◆ teachers (mainstream, next year's, ESL teachers, or aides)
◆ students
◆ parents

Administrators are faced with the issue of how and into what programs to place these students. They must know how much money, planning, and personnel they must commit to the education of non-English-speaking students, based on their numbers, learning needs, and literacy levels. They must know when and how to adapt to the changing populations that arrive and leave. They need to know that the programs they have implemented are the most appropriate.

Teachers need to know how they can plan instruction. They need to find out how much English these students know. They need to know whether their students can read or write when they enter the classroom. They also need to figure out whether students are learning or not, and, if not, why not? Teachers also need to know how to document what and how much students have learned in order to promote, graduate, or retain them.

Students need to know what they've accomplished, be aware of what they need to work on, and have a concrete record of what they have mastered so that when they go on, they can demonstrate what skills they have.

Parents need to know what their children are doing in school, what they are learning, and what the goals of the school are for their children.

Another important question is: why should we care? Why should we worry about these students when, in some cases, they are not graded or assessed until they are totally mainstreamed, or in others, they simply become the charges of the ESL teacher or the mainstream teacher until they become proficient?

The answer is very simple: the future of our students rides on our ability to make well-reasoned and appropriate decisions about their academic futures. Erickson (1981) writes:

> The consequences of misclassifications due to inadequate or inappropriate tests may include improper placement, insufficient instruction, and, as a result, lower academic achievement than would have been reached if appropriate instruments and proper placement had occurred. The ultimate consequence of such testing may include increased dropout rates and perpetuation of unequal educational opportunity for language minority students.

With so much at stake, we agree with Susan Morse (1990), who writes:

> When we are making life decisions for children...it is essential that we do so with great trepidation because we are presuming many things about

the future and capabilities of an individual. We must gather as much information as possible, seek as much assistance as is available, and presume that this child may be the undiscovered Einstein of this decade.

In the second place, the problem of adequate assessment of *all* students has become a major issue. The United States Department of Education has stated as one of its primary goals that "by the year 2000, American students will leave grades four, eight, and twelve having demonstrated competency in challenging subject matter including English, mathematics, science, history, and geography." Implicit in this goal is the assumption that schools can adequately demonstrate that they can teach these competencies. This means enormous pressure on schools and on you, the teacher, to help these kids succeed.

It's that simple: the assessment instruments we use must be able to tell us accurately and reliably how much a student knows upon entry, and how well he is doing in our classes.

WHAT EDUCATORS WANT AND NEED TO FIND OUT

You may or may not be faced with testing and placement decisions. Many teachers are and many others do not have that power or that burden. We feel it's important to present all the different types of questions asked, so that even if you are not responsible for these issues, you are aware that they exist. Somebody must make these decisions, and they must have certain kinds of information to make them wisely. They affect you in terms of who enters your classroom, the resources you are allocated, or the responsibility you are given for these students.

Stakeholders need answers to the following questions:

Which students come from homes where English is not spoken?
Identifying a child who comes from a home in which English is not spoken sends up a red flag announcing that he might need services. You need an initial sorting mechanism as a front-line device to alert administrators of special needs.

You can't assume that a child with a foreign surname will need special help with the language, or that someone with an English surname will not. Nathan Sims is the son of an American marine and a Panamanian. His mother speaks to him only in Spanish. Helga Rodrigues from Brazil is of Swedish-Portuguese ancestry. A home-language survey (see page 57) for each of them would be the first order of business to find out which language they speak primarily.

How much English does the student know? Does he speak enough English to be placed in a mainstream class? Or is his English so limited that he will need special attention?

Effective assessment allows the school to place those students who aren't proficient in English into programs and classes that are appropriate to their needs.

Eighth-grader Ichiro Fukuda's home-language survey reveals that his parents speak to him in Japanese. However, further investigation reveals that his father has been a professor of psychology for several years; that Ichiro is fluent in English and reads and writes English at grade level. His parents speak nothing but Japanese at home to instill respect for his culture and maintenance of their language. He goes to Japanese school every day after school.

Fifth-grader Richard Morales speaks and is spoken to in English at home. His parents insist, because they were told by a teacher not to speak their own language to their son. However, their English is slow and halting, and although Richard is in the third grade and is orally fluent in English, he can neither read nor write in either language.

How much content and what concepts has the student learned in his own language?

When you know that, you can decide where to begin and what to teach. Tenth-grader Martin, for instance, has been to school in Mexico City and reads fluently at grade level in Spanish. He has taken world history, algebra, and geometry. Sixteen-year-old Maria, on the other hand, has had less than two years of schooling and is barely literate in Spanish. Although they are both beginning speakers of English, it would be inappropriate to begin teaching Martin at the same level as Maria. Effective assessment allows you to make these kinds of instructional decisions about the student.

How much has the student learned since his arrival? How well is he doing? Are the methods currently being used working? Or should other methods be used instead?

James, from Taiwan, had been to school in his own country until he was ten and was far ahead of the class in math and science. Although he was quiet and didn't speak often, he understood what was said to him. And, while he read fluently in Chinese, he just couldn't seem to make the transition to reading in English. His tutor tried many methods—reading to James, talking about what they had read, having him read aloud, having him dictate stories—but James couldn't seem to put it together. Finally, they had to backtrack to a method that seemed to fit in with how he had learned Chinese characters: working on sound-letter correspondences with rhyming words and memorizing frequently used words. It went against many principles his tutor had learned in her whole-language theory classes, but it seemed safe and familiar to James. He found success with that, and they built from that small start.

Assessment, through careful observation of what James knew and what methods were successful, helped the tutor decide on a plan that eventually helped James acquire the skills he needed in reading.

How do you determine who has achieved enough proficiency in English to be reclassified? Who would continue to benefit from ESL or bilingual classes?

Margarita has made remarkable progress in just a few months. She speaks without an accent and can carry on a fluent conversation. Her mother has requested that she be mainstreamed. The teacher needs to be able to document just how much Margarita knows, and whether her reading and writing skills are strong enough for her to make the transition to a mainstream classroom.

How can you tell a student is progressing in the ESL and/or the mainstream classroom?

Tari is extremely shy and quiet. He fails the tests and doesn't turn in his homework. By these indications, he is failing his classes and has not learned anything. However, his science teacher notes that during lab work, he conducts the experiments competently. He draws well, and can demonstrate his understanding through drawing. He can also answer questions to the tests orally. By careful observation, allowing Tari alternative methods to demonstrate his understanding, and creating situations where he can contribute to class discussions and projects, his teachers can document that he is meeting the base-line competencies required for the courses he is taking.

How do you keep track of a student's progress after he has been exited from special programs? Is he functioning at grade level? Or has he slipped behind and not doing well in mainstream classes?

Effective assessment would reveal how well he is doing in relation to what is expected of him and his classmates, and what kinds of additional support he may need.

Loan, for example, had tested FEP (fully English proficient) and was no longer eligible for special services. She spoke English well, but had failed her English, history, and science courses. She could not cope with the content courses and eventually dropped out of school, saying that she had a job in a local factory.

A contingency plan could have been worked out to help her get through the content courses and meet the requirements for graduation.

Does a student who is not achieving have problems with language, or do his difficulties stem from psychological, physical, or emotional problems that would necessitate different programs and strategies?

Effective assessment, writes Alvarez (1991), helps distinguish between "real handicapping difficulties and transient difficulties the students might be having due to language, adaptation, or curricular mismatches."

Yebio was nine years old, in a third-grade class, and reading at a first-grade level. His teacher often gave him puzzles to do—that seemed to be the only thing that kept him occupied and out of trouble. The tutor who worked with him discovered that his attention span was, at best, five minutes on a good day. He quickly lost interest in anything. He dictated one letter to his father and wouldn't do any more. He typed one line and skipped off to another activity. He didn't like to read, and couldn't sit still to listen. His teacher finally resorted to doing simple activities with Yebio, such as taking walks and discussing environmental print, and playing Sorry. Yebio could not remember the rules from one day to the next; they needed to be explained to him every time they played, and he had great difficulty counting the correct number of squares during his turn. Months of individual work did not seem to make a difference in his progress. After careful questioning of Yebio's mother, the teacher learned that he had been in a refugee camp in the Sudan for his first four years of life and had had malaria from the age of eighteen months until he was three years old. Clearly there was more going on with him than language problems. After lengthy deliberation and testing, Yebio was referred to a special education class at another school.

◆

TC, nine when he arrived, was placed in kindergarten. His family had moved four times; he was shunted from school to school, placed in a fourth grade in one school, then dropped to third in the next. He was tested and labeled "borderline retarded." In his third state in three years, the ESL teacher tried everything she could think of to help him learn English and learn how to read. When he moved to another district he was retested as learning disabled. His interpreter and advocate believes that the schools have done him a disservice by misclassifying him; she feels that he should be in a regular classroom. But at sixteen he still cannot tell time, reads at a first-grade level, and cannot give directions from his home to school. He does not talk in complete sentences even in his own language.

After careful documentation of what ESL, mainstream, special-education teachers and tutors observed, and assessment by a team of teachers, Yebio was placed in a program designed to meet his particular needs as a learner. These measures have helped teachers at least begin to figure out how to help TC.

All these scenarios are based on the common theme: decisions must be based upon effective assessment. But what is effective assessment anyway?

EFFECTIVE ASSESSMENT

Effective assessment involves ways of obtaining enough essential and accurate information about your students.

Effective assessment depends on obtaining what Stiggins (1991) calls "good data." Good data contains the following features:

- **A clear target.** Know what it is you're looking for.

- **An appropriate sample.** Is the data you've collected truly representative of what the student is capable of? Is it enough?

- **Known sources of interference.** What gets in the way of your obtaining a good sample of what this student knows and can do? Is the test faulty? Are you looking in the wrong context? Are you current with the latest research concerning language learning and literacy development? For instance, research shows students learn large issues first and gradually refine grammar, and so on. A teacher who focuses on word endings or grammar errors and insists on perfection, while overlooking content, is focusing on the wrong issues.

- **Usable results.** Can you use what you have found in a way that is valuable to you (as the teacher planning the learning of your student) to other teachers, to parents, to administrators and to the students themselves?

CONCLUSION

ESL students bring a complex set of issues with them when they arrive at any school. To understand what a student knows and how much English a student understands, schools need to have assessment procedures that provide the stakeholders with accurate information. Being prepared for these students before they arrive means working out what it is you need to find out about them so that placement and teaching is as effective as possible. Beyond the required tests, how will the additional information be gathered? Placement needs to be appropriate, teachers need accurate methods of assessing and recording their students' development, and documentation needs to reflect the students' progress through and beyond any ESL program. Each assessment issue needs to be addressed. That is why understanding the difference between the role of testing and the role of alternative assessment is an important first step.

2

What Shape
Will We Use? Red!

TESTING VS. ALTERNATIVE
FORMS OF ASSESSMENT

In this chapter, we discuss

- why the traditional ways of testing and assessing are no longer adequate
- what the new ways of assessing have to offer teachers of limited English proficient students

THE HORNS OF THE DILEMMA

Juan is in a beginning literacy class for four semesters, and has not made any progress. He can barely finish 10 percent of the standardized placement test and is continually classified as nonliterate, non-English-speaking. Because he has already passed the age where he should have graduated from high school, counsellors and administrators are beginning to make rumbling noises about his "educability." He does not turn in homework and cannot read even the easiest of texts. His favorite sentence is, "I don't know."

Every day during spring semester, while driving through prune orchards to work, his teacher sees something different happening, and asks Juan, a migrant worker, about what she sees. Juan answers all her questions, showing a remarkable knowledge of how prunes are cultivated, harvested, and processed. His teacher has decided to abandon the class textbook and introduce projects on agriculture, reasoning this is what her students, mostly migrant workers, know best. And, although Juan needs a great deal of assistance, his project reveals just how much he actually knows. By capitalizing on his strengths, his teacher is helping him move toward literacy and proficiency in English.

◆

The California university system uses a test called the WEST to assess students' writing. To graduate, students must pass this test, which is holistically scored (writing is rated as a whole and scored within a range). Non-English-speaking students have trouble with this test, and many fail more than once; with each failure, their chances of passing wanes. For example, one student, a senior in engineering, failed thirteen times, and the WEST was the only thing standing in the way of graduating. One campus responded by giving nonnative-English speakers more time to take the test. But when Barb suggested reading the writing prompt to the students, the idea was rejected on the basis that reading and understanding the question was part of the test—this, despite the fact that many of these students spent more than half the allotted time just struggling through the writing prompt. One question on tree spiking was so far removed even from many American students' experience that the foreign students had little hope of responding articulately. Clearly there had to be another way to demonstrate that these students could write coherently.

◆

A local technical college, which has an ESL program, offers varying levels of ESL classes. However, to take regular technical classes, like mechanics, students must pass the Nelson Denny reading test, a mainly multiple-choice vocabulary test. Many ESL students, who are doing well in the classes and would like to get skill training at the school, cannot pass the test. They have neither the experience with that kind of testing nor the basic vocabulary the test assesses.

These stories illustrate the twin horns of the dilemma of testing and assessment: it frees us and it hogties us. Testing also serves as a gatekeeper, allowing those who can run the gauntlet in at the door, while effectively and anonymously barring others who would get in.

To be fair and reasonable, to show what students can do, assessment must be effective. Effective assessment is the key to finding the answers to the questions raised in chapter 1. Stiggins (1991) writes:

Important instructional and policy decisions are based on information about student achievement. If those decisions are made well, students benefit. If they are made poorly, students suffer. But those decisions can only be as sound as the data on which they are based.

But how do we do that? How can we keep from being biased? How can we prevent our own lack of knowledge, or personal feelings from getting in the way? How can we ensure that tests are selected properly, or read the way they were meant to be read, or used for the purposes they were intended for?

To make good, fair, reasonable, sound decisions we need to have the "good data" that we discussed on page 24, based on Stiggins criteria of a clear target, an appropriate sample, known sources of interference, and usable results.

Given these criteria for good data, then, what are our options?

How assessment differs from testing

There is an important difference between assessment and testing. Mitchell (1992) defines a test as a "single-occasion, unidimensional, timed exercise, usually in multiple choice or short-answer form." Testing is formal, and is often standardized, which means that "everyone takes the test under the same conditions." In other words, everyone is given the exact procedures for administering and scoring, the same test materials and items, and the same norms against which the student is compared. Assessment is a broader term. It implies evaluation based on a collection of information about what students know and can do. This means many ways and methods of gathering, at different times, in different contexts. Testing is a part of assessment, but as we demonstrate with the Quad (page 143), it is only one means of gathering information about a student. The focus in testing is on finding the norm. Assessment is broader; the teacher is looking at progress over time in a variety of contexts.

STANDARDIZED TESTS

Schools have long depended upon standardized tests to make their educational decisions. In fact, in the United States at least, "standardized multiple choice tests have come to dominate the educational landscape..." (Neill and Medina 1989). In the past several years these kinds of tests have come under fire, and as a result, nations such as Britain, the Netherlands, Germany, Sweden, and South Africa are moving ahead of the United States in education. The debate is heated, and nowadays "test-bashing" is in vogue. We do not ascribe to test bashing; we feel that, used properly, tests can provide some useful information. However, when they are used exclusively, tests cannot provide fair and useful information about students, particularly LEP (limited English proficient) students. We will attempt to clarify the issues through a careful discussion of tests according to Stiggins's four features.

Do they have a clear target?

Yes. Standardized tests are

- designed for what is called "summative" data. They are achievement tests to determine how much a student has learned.
- used to compare a student's knowledge against a set core of knowledge and skills that are deemed essential for students to know

Can you obtain an appropriate sample from standardized tests?

Many researchers say no for the following reasons:

- **Tests tend to fragment skills.** For example, reading tests focus on subsets of reading skills, and do not actually measure reading ability. Knowing vocabulary doesn't mean the student is able to read for comprehension. Knowing grammatical structures does not measure the ability to write.

- **Most test only lower-order thinking skills.** These include such thinking skills as memorization and recall, not higher-order skills such as inferencing and synthesizing.

◆ **Many tests cannot show whether the student knows the material or not.** This is especially true of those with multiple-choice answers. When a student can choose among answers, he has a good chance of randomly choosing the correct one. For example, Mark, a grade-eight student, was taking a standardized test. Barb watched with dismay as he simply ran his pencil down the page, randomly checking off answers. When she asked him why he didn't try, he countered "Why should I?" He wasn't a good student; he knew he had as good a chance of getting an answer right by hazarding a quick guess as he did by struggling laboriously over each answer (and probably guessing at the end, anyway.) This way, if he failed, he could save face by saying he hadn't tried.

◆ **Because standardized tests are "single-occasion" they are not necessarily measures of a student's competence (what he knows).** They are instead a measure of his performance (what he does at that particular time). In addition, they do not necessarily measure growth. Test scores cannot tell you a child has progressed from point A to point B.

◆ **From the test you cannot tell where exactly the student failed.** Conversely, you cannot tell what he does know. Because the scores are usually calculated by percentage points (for example, Nicholas scored 59 in math and 73 in English) and do not tell you where the student had difficulty, you as teacher have no concrete starting point to begin teaching.

◆ **Standardized tests test all language and thinking skills through the dimension of reading and writing.**

◆ **Standardized tests have no context.** Many vocabulary tests give isolated words or phrases with a list of other words to choose from. Instead of being absorbed in a task that is real and interesting, the student is confined to a desk marking little bubbles on a sheet of paper (see figure 2.1, page 32).

What are the known sources of interference? What gets in the way of a student performing well?

◆ **Standardized tests are linguistically biased against nonnative-English-speaking students.** This means that the tests cannot differentiate between wrong answers due to lack of knowledge or due to lack of proficiency in English. If a student cannot read English, he will fail—even if he knows a great deal about the subject. According to Baker (1991), these tests aren't designed to measure whether a student has a good enough command of English to succeed in school. Test makers have excluded the essential language skills that all native speakers possess to get along in society because these features do not separate the "haves" of knowledge from the "have-nots."

◆ **Standardized tests are culturally biased.** Norms are usually set for students from the mainstream culture. For many years this problem has been noted for populations other than white, mainstream students. It is even more a problem for ESL students. According to Hamayan (1991), "language tests are biased toward the culture within which they were developed. Through their construction, all language tests have unique cultural elements built in." This can be true even if the test has been translated

---

Vocabulary

Choose the word that has the <u>same</u> meaning, or almost the same meaning, as the underlined word.

11. at the <u>nearest</u> corner
   Ⓐ farthest
   Ⓑ latest
   Ⓒ closest
   Ⓓ widest

12. treated me <u>fairly</u>
   Ⓐ gently
   Ⓑ loudly
   Ⓒ justly
   Ⓓ surely

13. will be <u>delayed</u> again
   Ⓐ late
   Ⓑ hurried
   Ⓒ started
   Ⓓ early

14. <u>stroll</u> in the park
   Ⓐ plow
   Ⓑ dash
   Ⓒ work
   Ⓓ walk

Figure 2.1

into the student's language. For example, on one test, Chilean students were asked to complete the following: "You walk with your feet and throw with your _____ ." Since the dominant and most popular sport in Chile is soccer, many students completed this sentence with *feet*, a logical answer, since in soccer the ball cannot be touched or thrown with the hands except by the goalie. However, the test was

written in the United States where baseball and basketball predomi-
nate; therefore, the "correct" answer was *hands* (Hastings 1981).

◆ **Although standardized tests are meant to be summative, they are
often used for formative purposes.** In other words, they are used to
guide the curriculum. If a child does poorly on a vocabulary test, he
might be placed in a program that teaches sight words and vocabulary, even when lack of vocabulary might not be the reason he did
poorly.

Are the results usable?

Traditionally, test results have been used to measure whether or not
students have mastered that core of skills and knowledge, or to rank
students.

However, these tests have come to be used for many other purposes
for which they were not originally designed. Winograd et al. (1991)
write that they are used to inform the stakeholders—teachers, students,
or parents: "Instead, they provide administrative means of accountability that are used in the allocation of funds. Money, in part, makes
testing a 'high stakes' game which invites abuse."

Neill and Medina (1989) write, as we mentioned before, that standardized tests act as gatekeepers:

> **From preschool to college, they have become the major criteria for a
> wide range of school decisions. Test scores limit the programs that stu-
> dents can enter and dictate where students are placed. Test scores are
> used to assess the quality of teachers, administrators, schools, and en-
> tire school systems. Meanwhile, the content and format of standardized
> tests determine the shape of the curriculum and the style of teaching.**

These high stakes have had significant consequences for teachers, students, schools, and curriculums, even to the point, as Mitchell (1992)
alleges, of corrupting the teaching process:

◆ **Teachers begin teaching to the test.** Because the stakes are high and
teachers want their schools and students to look good, many begin to
focus on the items covered on the tests. California's Science Framework (1990) notes, "A truism in education is, 'What you test is what

you get.'" Students will focus their attention on the activities that determine their grades, placement, and career opportunities. Similarly, teachers will make decisions about instruction based on the criteria by which they and their students are evaluated. Principals will provide instructional leadership that is consistent with the basis on which their schools are judged. "Educators," notes Worthen (1993), "were quick to realize that targeting their instruction at the specific knowledge and skills to be tested would yield a jump in test scores."

As a result, the testing measures begin to drive the instruction, rather than the reverse. The curriculum has narrowed to focus primarily on this particular knowledge and set of skills; therefore, rote memorization has become the means of learning.

Furthermore, many students who are exempted from taking the tests because they are classified as NEP (non-English-proficient) have been losing valuable classroom time; the teachers feel they must devote time to those who are going to take the test.

These tests determine who will be placed in advanced programs, graduate, receive scholarships, go to prestigious schools. The consequence of this is a large number of students who place on the lower end of the scale on these tests—particularly ESL students (for the reasons outlined above)—are relegated to remedial or nonacademic tracks. They leave school dissatisfied, unhappy with their lot in life, relegated to failure.

◆ **Many nonnative-English speakers do poorly on these types of tests.** Writes Lieberman (1989), "because schools' average scores on any measure are sensitive to the population of students taking the test, these kinds of policies create incentives for schools to keep out those students who might lower the average scores." Schools have been known to place many ESL students in Special Ed; keep them in federally funded compensatory programs such as Title VII and Chapter I long after they should have been exited into the mainstream; not test; or worst of all, encourage them to drop out—because of the effect these students will have on overall scores.

Standardized language-proficiency tests

We have discussed the inappropriateness of using standardized achievement tests with LEP students. But there are other tests, specifically designed to measure the language proficiency of non-English speakers, that are used to place LEP students in the school system. Are they any better?

In the United States, federal and state roles in standardized testing are formidable. Some states, like New Jersey and California, mandate the use of at least one standardized test in the placement of students. The federal government holds the purse strings of programs such as Title VII and Chapter I that serve LEP students, and federal law contains explicit requirements for the use of objective test scores to determine the success or failure of the program. Schools are forced to use them, appropriate or not.

According to Baker (1991), two different commissions concluded there were *no* psychometrically acceptable language-competency tests in existence. Other analyses came to the conclusion that the ones in existence were neither reliable nor valid. "Nevertheless, both Texas and California produced lists of 'approved' tests for their schools to use. Thus, decisions about enrolling the majority of the language minority students in this country in bilingual education are made with tests that are known to be unreliable and invalid."

We can ask the same questions of these tests that we have of standardized achievement tests designed for native-English speakers.

Do they have a clear target?

Yes. They are designed to measure proficiency in English. One test declares outright that it is designed to measure achievement based on the basic skills found in most curriculum guides.

Can you obtain an appropriate sample?

No. The faults with these tests are the same as with other standardized tests:

◆ **They are single-occasion tests.** They only measure what the students can do at that particular time. These tests are often given during the first few weeks of school, at a time when a newcomer is liable to be the most confused, frightened, vulnerable, and most unlikely to give an accurate picture of what he is truly capable of doing. For example:

> Ahmer was having a bad day. He had arrived from Pakistan at midnight the night before. Even though he was exhausted, he took the exams because his uncle insisted. He did not do well and declared that his math and reading skills were rusty, as it had been a long time since he'd had to use them. He was capable of doing much better if only he had taken the tests on another day.

◆

> Hiro's mother registered him at school. When she left through the front door, Hiro bolted out the back. It took several hours to find him, several days to calm him down so that he could be left alone in the classroom without constant attention from the aide, and several weeks before he would speak. Testing would have been pointless on the day of registration.

Many school districts use the same test to make entry and exit decisions. Students become "test-wise" and learn, through several trials and through the grapevine, the right answers to the questions. Michael registered at the local university and took the ESL placement test. He wrote an essay with great fluency and ease. The problem: he had answered the question from last year's test.

◆ **The tests fragment skills.** One test measures grammatical knowledge with such questions as, "He is _____ carpenter." Mastery of the grammar of a language is only one facet of knowing a language, and a student's apparent success or failure of such a test is not an indication

Figure 2.2

1. Amy _____ her new dress to the dance last night.

   a) wear   (b) were   (c) wore   (d) went

2. The clouds looked threatening, but _____ the sun came out.

   (a) then   (b) when   (c) than   (d) where

of his ability to use the language in a different context, such as in a conversation or when reading a book.

For example, in figure 2.2, question 1, choosing *(a) wear*, does not necessarily mean that the student misunderstood the sentence. He may be unfamiliar with the past of that particular verb. He may have been tired and picked the first one that made sense. In question 2, the answer *(b) when* is logical if the student is not aware that placing it within the second clause produces a sentence fragment.

◆ **Tests isolate parts of speech and present them out of context.** Tests that measure the student's ability to hear the difference between *sheep* and *ship* or *thin* and *tin* have no relevance to the student. The words are removed from a meaningful context within which meaning would be apparent. In addition, the test is often given out of the context of meaningful conversations. Recent studies have demonstrated the vast differences between what a child can produce in the classroom, on the playground, and at home, and what he produces in response to stilted, isolated prompts in front of an examiner.

For example, one seventh-grader who did poorly on a proficiency test produced these sentences in the course of one recess on the playground:

Where you going?
Are you graduate this year?
What is you eating in the lunch yesterday?
When you go back to Mexico?
Why you not stay in Mexico?
Who broke pencil yesterday?
Will do you go to the park?
Who is not going to the store today?

Individually, the questions reveal that the student has not grasped English tenses. However, together, they reveal that his command of grammar—such as word order in question-making—is quite advanced. His final sentence is correct.

◆ **The tests have arbitrary cutoff scores.** Baker (1991) reports that the Office of Civil Rights decided to use the 40 percent cutoff to classify students needing services. When they were asked to justify the percentile cutoffs used, staff responded that they had picked a score that people seemed to agree would identify a student who was not doing well in school. Baker writes, "while that may very well be true, such a score does not tell us whether this student needs special language instruction, because a single score alone cannot differentiate among the several possible causes of a low score."

◆ **The tests don't show how the student reached the answers he did.** He may have guessed, he may have been savvy enough to find the answer without being able to read. For instance, in figure 2.3, the student could pick out the answer *(c) popcorn* simply by looking through the text, without understanding. Her score sheet tells simple that she did poorly, not why; nor does it tell what she actually *could* do.

Popcorn is a popular American snack. It is made from corn kernels that are heated until they pop. Most people add butter and salt to the popcorn before they eat it. Americans love popcorn so much that they eat about 450 million pounds a year.

The American Indians showed the first settlers how to make and eat popcorn. Some Indians used popcorn for soup; others used it for jewelry. Now it is mainly eaten, but sometimes children put popcorn on a string to feed birds or to decorate a tree or window.

1. Americans eat 450 million pounds of:

    (a) butter   (c) popcorn

    (b) salt   (d) soup

Passage 2: Popcorn ....

1. a
2. d
3. d
4. d

Figure 2.3:
Excerpt from a reading comprehension test with student's answers, inset

◆ **Tests do not tell us what we want most to know:** Can this student succeed in a regular English classroom? They lack "predictive validity." A student who gets over 40 percent isn't necessarily ready to compete with fully proficient students in the regular classroom, nor does a score of less than 40 percent mean he is not ready.

What are the known sources of interference?

These are nearly the same as with standardized tests with norms set for native-English speakers.

◆ **Linguistic bias.** Some tests are translated into Spanish, a few into a handful of other languages. If the instructions are not translated into the language of the student, the teacher has no way of knowing if he understood (see figure 2.4).

1. Minimal Sound Pairs

Student Instructions: We're going to listen to the tape now. When you hear two words on the tape, tell me if they sound the same or different.

Examples: coat, goat — different
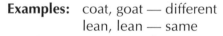
lean, lean — same

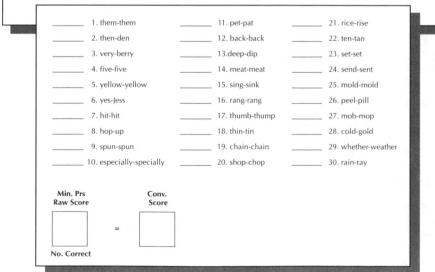

_____ 1. them-them	_____ 11. pet-pat	_____ 21. rice-rise
_____ 2. then-den	_____ 12. back-back	_____ 22. ten-tan
_____ 3. very-berry	_____ 13. deep-dip	_____ 23. set-set
_____ 4. five-five	_____ 14. meat-meat	_____ 24. send-sent
_____ 5. yellow-yellow	_____ 15. sing-sink	_____ 25. mold-mold
_____ 6. yes-Jess	_____ 16. rang-rang	_____ 26. peel-pill
_____ 7. hit-hit	_____ 17. thumb-thump	_____ 27. mob-mop
_____ 8. hop-up	_____ 18. thin-tin	_____ 28. cold-gold
_____ 9. spun-spun	_____ 19. chain-chain	_____ 29. whether-weather
_____ 10. especially-specially	_____ 20. shop-chop	_____ 30. rain-ray

**Min. Prs
Raw Score**

☐ = ☐

**Conv.
Score**

No. Correct

*Figure 2.4:
Can students
understand these
instructions?*

◆ **Cultural bias.** Asking children to identify pictures of frogs, or camels, or listen to a story about a computer—items that may not be within their frame of knowledge—does not tell us what they can do in English. They may not have words for apples or spaceships in their own language, and therefore would find it impossible to identify them (see figure 2.5).

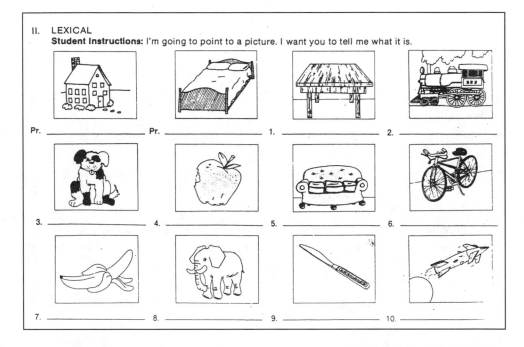

II. **LEXICAL**
Student Instructions: I'm going to point to a picture. I want you to tell me what it is.

Figure 2.5 Many children don't have couches or bicycles and have never seen an elephant or a locomotive. For example in figure 2.6, the correct answer was *barber*. One child answered, "Lice checker."

Are the results usable?

To a certain extent. These tests can give a basic picture of the student, a ballpark classification of his language capabilities, such as NEP or LEP or "limited

Figure 2.6

reader." However, since they are often used again and again to classify and reclassify students into and out of programs, the results may not be usable. A child who is labeled FEP (fully English proficient) is no longer eligible for services, but he may be classified FEP simply because he passed the oral component of the test, not because he is proficient. Baker (1991) points out that "language proficiency forms a continuum ranging from no proficiency to fully proficient. How far along this continuum does a student need special language help?" The experts cannot agree.

Many say not only are such tests unusable, they are dangerous. The United States Department of Education administered a test called the Language Measurement and Assessment Instrument (LM & AI) to a nationally representative sample of native-English-speaking children and classified 42 percent of them as LEP. Other researchers found incidents where only 33 percent of LEP children in a district were more fluent in their home language than in English, and another where almost 40 percent who were classified LEP did not speak the language of their parents.

Many teachers confide that since the tests are mandated and they must use them to gather information about a child's proficiency, they pay more attention to *how* the child takes the test and what he does while taking it than to the actual scores. As we point out throughout this book, watching a student's strategies for finding answers or listening to the accuracy of his language can reveal a great deal.

Testing is here to stay

Even with major shortcomings, testing is a major institutional practice that is not about to go away. Tests are a given, and will be for a long time, for several reasons:

◆ **Reluctance to change.** Schools, districts, states, and nations are not about to abandon testing in favor of newer methods (which produce what many regard as "soft" evidence) until these methods are sufficiently refined and standardized. Administrators have to be reassured that they are a better means of assessing performance. There is much that is subjective about assessment, which is based upon the teacher's observations. It is unlikely that standardized tests will soon be supplanted, because of the following unquantifiable factors that can skew validity and reliability:

- how much the teacher likes or dislikes an individual student
- how much training the teacher has received in alternative assessment
- the differences in the contexts in which the new types of assessment are given
- how much time individual districts put into developing methods to fit their curricular needs
- how much schools value alternative methods

Carl Braun (1993) writes:

> ...test-score talk reigns over common sense when the heat is on. It also underlines the distrust in teacher's abilities even to manage a test. The resistance to change generated by public pressure, then, is motivated partly by firmly ingrained beliefs about the mystical powers of commercially packaged tests....That these instruments tell blatant lies about children's learning, or at the very least, distort the truth about what they have learned (what teachers have taught) is rarely considered. And when teachers do raise the argument, it is looked upon as professional self-defense against poor teaching. The validity of the objections is swept under the carpet.

- **Accountability.** Whether legitimate or not, schools use standardized tests, such as the SAT or the CTBS, to measure their success against other schools. In early 1993, *Newsweek* reported that the superintendent of one of the largest school systems in the United States resigned his post. Cited as one of the three major reasons for his resignation was "his failure to raise test scores." *Newsweek* went on to say that among the school system's greatest woes was the fact that "49 percent of sixth graders scored in the bottom quarter of a national test of basic skills." Schools must have a means for judging if they are succeeding at their jobs; tests that are designed to measure a basic set of knowledge and skills are perceived to be a rational means for doing so. The federal government wants an accounting of whether the money it spends on programs is money well spent.

◆ **Competence.** At one time or another, all students must demonstrate their academic competence. A test of predetermined skills, standardized to a norm, will show—to some extent—whether they have or not.

◆ **Tests provide information stakeholders need.** Norms are important. Children's growth has to be compared against what is considered a normal range. Administrators and teachers need to know where the school and the curriculum measure against a standard. Whether or not it's true, standardized tests are viewed as the best way to evaluate the relative success of the school and its students.

ALTERNATIVES TO STANDARDIZED TESTING

Since we began writing this book, there has been an explosion of interest and research favoring alternative assessment—assessment that's based on a child's performance over time. We don't need percentile rankings; we need to be able to look at students and show them to the best of their abilities.

Alternative assessment is not a new idea. Worthen (1993) writes:

> ...insightful teachers recognize that [it] has long constituted the core of their methods for assessing student learning in the classroom. Elementary teachers were keeping anecdotal "running records" and folders of student work long before such records were legitimized and refined....Student performances or sampling of student products have long been the basis for teachers' evaluation of student outcomes in areas as diverse as music, drama, debate, art, shorthand, creative writing, and physical education....In short, our nation's classrooms have been quietly awash in such performance-based assessment for decades.

Trusting teachers

Many researchers and teacher advocates such as Kenneth Goodman have long alleged that standardized testing was, among other things, instituted because administrators, districts, and governments did not trust or value the individual teacher's judgment; we as teachers were too subjective to make accurate assessments of student progress and achievement. Although responsibility and accountability have remained, the power and the ability to determine futures was essentially taken out of our hands.

The consequences of this, according to Braun (1993), have been severe:

> Unilateral edicts and mandates affect the dignity of teachers and ultimately the lives of children. The message to teachers is that their judgment means less than the marks children make on paper—that in spite of their day-to-day observation of children, when decisions are being made, their judgment doesn't amount to anything....The most blatant corrupting consequence is that tests reduce opportunities to teach and to learn, certainly in any creative sense.

Research shows, however, that teacher's knowledge of children and their strengths and weaknesses is more accurate and sound than testing. Ulibarri (1991), for instance, did a study in which nine hundred children were given standardized achievement and proficiency tests. He also gathered the teachers' assessments on the children's English proficiency, competency in reading and math, and chance for achievement if taught in English. His study and several others found that the teacher's judgments and predictions were more accurate than tests. Baker (1991) articulates what many of us have been thinking: "What is the point of prescribing elaborate surveys and testing programs to replace teacher judgment when the empirical literature indicates that teacher judgment is more accurate?"

Why indeed? The movement toward alternative assessment is, in part, a movement toward empowering not only students but those of us in the trenches by giving the power to make decisions and judgments about children back to those who know them best: the teachers.

Alternative assessment is appropriate

The questions with which we scrutinized standardized testing are also appropriate to ask of alternative assessment:

Does alternative assessment have a clear target?
The answer is clearly yes. In addition to determining *how much* a student has learned, alternative assessment is used to find out

- how the student learns
- the strategies he uses
- how much progress he has made over time

Can you obtain an appropriate sample?

The answer is, again, yes. Alternative assessment can

- reveal "higher-order" skills. A teacher can directly determine whether the student has synthesized information or made proper inferences about material
- demonstrate whether the student actually knew the material or not

Because many types of alternative assessment are used to collect information over time, it can

- show growth
- differentiate between competence and performance. If the child cannot perform a task on a particular day, the teacher has the time and the opportunity to discover whether he can perform the task at a different time, in a different situation.

Alternative assessment is developed within a context. It is designed to be done within your classroom, as a normal part of the everyday social structure, events, and curriculum of the class. This makes it easy to be responsive and to measure the student's strengths in different areas and different situations.

What are the known sources of interference?

Unfortunately, this question is the major hurdle that must be addressed and answered by proponents and designers of alternative assessment. Following are some of the problems:

- **Cost.** One major advantage of standardized tests is they are inexpensive and easy to administer. Alternative assessments can be laborious: they require extensive training and a great deal of time and energy on the part of the teacher. In addition, many methods recommend more than one teacher or professional to provide input, whereas with standardized testing, the machine can do the work.

- **Cultural bias.** Just as standardized tests are known to be culturally biased, so too can the assessment of non-English-speaking students by untrained, insensitive, or ignorant teachers. Misunderstanding of ways of speaking, turn-taking rules, norms for politeness, or simply a bias against an ethnic group can lead to avoidance, lowered expectations, or rejection of the student. This can lead to failure for reasons divorced from the student's abilities.

- **Linguistic bias.** A student's English proficiency and a teacher's ability to understand his attempts can have a profound effect on what she sees and interprets.

  In figure 2.7, for example, the teacher comments "Makes no sense." While it is true that the essay is difficult to follow, and it's obvious that the student is struggling, one can make some sense of the essay. The writer seems to discuss each topic separately: (1) his school day consists of study and lunch; (2) he compares his previous school to the new one. This is a classic example of the effort it takes to reach meaning. The base-line assumption should be that meaning was attempted; it's in there somewhere.

Figure 2.7: Student writing exercise

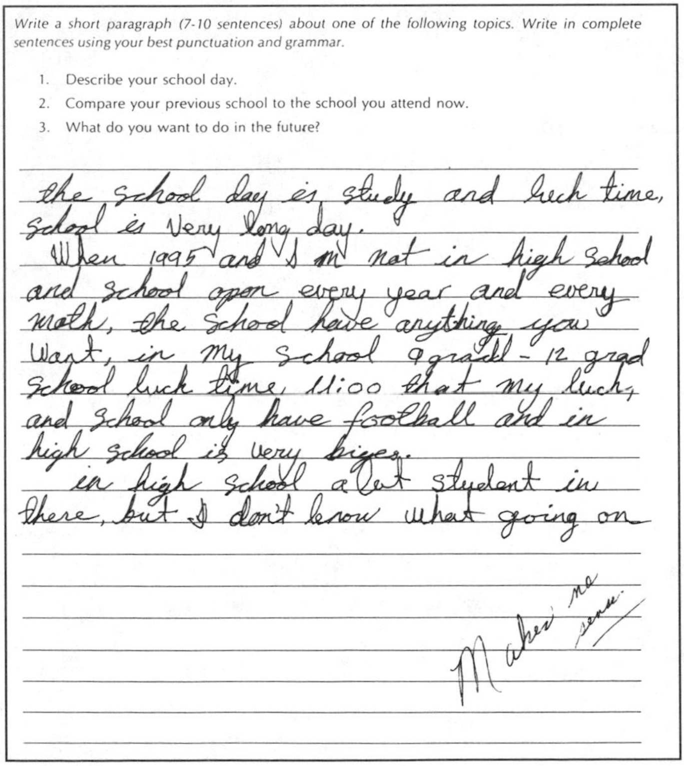

Write a short paragraph (7-10 sentences) about one of the following topics. Write in complete sentences using your best punctuation and grammar.

1. Describe your school day.
2. Compare your previous school to the school you attend now.
3. What do you want to do in the future?

the school day is study and luch time, school is very long day.
When 1995 and I m not in high school and school open every year and every moth, the school have anything you want, in my school 9 gradl - 12 grad school luch time, 11:00 that my luch, and school only have football and in high school is very biger.
in high school a lot student in there, but I don't know what going on

Makes no sense.

- **Asking the right (or the wrong) questions.** The paradigm you use to look at your students is critical in determining the answers they find. For instance, a teacher who does not understand the place of errors in second language learning, or who believes that language should be learned by memorizing grammatical rules in sequence, will measure the students against those yardsticks and find the students wanting.

For example, in figure 2.8 the writer was saying:

> I like school life because in America, playground is very big. In school class I would like to learn English fast so I can talk to my American friends. Writing is the hardest. Speaking is too.

A teacher tuned into the idea of language learning as a continuum, in which a student is grappling simultaneously with syntax, vocabulary, and transcription in a language he's not proficient in, will be able to see through the errors to an

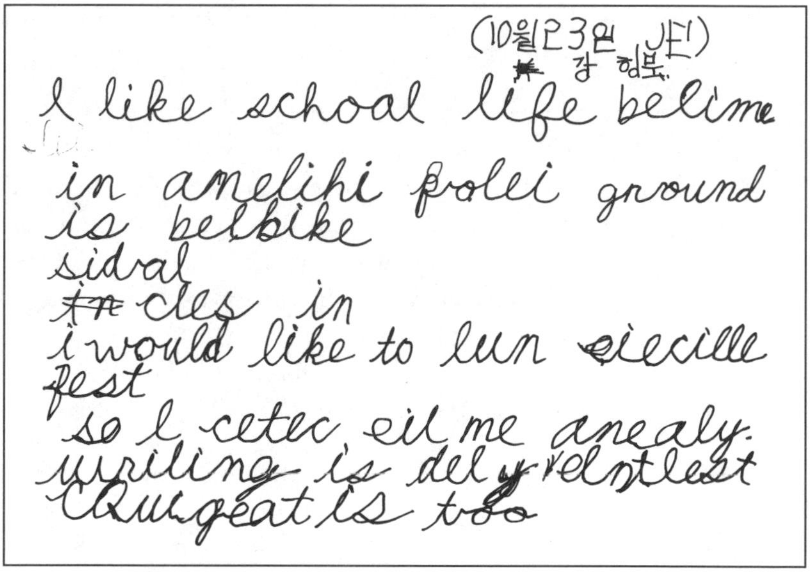

Figure 2.8: Student writing sample

admirable attempt at conveying meaning, rather than a woeful lack of proficiency in spelling and grammar.

The school that espouses the drill-and-kill method of teaching will have a difficult time using assessment to accurately measure real progress in learning.

- ◆ **Validity and reliability.** The problem of ensuring reliability and validity is especially acute with alternative assessment. Coaching or not coaching, making allowances, or giving credit where credit is not due are critical issues that have yet to be addressed; we simply do not have the answers yet.

For example, when Mary is working with Stan, and the history teacher gives her a test to work on with him, she has to tread a fine line, judging how much to tell him and what to expect from him. What if he needs the context? He didn't grow up in North America and has many gaps in his background. How much does she tell him? How much doesn't she tell him? Is this coaching?

In another example, Rogelio's English teacher grades down for spelling errors. Rogelio, whose first language is Spanish (with its very regular spelling), is having a very hard time. Mary, his tutor, who can see through the errors to the message, simply corrects the spelling for him. With limited time on her hands she doesn't want to waste it on surface errors. Is this cheating? We don't think so, but where do we draw the line?

◆ **Standardization.** Although alternative assessments are meant to measure—and treasure—the diversity of students and their learning, researchers strongly suggest that a lack of standardization could render the results useless for the needs of administrators, legislators, and governing boards. Worthen (1993) writes that the task of standardizing criteria and performance levels "sufficiently to support necessary comparisons, without causing them to lose the power and richness of assessment tailored to the student's needs and achievements, remains a daunting issue."

◆ **Manageability.** If you are already "taxed to the max" with other duties, you must be able to incorporate assessment into your classroom schedule and do it justice. Assessment must be do-able, manageable, readable, and valuable to the next teacher and to the parents who question what their child is doing.

Are the results usable?

Again, yes. Alternative assessment focuses on the strategies a student employs, an inventory from which new strategies and new learning develops. With results, you can make appropriate decisions about what to teach next, what to focus on, what areas need intensive work as opposed to what the student has already mastered.

Students can leave school or go on to the next grade with a record of what they *have* mastered and *can* do, rather than with a simple list of scores that reveal only failure to succeed on one type of assessment.

Results of alternative assessment

♦ give a fuller and fairer account of a wider range of experience than standardized testing can
♦ recognize types of achievement that don't lend themselves to conventional methods of assessment
♦ can be adapted to different teachers, styles, classrooms, purposes
♦ foster a "learning-through-success" pedagogy that provides a continuous record of tasks that the student has achieved

Final outcomes

When alternative assessment is implemented properly, the stake-holders—educators, parents, students, and the public—will have certain concrete things by which to judge the student's success. You, the teacher, will have

♦ a clearer picture of the student's proficiency level and capabilities
♦ data on which to base decisions about curriculum, matriculation, retention
♦ a course of action you can follow
♦ "do-able" options

Students will have

♦ a clear picture of their own capabilities and levels of proficiency
♦ a positive record of what they have accomplished
♦ a sense of control and power over their own education and their future

Parents will have

♦ a concrete record of where their child is in terms of learning and capabilities
♦ an awareness of the level their child is functioning at *now*
♦ a sense of direction for their child
♦ expectations

Administrators will have

- a concrete record of each student's accomplishments and proficiency level
- a set of records from which to base larger programmatic and curricular decisions
- clear data that either supports or refutes the model upon which the programs are built
- a sense of security that children are going to benefit because they feel good about themselves

CONCLUSION

Alternative assessment has a long uphill climb ahead of it to iron out its inherent difficulties. Worthen (1993) ventures that it may be a decade before we have workable, usable, standardized, valid methods. However, he goes on to say "district, state, and national assessment efforts should follow the lead of the National Assessment of Educational Progress in using performance assessment tasks whenever feasible, especially in low-stakes settings that are more accommodating of experimentation." This includes the relatively "low-stakes" settings of the classroom where tasks can be adapted and refined to the needs of the individual teacher and school.

Low-stakes settings for high stakes. With pressure from the federal government (in the form of Education 2000), states are moving again toward base-line competencies. Wisconsin has already mandated testing in grades ten and twelve, exempting only low-level English proficient students. Other states are considering mandating that no child pass the sixth grade without reading at grade level. These are frighteningly shortsighted standards. Until the programs are in place to ensure all students can read at grade level, until funding is available to bring LEP students up to speed, and unless there are legitimate, fair, and accurate ways to assess proficiency and competency, many students will lose. Newcomers will lose the most.

Therefore it is not only critical, but imperative, that we push for alternate means of assessment. In the following chapters we discuss how to implement these methods.

Determining the Navel Assigned to the Factor:

INITIAL PLACEMENT

In this chapter we discuss

- how to identify students whose first or home language is not English
- ways to assess the language proficiency
- ways to determine academic level
- issues to consider when placing students

"We've got two more," called the secretary gaily, waving the enrollment forms of two small newcomers above her head, as if placement were a form of lottery. "Who wants 'em?"

◆

Daniel, Martha, and Elsie were brought to the middle school. Barb was summoned from the "Boogie Room"—the tiny windowless classroom that she'd been assigned to, found along an unlit corridor on the second-floor landing. Standing in the hallway outside the office with the principal and the counsellor, she had to make an on-the-spot decision about where to place the three newcomers. According to their father, Daniel and Martha had had a solid foundation in learning, and he thought they would do well in seventh and eighth grade respectively. Elsie ought to be in sixth, he said. Everyone took his word for it. No one had any idea how to find out at what grade level they were or how much English they knew. Besides, the older two looked mature enough. So that decision "felt" right. But then Barb looked at Elsie. She was very tiny. She looked nine, not eleven. She hid behind her father, peering at Barb with large frightened eyes. Instinct told Barb that Elsie would do better at the elementary school. But Daniel and Martha were going to be at the middle school. Maybe it would be better to keep her with her brother and sister. She might feel safer here. Stifling her apprehensions, Barb agreed to place her in the sixth grade—with the other eleven-year-olds.

◆

Zer walked in the front door of the school along with his parents and an interpreter. The secretary asked how old he was. When told he was eight, she decided he belonged in the third grade, consulted the class rosters, and determined that Mrs. Hardesty had room. The parents left, and the secretary escorted Zer to his new class. It would be three weeks before Norma, the traveling ESL teacher, could get to him to test him for skills and proficiency. In the meantime, Mrs. Hardesty was faced with one more student—a terrified little boy who spoke no English.

◆

When fifty new students arrived unexpectedly on the doorstep of the school district, all the ESL teachers at elementary, middle, and secondary levels had to drop everything to test them. Students already enrolled sat in their classrooms, while desks lined the hallways as teachers tried to give the new students fair and accurate placement tests.

None of these scenarios is as it should be. However, each is a real story that illustrates the haphazard way many students are tested and placed. Some districts are well-prepared for the influx of new students, and have placement issues and procedures well-defined, the responsibilities designated, and the testers trained. Others, like the ones above, leave it up to the ESL teachers, or worse, to secretaries who have little or no training in the area of placement.

Zer did well and succeeded. Somehow the fifty students got tested and placed. In Elsie's case, however, Barb's instincts were right. Sixth grade was too much, she was too immature, her academic background too spotty. As a tiny eleven-year-old all she did was smile shyly and whisper. Two years later she was still smiling shyly and whispering, but she had grown into a very large girl whose helplessness and unwillingness to try drove everybody crazy. She never seemed to pull it together and floundered for all the years she was at the middle school, only to return to who-knows-what in her own country. Barb has been haunted by the sense that if she had to do it over again she would have done it differently.

If she had known about Elsie's background, about her level of reading ability, her grasp of basic academic skills, Barb would have asserted her apprehensions, articulated her rationale, and taken stronger measures when Elsie didn't begin to make progress.

Information is the key—adequate information with which to make reasoned, well thought-out decisions. Schools need to collect, then share pertinent information about each student. Only then can teachers make sound decisions on placement.

In this chapter, we give you an ideal that you can work toward or point to as a method of decision making that removes much of the guess work. We show you how to make decisions grounded in solid information. Each step narrows the field and focuses more closely on the student, on his abilities and level of proficiency, so you have enough information to make decisions that will benefit the student.

BEFORE STUDENTS ARRIVE: A PROCEDURE

Most districts prepared for incoming non-English-speaking students have two procedures in common. First, they have an established sequence for testing and placement. Second, they use a battery of assessment instruments to gradually sharpen their focus and profile each student, making placement in programs and grades as accurate as possible.

Your school needs to be clear on the who, what, and where of intake procedures. It is critical, therefore, to establish a standard district-wide process, which all personnel can follow. This includes

- a list of available interpreters
- a designated person (or persons) responsible for overseeing intake, administering tests, keeping records, requesting records from previous schools, placing the students, and ensuring that teachers receive appropriate information
- a home-language survey
- a list of tests or assessment instruments to be used in the initial placement decision
- a set procedure

When your school is clear about what is supposed to happen when the student arrives, the panic level decreases and decisions for placement are based on real information and agreed-upon procedures—not someone taking a shot in the dark as to where the student should go.

Figure 3.1:
Initial
identification
and assessment
procedure

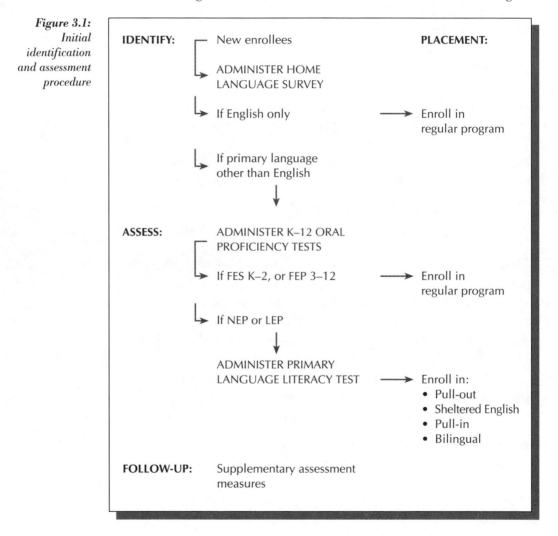

IDENTIFY: New enrollees   **PLACEMENT:**

ADMINISTER HOME
LANGUAGE SURVEY

If English only ⟶ Enroll in
regular program

If primary language
other than English

ASSESS: ADMINISTER K–12 ORAL
PROFICIENCY TESTS

If FES K–2, or FEP 3–12 ⟶ Enroll in
regular program

If NEP or LEP

ADMINISTER PRIMARY
LANGUAGE LITERACY TEST ⟶ Enroll in:
• Pull-out
• Sheltered English
• Pull-in
• Bilingual

FOLLOW-UP: Supplementary assessment
measures

Here is a sample procedure:

Step 1: Identify
WHO: all new students enrolling in K–12

WHY: to establish who is potentially eligible for services

WHAT TO USE: home-language survey

WHEN: before students are placed in school or class

Step 1a: Decide
Register students who speak English only in regular program. For students whose primary language is other than English, go to step 2.

Step 2: Assess oral proficiency
WHO: all whose home-language survey reveals they are not native-English speakers

WHY: to determine the language proficiency of each student

WHAT TO USE: oral interview using rubric such as SOLOM, or a standardized form such as IPT (Idea Proficiency Test)

WHEN: before they are placed in class

Step 2a: Decide
For students entering grades K–2, if fluent (FEP) in oral English, enroll in regular program. For all others, go to step 3.

Step 3: Assess literacy
WHO: all students in grades 3–12

WHY: to determine the level of academic assistance each student will need

WHAT TO USE: Mandated standardized test, such as the LAS (Language Assessment Scale), that include reading selections and writing samples

WHEN: before placement in classes

Step 3a: Decide
Enroll those students who are fluent in written English in regular program. For those students NEP or LEP in written English, go to step 4.

Step 4: Administer primary-language literacy test

Who: all students who are NEP or LEP in written English

Why: to determine if each is literate in any other language

What to use: standardized test in language (e.g., Bilingual Syntax Measure, or BSM) or, if no literacy test in a student's primary language is available, take an informal inventory

When: before placement in class

Step 5: Tentative placement

This is subject to ups and downs and involves moving students should you find that they are too advanced or too limited in proficiency or content knowledge.

Step 6: Supplementary assessment

Who: all NEP, LEP, and FEP students

Why: to determine what strategies they use in reading and writing

What to use: Boston Cloze, RMI, Concepts of Print Test, observation

Where: in the classroom, during interviews, additional testing situations

When:

- before or after tentative placement
- when teachers feel students are ready for exit from special programs
- when students are making exceptional progress or not making expected progress

STEP 1. INITIAL IDENTIFICATION

When a student arrives in the school or district there are certain basics you want and need to know about him:

- Does he speak a language other than English?
- Does he speak any English?
- Can he read?
- Can he read in English?

◆ Can he function on his own in the mainstream class, or does he need help?
◆ How much help does he need?

The home-language survey

The first step in assessing the ESL student is finding out what language(s) the student knows and speaks at home. In the United States, federal law requires that all students coming from a non-English-speaking background be surveyed to determine whether they speak a language other than English. Five standard questions in a home-language survey are:

1. Which language did your child learn first?
2. Which language does your child use most frequently at home?
3. Which language do you most frequently speak to your child?
4. Does the child know any other languages?
5. What language does your child speak most often?

In California, surveys such as this are routinely given to all incoming students when they enroll. Some states send the survey home to parents, but it often doesn't get returned. We recommend having parents do it at the same time they enroll their child. (Have the survey translated into as many languages as you anticipate your students will speak.)

Why is the home-language survey important?

The survey gives you a base-line figure of *potential* LEP students. The survey's information is a "quick sort" mechanism that tells you who is a native-English proficient speaker, and who is not. This is your starting point. The survey

◆ is an initial bell-ringer to sort out who needs testing and who is competent enough in English to be immediately mainstreamed. For example, you do not need to waste time screening Mara when you know she comes from an English-speaking background and can be placed immediately. You can then focus your attention on Vladimir who is not fluent and needs to be screened for his capabilities.

- helps you get a lead on what resources you will need to work with the student. It gives you notice so you can begin amassing materials in the student's home language.
- helps you find out which language group to alert. For example, a school district in the Sacramento area saw the beginnings of a trend in Russian-speaking students; immediately it began to search for interpreters *before* the wave hit. This way, when the need arose, the school district already had resources to contact for translation purposes.

What does the home-language survey tell you?

The survey tells you

- your student's first language
- what language(s) the student can speak. Sometimes you can tell what nationality a student is. Sometimes you can guess their native language by their last name. Other times you can't. Michael Young might be Chinese, he might be Dutch. Ahmed Mahjour, for example, has a Persian name; his Iranian father speaks Farsi, but his mother is Japanese, and he has reached school age fluent in Japanese with only receptive proficiency in Farsi.
- how much English the student hears at home, and whether or not the English he hears at school is the extent of his exposure
- whether the student has knowledge of other languages. This information is useful when you don't have someone to interpret a student's first language. For example, you may have a student who speaks Khmer, for which you have no interpreters, but he may also speak Thai because he grew up in Thai refugee camps. When you know what other languages the student knows, you can try to find an interpreter who has some common ground.

What doesn't the home-language survey tell you?

The survey cannot reveal

- how much of any language the student knows
- which language the student is dominant in

- which language the student prefers to use
- which language the student was schooled in
- whether the student is fully proficient in English

The survey tells you what language is used at home; it doesn't tell you how it is used, by whom, for what purposes, and so on. Baker (1991) cautions:

> ...since there are large intergenerational differences in language use in immigrant groups, knowing that a child's parents or grandparents speak Spanish, for example, provides no information as to what language the child speaks. A monolingual English-speaking child could answer *yes* to the question whether someone in the home speaks a language other than English.

The wording of the questions is, therefore, important. In addition, it is critical *not* to assume the student speaks other languages that are spoken in the home. For answers to the above issues, and to determine whether or not the child is dependent on a language other than English, we must look further.

STEP 2. ASSESSING ORAL PROFICIENCY

The home-language interview

The next step in the placement procedure is to determine the language proficiency of each student. You may wish to do a home-language interview to help establish the dominant language. We adapted the questions in this interview (figure 3.2) from Malherbe (1943) who recognized the difference between the home language and the language(s) used in public, and the impact of preferences on the student's proficiency in those languages.

Figure 3.2:
Home-language
interview

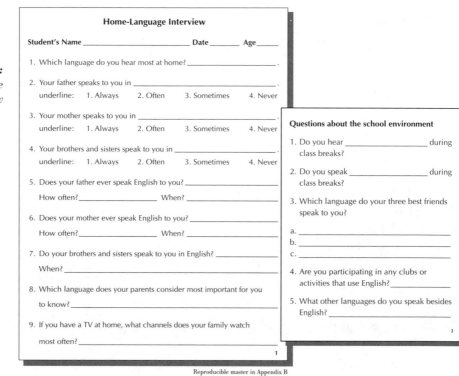

Reproducible master in Appendix B

Why is the home-language interview important?

This survey can be administered either orally or written, in English, or in the home language.

What does the home-language interview tell you?

The home-language interview will tell you

- which language the student prefers to communicate in
- which domains the student uses his language(s) in. (Samia's home language survey, for instance, revealed that she spoke Arabic as her native language, her parents spoke it exclusively to her at home, but that she had only English-speaking friends.)
- basic conflicts between parental wishes and students wishes. If Chinyeri speaks English and prefers it, but her parents are adamant about maintaining Yoruba because they intend to return home

soon, then trouble may be looming on the horizon, and you may be able to find materials to help maintain and promote her native-language learning.

What doesn't the home-language interview tell you?

It will not tell you which language the student is academically strongest in.

Oral assessment options

You want to engage students in as natural a discussion as possible. This is tricky. As Underhill (1987) notes:

> ...two people having a conversation on a topic of common interest...is also the hardest to make happen in the framework of a language test; it can only occur when both parties are relaxed and confident and something sparks between them...the oral test then reaches its highest degree of authenticity by no longer being a test.

The reality of many ESL testing situations is that they are done in an office with secretaries walking by, phones ringing in the background, and time constraints. So you need to take some steps to create a relaxed setting. Try choosing a nonthreatening environment: an office with a window that looks out onto a natural setting, or a room with few desks and nice posters, away from the hustle and bustle of the front office. When you are in the testing situation, limit your talk so students can participate and allow them time to hesitate so they can sort out what it is they are trying to say.

THE QUESTION/ANSWER FORMAT

If you know your student is no higher than an intermediate level, you may have more success with a question/answer format. Be aware that the English elicited by this method is controlled by the kind of question asked. If your student shows the potential, you can expand a question into a discussion. Underhill suggests that you start with easy questions and build to more complex ones, stopping when the student indicates that he cannot handle any more progression.

Here are a few examples of Underhill's questions, beginning with the easiest structures:

What's your name? Can you spell it?
How are you?
Tell me a little about your family.
How/where did you learn to speak English?
What will you do when you leave school today?
Can you speak any other languages?

Underhill suggests asking questions of different types (in order of ascending difficulty) to learn more about the speaker:

- Yes/no
- Tag (It's hot, isn't it?)
- Either/or (Do you take the bus or do you walk to school?)
- Simple factual (What will you do after school today?)
- Descriptive (Can you name three things in this room and tell me what they are used for?)
- Narrative (Can you tell me about your move to this country?)
- Speculative (How long do you think winter will last?)
- Hypothetical (What would you do if your house was on fire?)
- Justification of opinion (Why do you think so?)

Explore how well your student can ask you questions. Suggest the student ask you about the school routine, your family, a hobby, or something general about you. Also, observe how your student responds to your answers. Can he respond with a statement of his own? For instance, when Ben, an exchange student from Peru, was asked, "How does your mother feel about you coming here?", he grinned: "She said, 'Oh, my baby son,' and cried a lot." What the student says, how he says it, even what the student does physically (continually shifts in the chair), reveals much and gives you data to support your instincts.

STEP 3. ASSESSING LITERACY

Standardized testing options

The next step in the placement procedure is to determine the student's English language capabilities and educational background through testing. Most districts use a standardized proficiency test. A number of these tests are available to help determine the English capabilities of ESL students. The most common are the LAS (Language Assessment Scale), BINL (Basic Inventory of Natural Language), BSM (Bilingual Syntax Measure), and IPT.

Why is standardized testing important?

Even though standardized tests have major limitations, and are often misused, they can be useful:

◆ A test keeps you focused strictly on the language capabilities of the student.

◆ Using one test keeps the entire district and its schools in agreement as to what each level of proficiency is. If, for instance, Patty at Meadowview perceives that a "level one" is different from Cathy over at Riverdale, Patty may keep a student in an ESL program or a bilingual program whereas Cathy would have exited this student long ago.

◆ Programmatic decisions are tied to the level of functioning at which students enter. For instance, Brunswick East High School in Australia experienced a decline in the number of newer arrivals with little or no English, and as a result, shifted its focus and its teachers from teaching survival English to helping students succeed in academic courses. In Canada, Ottawa schools, enrolling large numbers of Somalis who are largely illiterate, are focusing their efforts on early literacy.

◆ Funding is tied to testing. These tests have everything to do with where students are ranked, what program they are placed in and whether that district is entitled to funding from outside sources or categorical programs. For instance, Ulibarri (1991) reports that the Bilingual Education Act requires that applicants for grants evaluate the achievement levels of their students by comparing their scores with standardized achievement test norms (Code of Federal Regulations, Title 34, Part 500.5 and 500.52, 1987.58).

What do standardized tests tell you?

These tests tell you, in a general way, how much English a student knows—whether he is literate, has any command of English grammar, idioms, or Western culture. Their intent is to give a *broad view* of what the student is capable of in English.

What don't standardized tests tell you?

Because they are linguistically and culturally biased, and norms may have been set for a different group, the tests will not

◆ tell you a student didn't get an answer because he doesn't know the concept, doesn't know the language, or doesn't have the content-based or cultural vocabulary

◆ give you all-important information about the strategies the student is using to gain meaning from the test. They only label right or wrong.

◆ tell you in which language the student is dominant in terms of academic skills

USING THE TESTS FOR YOUR OWN PURPOSES

One teacher in charge of assessing the new ESL students for her district told Mary that she often senses a student knows more than the standardized tests demonstrate. Our intuition raises the flags for us to further investigate. Because standardized tests do not accurately reflect what a student is capable of, it is often more instructive to watch *how* the students takes the test, and the strategies he uses to gain the information you need.

For example, Mary Marcus administered a test to a small boy named Hue. (She reports that during their five-year acquaintance she has learned never to ask questions such as "Who does this belong to?" Or "Who wants to erase the chalkboard?")

Mary gave the test at her house. After a tour of the house and a trip through what he observed was her "very messy" basement, Hue took the LAS Reading and Writing Assessment 2B (see figure 3.3). He had no trouble understanding the instructions to the test. Mary noticed that he understood punctuation, but had trouble with *s* and *ly* endings. He achieved a total score of 78, "Limited Reader/ Limited Writer," but as she watched him take the reading section she saw that he was able to

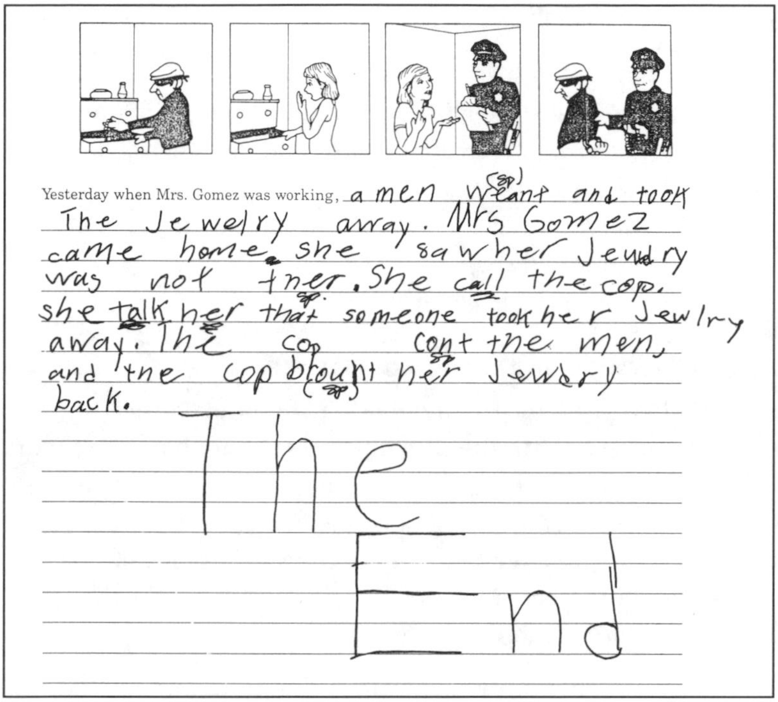

Yesterday when Mrs. Gomez was working, *a men weant and took The Jewelry away. Mrs Gomez came home, she sawher Jewdry was not tner. She call the cop. she talk her that someone took her Jewlry away. The cop cont the men, and the cop brount her Jewbry back.*

The End

Figure 3.3:
Hue's writing
sample

look back at the story for information—a useful and important strategy. He also announced that he was going to guess on some questions; those lucky guesses brought up his score. When he was just about done with the reading section, he asked, "When I finish this, am I done?" Mary explained that there was another section and he grinned, "Oh, me and my big mouth!" His huge *The End* at the close of his writing shows not only that he was tired, but that he is familiar with English "story grammar." His spelling errors, lack of past tense, and word endings lowered his writing score. Afterwards, Mary let Hue and his sister Zoua play the piano. When Zoua complained of the noise and asked why he was thundering so loud, he said, "To make your life miserable." Mary took them to Pizza Hut afterwards, an experience he had never had before, and a situation in which he was clearly uncomfortable. He would not take off his jacket, and asked if they could eat in the car. When the waitress was slow, he wondered if they could just call out "Waiter! Waiter!" so they would be served quickly.

Aside from the "official" test results, Mary learned

- Hue is familiar with test situations
- he has several useful strategies for getting meaning from text
- he does not perceive or hear many word endings, such as tense, plural, and adverbial endings
- his oral command of English is much stronger than the contrived testing situation would suggest
- he can write a story using correct sequencing

LEARNING MORE: NARROWING THE FIELD

As tests are often given by personnel other than the teacher who is going to work directly with the student, you may not have the luxury Mary Marcus had in watching Hue. (She also had the advantage of a good relationship with him, and a comfortable testing situation.) Hue's score of 78—limited reader and limited writer—is not very helpful for the receiving teacher. A teacher also needs to know the following information about a student:

- his ability to communicate in different situations and contexts
- his reading strategies
- his ability to write using English conventions
- his ability to organize prose
- his command of grammar
- language he is most comfortable with academically

STEP 4. DETERMINING PRIMARY-LANGUAGE LITERACY

Home-language literacy

Determining the student's literacy in the home language provides further valuable information about his background. If the student is literate in the home language, it is a safe bet he will be able to transfer those skills to the second language. You are also able to learn what the student can do when lack of proficiency in the English language is not an interference. The student can demonstrate what he or she has learned up to this point in the content area; this provides the classroom teacher with a starting point to begin instruction.

Judy Lewis of Sacramento tries to assess all incoming students in their dominant languages. She learns volumes just observing the students take the test. The Folsom Cordova School District uses this prompt:

> **Write an essay or story of at least ten sentences in your primary language. Choose one of these topics:**
>
>   **A. My best friend**
>
>   **B. Coming to America**
>
>   **C. Things that are green**

These topics could, admittedly, be criticized because they are not whole language or contextual, but they do give a broad view of the student's capabilities. We want to know if he is literate. The strengths of this test are: (1) it is a relatively simple task to get this translated into other languages because it is short and to the point; (2) you do not need to be proficient in that language to note whether the student is literate or not; and (3) you can quickly establish whether the student is literate, of limited literacy, or nonliterate in his own language. Even if you don't have a particular language translated, you can make a determination based on how the student responds to a paper-and-pencil task.

For example, Thanousi arrives. Judy has no formal tests translated into Lao, so she gives him a piece of paper and, through gestures, asks him to write a short sample in Lao. He takes the pencil tentatively and holds it awkwardly. After much hesitation he scrawls a few symbols. The simple maxim, "If he can write, he can read," applied to Thanousi. Thus, even though she can't read what he wrote, Judy knows that he is a beginner in literacy in his own language. She is also certain he will not be able to read or write in English. She can make a confident placement based on this very basic test.

Figure 3.4:
Informal
questionnaire for
primary-language
literacy assessment

The Primary-Language Literacy Test

If you know that a student can read and write in his language, you can gather more concrete evidence from the questionnaire in figure 3.4, adapted from the San Francisco School District.

Primary-Language Literacy Questionnaire

Student's name _____ Date _____ Age _____

Primary Language _____

Interviewee's name _____ Relationship to student _____

1. How many years of formal education has the student completed

   in _____ ? Number of Years _____
            Country of origin

2. What language was used for instruction? _____

3. How long has it been since the student received instruction in the

   primary language? _____

4. Did your child attend school in another country while en route to the

   United States?   No _____ Yes _____

   If yes, which country? _____ How long? _____

   Language of instruction _____

5. Does your child read books in his own language at home? No _____ Yes _____

6. How well does your child read compared to other children of his age?

   (a) very well   (b) the same as   (c) not as well

   (d) cannot read   (e) don't know

7. Does your child write to friends or relatives?   Yes _____ No _____

   In what language? _____

8. How well does your child write compared to other children his age?

   (a) very well   (b) the same as   (c) not as well

   (d) cannot write   (e) don't know

Reproducible master in Appendix B

Higher-level measures of literacy

There are several other options that give you a fairly accurate sample of a student's ability to read and write. These consist of cloze tests and writing samples. Tests that simply have students fill in blanks or answer questions do not give you as much insight into the student's actual performance capabilities in reading and writing as does just asking them to read and write. Finding out how much they are capable of producing, and how difficult a passage of text they are able to understand, gives you more focus on what level they are operating at.

CLOZE TESTS

Cloze tests consist of small passages of text from which a set number of words, such as every fifth, seventh or tenth, have been deleted. Students read the text, then fill in each blank with an appropriate word (see figure 3.5). This is a higher level test, not for beginning readers or for real newcomers; eliminating words from a passage makes it substantially more difficult, demanding a certain level of proficiency in reading. Cloze tests provide a window into the strategies the student is using to gain meaning, as well as insight into how sophisticated his skill level in English is. Some commercial cloze tests, such as the Boston Cloze, allow only one answer. However, there are a range of answers that are syntactically or semantically correct. Again, "right" answers alone do not give insight into the test takers' thinking process. In addition, errors in tense, incorrect spelling, and using the wrong part of speech, such as adjectives instead of adverbs, do not make an answer wrong; these are issues separate from comprehension.

After you have corrected the test, an effective strategy is to review it with the student to find out why he made the choices he made.

Figure 3.5:
Cloze test

Story 5

For a long time television seemed to be a world of men. But it's not that way now. ~~men~~ and more women are working in _groups_.

Dee Morales is a TV news _statin_ in charge of a big city _Quality_ beat.

If something big is about _to_ happen, someone calls to tell her _about_ it. She must then try to _write_ out the details, either in a _an_ interview or videotaped for later broadcast. _Writer_ will tell you it's not always _good_ to get enough information because some _people_ don't want to say much, especially _when_ a reporter with a television news _camera_. So in Dee's job, getting along _with_ people is as important as getting _The_ story. If people like her, she _has_ a better chance of getting the _stories_.

Even though there are not many women working in television, more and more are training to work in a TV career.

Holistic measures of writing

More and more, standardized tests are including writing as a portion of their test. This is because a writing sample gives you a good look at a student's productive proficiency and grasp of English syntax, vocabulary and conventions, and organizational skills. The choice of topics should ideally be a genuine response to a subject he has an interest in or experience with. In Appendix A, page 281, we give a rubric for scoring. Figure 3.6 is one example of student work.

- -

Figure 3.6:
Student writing
sample

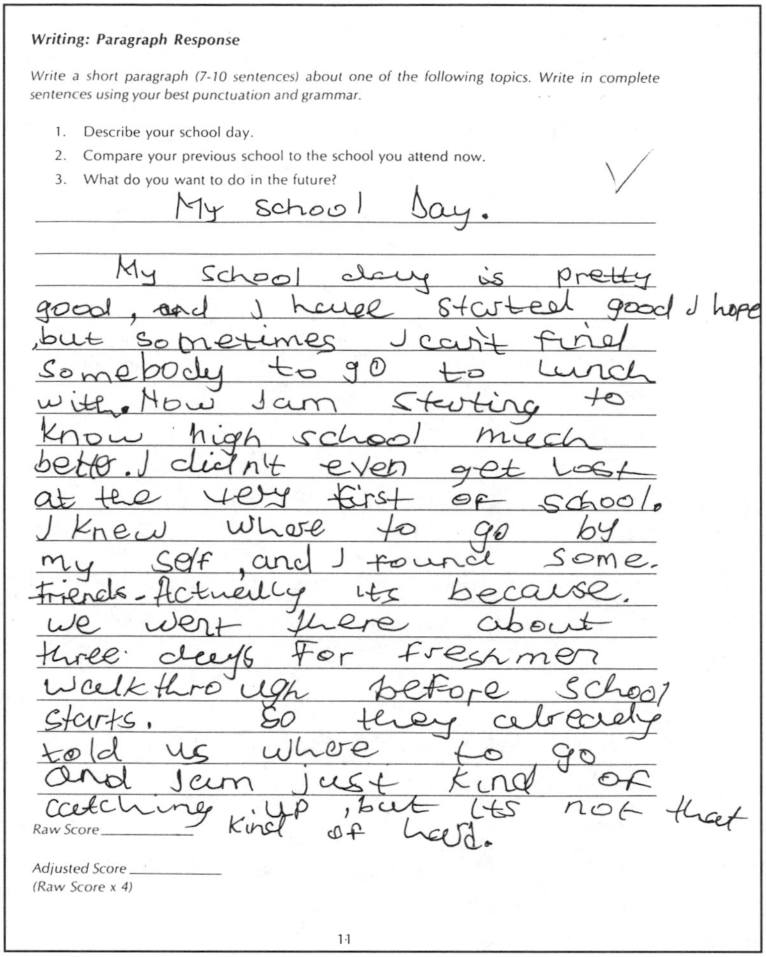

Writing: Paragraph Response

Write a short paragraph (7-10 sentences) about one of the following topics. Write in complete
sentences using your best punctuation and grammar.

1. Describe your school day.
2. Compare your previous school to the school you attend now.
3. What do you want to do in the future?   ✓

My school Day.

My school day is pretty
good, and I have started good I hope
, but sometimes I can't find
somebody to go to lunch
with. Now I am starting to
know high school much
better. I didn't even get lost
at the very first of school.
I knew where to go by
my self, and I found some.
friends. Actually its because.
we went there about
three days for freshmen
walkthrough before school
starts. So they already
told us where to go
and I am just kind of
catching up, but its not that

Raw Score_____ kind of hard.

Adjusted Score_____
(Raw Score x 4)

11

You may, in addition, want to see how much information a student
can extract from a text. On the following page are two examples of
student responses to a small selection from the *Autobiography of
Malcolm X.*

Response Sheet for Malcolm X Essay

Figure 3.7:
Student responses

Name

1. Read the essay.

2. Describe as carefully and completely as you can, the significant point or points Malcolm X is making in this essay.

3. As carefully and completely as you can, write about whatever in the article is significant to you. Be sure to explain why it is important or significant.

2: The best way to study and learn some words is to get hold of a dictionary that is like a miniature encyclopedia.

3. As carefully and completely as you can, write about whatever in the article is significant to you. Be sure to explain why it is important or significant.

2) I think he wants to show us the important to be decide in our lifes; if we really want to do something we can do it, no matter what is the problem.

3) Is important to me see how a man who wor frustated to write or to express, doesn't bogged dou or lost his way; he keep doing the things well, no matter if is in the jail he found the right way to learn. It was copying, reading and thinking about those words in the dictionary.

STEP 5. TENTATIVE PLACEMENT IN THE PROPER GRADE

The reality of the placement issue is that it is often rooted in the hazy realms of intuition or judgment calls. Even states such as Illinois, whose administrative code requires "each student who scores below the fiftieth percentile on [a test of reading and writing proficiency] shall be considered as having limited English proficiency," (Illinois CH. I, S.228.15) cannot, according to Ulibarri (1991), be assured that

- teachers know what students know and can do
- what students' true percentile is
- how best to teach them
- a student will be successful in a mainstream classroom if he achieves above the fiftieth percentile and is therefore ineligible for services

Successful programs take the following issues into consideration:

- **The student.** Age is a primary consideration. The student can be placed up or down a year depending on literacy, maturity, and educational experience. These factors provide the basis for the next level of decision making.

- **The resources available,** including
  - *Programs.* A school system with a number of programs and options for ESL students obviously will have more options to consider. Basically the school can choose a bilingual program, ESL pull-out, sheltered English, immersion, and so on.
  - *Numbers.* How many students of a particular language background attending the school and program will affect the resources invested.
  - *Personnel.* Coordinators also take into account how experienced the teacher is at working with ESL kids; how impacted the school and classroom are; how receptive (or potentially hostile) the classroom teacher is in working with ESL students.

Placement Scenarios: Three Students

To illustrate the assessment and placement procedures as well as the real dilemmas that greet teachers, we use three hypothetical students in a town we'll call Elizabeth Arbor. Elizabeth Arbor is a moderate-sized city, which has experienced a steady number of newcomers over the years. The school district has two ESL teachers who serve nine schools at the elementary level, a bilingual Spanish program, and a half-time ESL teacher at the middle school where all middle schoolers and high schoolers are bused for ESL.

The three students are Boris, Elsie, and May. We are attempting to demonstrate that the choices teachers often make are not good choices, but choices they are forced to make in the real world when school districts do not have a program or a plan.

BORIS

Boris, seventeen, and his father show up at the principal's office unannounced, and since Eloise, the ESL teacher, is teaching her home economics class, the secretary has them fill out a home-language survey (HLS) (see page 57).

His HLS reveals Boris was born in Russia, learned Russian as a child, and his parents speak Russian exclusively to him.

When Eloise arrives, she asks Boris to take some tests. His father says, "I'm not really sure that's necessary." Upon questioning, his father reveals he is an engineer in a local firm who emigrated from Moscow. The family speaks English fluently. Boris's parents, who want him to retain his Russian, have imposed the rule that only Russian be spoken on the weekends when all are home together. Eloise decides to abandon her agenda of formal testing and, instead, asks Boris a few questions. He is at ease, slightly cocky, and sits back in his chair with his arm dangling casually over the back.

ELOISE: Were winters pretty hard back where you grew up?

BORIS: Well, it got below zero Fahrenheit by November. So I'm pretty used to the cold.

ELOISE: What kinds of things did you study in your last school?

BORIS: Everything. I think this school will be too easy for me.

ELOISE: What kinds of things do you like to do for fun?

BORIS: I like soccer. I'm pretty great at it. I was captain of my team.

ELOISE: Would you like to ask me some questions?

BORIS: I heard the soccer team here really sucks.

Boris's main problem seems to be a rather large chip on his shoulder. Although he has a marked accent, his English is decidedly fluent, even colloquial.

Boris has brought with him a cumulative file of his school records. Eloise consults *The Country Index: Interpretations for Use in the Evaluation of Foreign Educations Credentials* (1986) to determine whether the courses he has taken in his country are equivalent to the required courses at this school. Most of them are, but he still must take U.S. history, civics, family life education, as well as several math and science courses. She suggests a course or two at the grade-nine level in English, but his father objects; he insists that Boris can handle higher level requirements.

In response to a writing prompt, "What are your goals in life?" Boris writes a rather poignant essay that gives Eloise a clear view not only of his capabilities, but of Boris himself:

> Our life is a very short period of time given to us by God and probably everyone drims about a better place in it.
>
> Everyone has the right to be born and to die, but people who are born in the state of Russia seem to be extraordinary because from their birth, these rights were taken off them by the leading group of the country. And then appears the feeling of struggle, struggle for just a normal human being existance, for just a quiet, peaceful life and love. And that straggle continues all their life. They suffer a lot, they seem to be heroes for themselves, but their shout is a shout in silence of dark system.
>
> As to me, I always was one of these and straggled a lot for reaching a better life, I and my father, and he did everything possible in order to overcome all the difficulties in order our dream came true. He did a lot for that, he seemed to be a silent hero for himself. He overcame all the tense relations with officials, sometimes with close people that refused to understand us, but we saw the right of our purpose ahead of us and in spite of all opsticals we went to it and now we are here.
>
> Now I have another goal in my life—to occupy a better place in a social staircase of American society and to be happy man and citizen of this country.

Eloise wants to be sure that Boris can read content at grade level, so she gives him the Malcolm X selection. Here is his answer:

> So I have read Malcolm X essay and I can say that I completely agreed with his point of view. They are a lot of examples that can tell us how people have changed of reading books. I think he had done a good job. Also it

was very difficult. But I can say I found this article very interesting. When I read this article I finded his way of learning very alike to me. I know that people can have different ways of memory. For me it is very similar because I always learn words in such a way. I find it more progressive. Another point is that the author wanted to say that if you want to do something (to learn, to get job, to have interesting life,) you must always try to do this, even if it will be difficult for you. And I think the third thing is that all the time when he saw that he made progress, he got more real to do it more, to make higher his knowledge.

As a result of the writing sample, Eloise can see that she has a student who can write not only capably, but with power and passion and the ability to move his reader. This is more than we see in many of our English-speaking students. Boris is a young man with a superior grasp of English and real abilities. In addition, he can read for information and articulate the important ideas in a reading selection. Eloise decides that mainstreaming is the best choice.

MAY

May is fifteen and in the tenth grade when she arrives in Elizabeth Arbor. May's parents speak no English, so when she arrives with her four elementary-age siblings and three cousins, she acts as spokesperson. Since the parents can not fill out the HLS, another version, which directs questions to the student, is administered.

Eloise had advance warning that these students were coming, and since their last name was Laotian, she had attempted, unsuccessfully, to find a Laotian interpreter. To her surprise, they all answer that their first language was Hmong. (Unless an interpreter could speak Hmong as well as Lao, he would have been useless. In addition, attempting to amass materials in Lao would have been a mistake.) May explains that their grandfather had been a freedom fighter for the French and had taken a Laotian name.

Eloise gives May a home-language interview (see figure 3.8) followed by several questions about the school environment.

Figure 3.8a:
Part one of
May's home-
language
interview

Home-Language Interview

Student's Name ___May___ Date _Feb. 14/95_ Age _15_

1. Which language do you hear most at home? _Hmong_ .

2. Your father speaks to you in _Hmong_ .
   underline: 1. Always   2. Often   3. Sometimes   4. Never

3. Your mother speaks to you in _Hmong_ .
   underline: 1. Always   2. Often   3. Sometimes   4. Never

4. Your brothers and sisters speak to you in _English_ .
   underline: 1. Always   2. Often   3. Sometimes   4. Never

5. Does your father ever speak English to you? _No_
   How often? _____   When? _____

6. Does your mother ever speak English to you? _No_
   How often? _____   When? _____

7. Do your brothers and sisters speak to you in English? _Yes_
   When? _All the time_

8. Which language does your parents consider most important for you to know? _English_

9. If you have a TV at home, what channels does your family watch most often? _8, 5, 12_

1

Although she speaks it almost exclusively to her parents, May's answers reveal she is more comfortable speaking English than Hmong. May spent several years in a camp in Thailand and was taught some basic English. Then, once she arrived in the country five years ago, she received ESL training.

Eloise administers the IPT and the LAS, which rate her as "limited proficiency."

Eloise reads May the fable *The Crow and the Pitcher* and asks her to retell the story. May's response is, "He's looking for water...she...He saw a pitcher looked like a water. Find water...He drink he go...She go." This tells Eloise she understood at least part of the story, even if she was not able to articulate what the crow did to get water.

Questions about the school environment

1. Do you hear ___*English*___ during class breaks? *Yes*

2. Do you speak ___*English*___ during class breaks? *Yes*

3. Which language do your three best friends speak to you?
   a. ___*English*___
   b. ___*English*___
   c. ___*English*___

4. Are you participating in any clubs or activities that use English? ___*Yes*___

5. What other languages do you speak besides English? ___*Hmong and Thai*___

Eloise gives May the Boston Cloze Test (see figure 3.9). She partially finishes the first story, then gives up, saying it's too hard. The first story is at an instructional level of second grade.

May's answers show comprehension. Each blank, although not technically correct, shows logic and understanding. For instance, in blank one she inserted a verb; *then* is not correct, but fits syntactically and semantically.

Figure 3.8b: Part two of May's home-language interview

Once a family of ants lived on a hillside. The ants were very busy. They _were_ good care of the baby ants, _Then_ they stored up food for the _Winter_. Nearby in a grassy field there _____ a grasshopper. He never worked. All _____ long he played happily. When he _____ the ants hard at work, he _____, "Why do you all work so _long_ ?" "_____ must get ready for winter when _snow_ is on the ground. We cannot _get_ food then." "I have never gone _____ yet," said the grasshopper. Then he _go_ away. "You'll be sorry when it _____ too late", said the family of _ants_. By and by winter came. The _ants_ were very cold, the long grass _____ stiff with frost. The ants ran _inside_ their house and shut the door. The grasshopper could not find any food so he was hungry all winter.

Figure 3.9: May's cloze test

Eloise gives May some dictation sentences at the third-fourth and fifth-sixth grade levels (figure 3.10):

> When we go to the zoo/ we always see a lot of monkeys. / Last week we went on a field trip / to the zoo. / We decided to count the monkeys./ We counted 37 of them.

> Thomas Edison was a very smart person./ When he was a little boy/ he was very curious./ His parents often got mad at him / because he would take things apart / to find out how they worked.

These demonstrate that she had instruction in sound/spelling correspondence because she sounded out the words as she spelled them.

Figure 3.10:
May's dictation

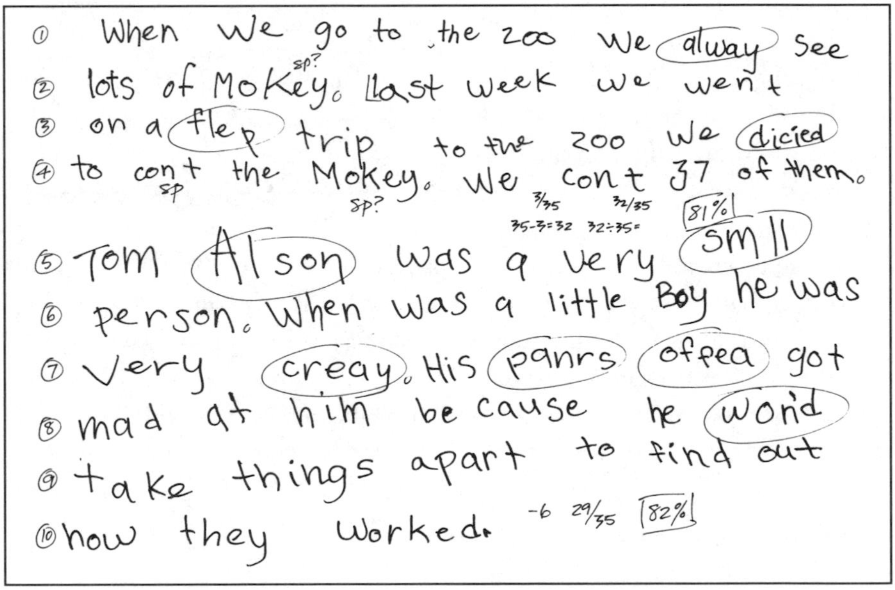

Eloise then gives May a writing topic: her first day of school.

The writing sample (figure 3.11) shows that her knowledge of grammar and sentence structure is limited and her organization meanders. She is writing at an elementary level, not at the level one can expect of a tenth grader in the regular curriculum.

> I Happy to have school I like school very very much I wish we will have school all the time always When I get to school I have school Mate and shoes on and skool on. and take bath very day whe I come to school and brsh my hair too and put closeing on then the morning I put eury thing on me I walk to school.

Figure 3.11: May's writing sample

From these samples, Eloise can see that May is reading and writing at a very low level, between second and fourth grade. For Eloise this creates a dilemma about where to place May.

The state in which they live has clearly delineated levels, which solve many programmatic and instructional issues:

Level I: Does not understand or speak English

Level II: Understands simple sentence in English, but uses only isolated words or expressions in English

Level III: Speaks English with difficulty, converses in English with help, understands at least parts of lessons and follows simple directions given in English

Level IV: Understands, speaks, reads, and writes English with some degree of hesitancy which may be due to language interference because of a foreign language or nonproficient English spoken at home.

Level V: Understands and speaks English well, but needs assistance in reading and writing in English to achieve at a level appropriate for his age or grade.

According to these levels, May is at a low Level III. If they had lived in a city where there was a fully developed program, with instruction at all levels, Eloise could have placed May in content-area classes geared to her level of functioning. But in this town, Eloise herself is the only ESL teacher at the upper levels. In reviewing her transcripts, Eloise finds that May had sheltered classes in biology and history at the beginning literacy level. She had taken no mainstream courses except for art and music and has finished most of those requirements for graduation. What's left are the "heavy-duty" content courses of government, history, science, and English.

Eloise consults the counsellor, Carol, who recommends what most students call "flunky English." But Eloise knows that plowing through *Tess of the D'Urbervilles* is not what May needs. She doesn't have the proficiency in reading or writing to benefit from a class for regular English-speaking students. She needs lots of work focusing on literacy skills.

"But what about college?" protests Carol.

Eloise has witnessed this problem before. The school system professes to want all students to go to college, but everybody knows that students like May are going to take much longer than the years allotted to make it, if at all. It's going to take May much longer to acquire the level of proficiency to function and compete at the level the district expects of its students. What she needs is time, and time is what she hasn't got in the regular school system. College is an unrealistic goal, and typically the school has "bailed out" in terms of responsibility by giving up when it comes to students like May.

Statistics show that many schools place such students in special education classes. There have been many lawsuits in the higher courts about this phenomenon. But Eloise considers it carefully because for May this would mean what it has meant to all other students in her situation: small classes and attention to her individual needs. In the end she abandons the idea, because although special education teachers do know how to adapt curriculum to the needs of special students, the teacher in this district does not know about the problems and issues of working with ESL students. In addition, Eloise knows that what May needs is meaning-based language activities. Her problems are related more to gaps in her knowledge base, not to disabilities inherent in herself. Eloise also decides that the potential risks of special education outweigh the possible benefits.

Eloise is troubled about where to place May and her cousins, who also test in about the same range. She knows that, realistically, the school system, even though well meaning and concerned, is not about to mount a special program and hire teachers until the number of students at this level of proficiency and literacy reaches a critical mass. Therefore she has to cope with them herself.

Eloise has not had experience with this low level of literacy before either. She decides to get help, and calls a school system in Ontario to get advice. Verna and Helen, administrators there, are very helpful. With their help, Eloise can think her way through to realistic goals for May.

The two main goals for May are: (1) to develop her skills so that her limited proficiency won't be a barrier to achieving her own personal goals; and (2) to help her acquire the basic academic skills for continuing her education beyond high school if she chooses to do so. With those goals in mind, Eloise elects to schedule May for as much ESL help as possible, as well as time with the reading specialist. She finds a buddy to tutor her in study hall, and schedules her for health, computers, and home economics. She has to choose a course that has expectations that are neither too high nor too low for a girl who arrives at the eleventh hour.

ELSIE

We discussed Elsie at the beginning of the chapter. Elsie and her siblings, Daniel and Martha, arrived from Ethiopia at the middle school, and Barb had to make an on-the-spot decision about placement. Since Elsie's story has haunted Barb for so many years, and since the issues and problems confronting the school were so complex, we decided to recreate Elsie and a "what-we-might-have-done-if-we'd-known-more" scenario. There are no "what-ifs" in the real world, and there is no turning back the clock to straighten out a life that's taken a wrong turn. Her unfortunate story is a combination of a lack of knowledge on the part of the school system, a profoundly disrupted school and home life, and a small girl who would not or could not take ownership of her own learning.

In our re-creation, however, the first step in the placement process is a home-language survey (see page 57).

The IPT is administered to Elsie. She responds correctly to only two questions: her age (in a barely audible whisper) and the word *banana* when shown a picture. The test registers Elsie as NEP. Had Eloise accepted the results, she would have concluded Elsie did not know the English words for *mother, clock, foot, bunny,* and so on, or that she did not yet understand simple English instructions, such as "Put the pencil on the table" or "Raise your hand." (Daniel and Martha breeze through the IPT, and place quite high in reading and writing. The test indicates that they need assistance, but they are ready to tackle many of the classroom tasks.) Eloise tentatively follows Elsie's father's wishes and places Daniel and Martha in seventh and eighth grade.

Eloise speaks to the father in an attempt to learn more about Elsie's schooling background. She finds out he had been in Oklahoma studying when Daniel and Martha were preschoolers, and so they had all learned English. Then they returned to Ethiopia. Daniel and Martha had a good start in their formal schooling and learned to read and write in their own language. When Elsie was just beginning school, fighting broke out. Her formal education was disrupted, and much of her schooling consisted of marching and singing patriotic songs. Several times they had to flee their home. Their mother was still in Ethiopia, literally held hostage to ensure the father's return.

Elsie's father fills out a primary-language literacy questionnaire so Eloise can have a better idea of Elsie's background (see figure 3.12).

Later, Eloise goes to the Kebede's apartment and starts with some very basic testing. She uses an oral interview, a dictation, and the Test of Print Knowledge (an assessment designed to reveal what learners know about literacy materials).

The oral interview is not very revealing. It's hard to tell whether Elsie doesn't know or is just extremely shy. For instance:

ELOISE: What will you do after school today?

ELSIE: Play.

ELOISE: What would you do in case of a fire in your home?

ELSIE: I don't know.

Primary-Language Literacy Questionnaire

Student's name _Elsie Kebede_   Date _Oct. 9/95_   Age _11_

Primary Language _Amharic_

Interviewee's name _Mr. Kebede_   Relationship to student _father_

1. How many years of formal education has the student completed

   in _Ethiopia_ ? Number of Years _three_
         Country of origin

2. What language was used for instruction? _Amharic_

3. How long has it been since the student received instruction in the

   primary language? _6 months_

4. Did your child attend school in another country while en route to the

   United States?   No ✔   Yes _____

   If yes, which country? _____   How long? _____

   Language of instruction _____

5. Does your child read books in his own language at home?   No ✔ Yes _____

6. How well does your child read compared to other children of his age?

   (a) very well   (b) the same as   (c) not as well

   (d) cannot read   (e) don't know

7. Does your child write to friends or relatives?   Yes _____   No ✔

   In what language? _____

8. How well does your child write compared to other children his age?

   (a) very well   (b) the same as   (c) not as well

   (d) cannot write   (e) don't know

ELOISE: How did you get to school this morning.

ELSIE: Bus.

ELOISE: Tell me how to get to your house from school.

ELSIE: Close to school.

Figure 3.12:
Elsie's primary-language literacy assessment

With her father translating to be sure that Elsie understands the questions, and the test actually checking her skills, not her English, the Concepts About Print test (Clay 1979) is very revealing. We have reproduced a large part of Elsie's test here:

ELOISE (*Showing her the book*): What's this called?

ELSIE (*Tentatively*): Book.

ELOISE: What do you do with it?

ELSIE: Read it.

ELOISE: What's inside it?

ELSIE (*After a long delay*): Letters, picture.

ELOISE (*Gives Elsie the book upside down*): Show me the front of the book. (*Elsie finds the front cover and turns it right side up.*) Show me a page in this book. (*Elsie points to a page.*) Read this page to me. (*Elsie shakes her head. Even with encouragement from her father she won't attempt it. Elsie is able to show the top and the bottom of the page, and the exact place where Eloise should begin reading, and which direction Eloise should move her eyes as she reads the page.*) Now I want you to point to the story as I read the page to you.

Up until this point Elsie has been doing fine. However, as Eloise begins to read, she sees that Elsie is not matching the spoken word with the written word. She moves her finger smoothly across the lines on the page, not noticing that her finger is not on the correct word. She is finished sweeping her finger across and down the page before Eloise has completed reading the second line.

This tells Eloise that Elsie understands that print has meaning, and knows how to use a book, but is not at the stage yet where she is actually looking at the words. She has not "connected" the print to the meaning yet. This means that she is still an emerging reader. She has a long way to go before she can begin work at the sixth grade level.

Eloise now has to decide whether to place Elsie in the middle school or to place her at the elementary level. The district has an early-exit bilingual program for the Spanish-speaking population located at three of the elementary schools in the district; this is a good program, but Elsie doesn't speak Spanish, so Eloise needs to look elsewhere. There are interpreters and tutors for Spanish, Japanese, and Vietnamese, but not, to anyone's knowledge, for Amharic.

The closest elementary school is Lange Street Elementary. There are three fifth-grade classes. One is a split-contract fifth, with two teachers each working half-time. One of the teachers has taught sheltered English before in pull-out classes; but she is pregnant and will be on maternity leave beginning in December. Her partner is a good enthusiastic teacher, but this is her first year teaching.

The second fifth-grade teacher here has an excellent reputation. He is a creative individual and has had great results with the mainstreamed students. He has no ESL experience and already has enough students. His hands are full as he has a number of special day students and a few students with challenging home problems.

The third fifth-grade teacher is low on the list of options for fifth grade. She is ready to retire at the end of the year and has made it known she is not taking on any new challenges. She really does not have the experience or the flexibility for someone like Elsie.

Austin Elwin Elementary, located within walking distance of the middle school, has a combination of East Asian and Latino students, so teachers are experienced. The itinerant ESL teacher provides pull-out ESL classes and newcomer initiation for the NEP and LEP students.

Another choice is Rowland Elementary, eight miles southeast of the middle school. This school has two Latino students and one from Eastern Europe. The ESL teacher, with her heavy schedule, may make it there three times a week for an hour. However, this site has a fifth-grade teacher who has had LEP students in the past. He has a great reputation and is receptive to taking on a student like Elsie.

Meyer Middle School covers sixth through eighth grades. There are seven period classes so the school has begun to provide a few sheltered-English classes for the LEP students. These consist of content classes (science, math, and so on) organized for non-English-proficient students and designed to teach the language an content concurrently. The eighth-grade science teacher is teaching life science, and Eloise is teaching two sheltered-English language arts classes. These are not too large (some fifteen students), and she could provide support for Elsie at the middle school level. Elsie would be attending the same school as her brother and sister. They would provide some emotional security for her, as well as help with translating, if needed.

Faced with these choices, Eloise knew that there are no clear answers to proper placement. It all boils down to priorities. Proper placement is critical and each placement must be made according to the specific needs of the student.

The drawbacks to placing Elsie in the middle school are her young age and the sheer intensity and immensity of a seven-period day; handling all the content classes may be overwhelming. The sheltered English may be helpful for Elsie, but the language and content may be too difficult. Elsie still needs many basics; sheltered English is really designed to make content classes more understandable. If Elsie was in this class, the teacher would have to spend a good deal of her time trying to fill in all the gaps, which is not the intent of a sheltered class.

Eloise decides to place Elsie in Austin Elwin Elementary. That extra year at the elementary level will give Elsie much needed time to catch up with her peers. It could provide the individualized services that Elsie will so desperately need. The school is not too far from Elsie's siblings, so she can ride the bus with them before and after school. It is a drawback that she will be removed from class for some of her day. She will, however, still have time in the classroom, and if she is going to make the strides she needs to before middle school, time is of the essence. The experience of the staff, plus the possibility of a newcomer program, seem to outweigh all the other advantages of the other schools. Elsie has much ground to gain not only in English, but in content and literacy. As well, with Elsie testing NEP, she would be eligible for tutoring; someone would be hired to help implement what the teachers set up for her. Because the dropout rate is so high among secondary students who have a weak educational background, Eloise feels that the extra elementary year tailored specifically to Elsie's needs will be the best for her.

No environment has the perfect solution. Once the pros and cons are judged, the school *and* the parents need to decide the best placement situation. This means the parents' priorities and issues must also be carefully considered.

STEP 6. FOLLOW-UP ASSESSMENT

Tests often show the student's abilities to be lower than they actually are (as, for example, with Elsie). For one thing, many new students are nervous in a testing situation. They may not even attempt to answer questions if they are not certain of the answer. For writing samples, they may write as little as possible because they are afraid of making mistakes.

It is important, therefore, that the teacher testing the student keeps in touch with the classroom teacher *after* the placement is made to ensure the placement and support procedures are appropriate for the student's needs. All too often, the student gets placed and forgotten.

Mary interviewed students in a school with few ESL students. One of the students being tutored in English, Tomas, tested NEP on the IDEA proficiency test. After a few weeks, it was evident that he was more proficient in English than the test reflected. He was capable of staying with his grade for some of the content classes, but because of the official NEP status, his program was never reassessed. Much to the chagrin of the ESL teacher, he was even pulled out of the content classes that she was sure he could succeed in.

SECONDARY PLACEMENT DILEMMAS

More and more, secondary schools are getting ESL students with little English and little literacy/content background. These schools are experiencing frustration and confusion. The issues of placing an ESL student at the secondary level are complex. The school must juggle a variety of schedules, teachers, classes, credits, competencies, and so on (for example, finding a class for Geraldo at first period, then making sure the ESL teacher is available at a certain time so he won't miss his only math class by going to ESL).

According to Berman and Weiler (1992):

> **The departmentalization of most secondary-school faculty and content areas has major repercussions for the programs of LEP students...no one is in charge of a comprehensive approach to LEP student programming...The impact of the nature of secondary programs on LEP**

**students is that many students do not receive instruction in academic
content areas. This limits their ability to graduate (by not meeting course
requirements), go to college, or be prepared for employment opportunities. School staffers feel that many LEP students drop out of secondary
school.**

While no school has hit on any one "magical" solution to the problem
of placement, some new methods for coping are being tried. For
example, some schools allow ESL students a year longer to complete
their requirements; others coordinate the curriculum with that of the
adult education program, so ESL students can continue to earn their
credits in the evening. Saturday schools, intersession classes, five-year
programs, and summer schools are providing some options. Some
districts are allowing students to enroll in high school up to the age
of twenty-one (and some teachers, without announcing, have enrolled
students older than that) because there are no other options for them.
Finding the answer for your school or district takes strong leadership
and commitment from everyone.

The solutions for accommodating secondary ESL students are new
because until recently, most secondary schools simply did not have to
cope to the degree that they must today. ESL students were largely
confined to the elementary schools and the higher grades were able
to "get by." Now these schools must find creative, workable answers
to the growing numbers of ESL students in middle and high schools.
Ignoring this problem means that a large number of students fall
through the cracks and eventually drop out, which is exactly what
Elsie did by the time she reached the ninth grade. Everyone involved
must see the writing on the wall and find ways to make placement
work for their population. This takes strong leadership, from the
administrative levels through all personnel at the school site. Everyone must accept these students as their responsibility. This means
devising creative approaches to the schedules and finding new ways
to make the system work.

CONCLUSION

Placement procedures need to be clearly defined so that no matter what kind of situation exists in your district, you are prepared to deal with the incoming ESL students efficiently and humanely. The plan needs to be agreed upon by all the levels of personnel so everyone knows the who, what, and where of the procedure. Most important, all members of the team—from the administration, the teachers, through to the office personnel—share the responsibility of helping the student make the transition to English. The placement procedure depends on all levels working as team. Communication and knowledge of available resources are critical before an informed and logical decision can be made.

Proper placement is one of *the* most critical issues facing schools today. When the students are in the best place possible for them and there is care and concern that they succeed and improve, then the school's ultimate goal—to educate all—is met. When all levels aim to place the student where success is most possible, then success is likely. However, the opposite is also true. When placement is haphazard and no one takes responsibility to foster the student's success, then the likelihood of the student falling through the cracks and eventually dropping out is far, far greater.

Our aim is to prepare all students to participate fully in our society. This goal can appear to be overwhelmingly idealistic when we come up against the realities of the students we serve. That is why a clear, unified plan, supported by the staff, is the best hope for meeting the challenge.

4

We're Working Hardly:
EMERGING LITERACY

This chapter deals with the first step in assessment—how to look at the broad view of the learning environment: the student, the context, and the language learning continuum itself.

In this chapter we

◆ discuss the importance of context
◆ discuss the concept of emergence
◆ demonstrate the levels of emerging proficiency and literacy
◆ show examples of student work
◆ suggest activities to enhance each level of emerging proficiency and literacy

Miss Nguyen is the bilingual teacher at Sherwood Park School. She has forty children of non-English-speaking background. Most are Vietnamese, but recently several Russian children have enrolled in the school, and she has taken over responsibility for them, too. The children, from first through fifth grade, come and go at various times of the day, in what to an outside observer seems an extraordinarily complicated system of groups and individual programs.

When asked, "How do you decide what groups they belong in?", Miss Nguyen says, "I watch them."

"How do you know when they can be mainstreamed?"

"I watch them."

"What do you look for?"

She shrugs. "English competency. Readiness."

Though the answers she gives sound vague, Miss Nguyen is observing all day, every day. She knows what each child can or can't do, and whether they will be able to succeed on their own in the mainstream class.

All teachers observe. Every teacher watches her students and can tell where they are and what they are capable of doing. Observation and ongoing assessment and reassessment are a part of every teacher's daily role.

However, Miss Nguyen's situation brings up two key issues that we need to address:

1. Teachers see what they believe. How you view the learning process depends on what you believe about it.
2. In today's world, with the emphasis on accountability and the press for inclusion, vague answers (such as those given by Miss Nguyen) are not sufficient and will not satisfy principals, ESL teachers, nor classroom teachers who want to know how well their students are doing outside their own class.

WAYS OF SEEING

No matter what role you may play in your ESL student's learning—whether you are the classroom teacher, the ESL specialist, or the provider of some other support—you need to assess your student with an understanding of the language acquisition process. This process has qualities as unique as each individual who struggles to acquire the language. Therefore, before we can discuss how to document what your students are doing, we need to consider the big picture, what we see when we work with the students who learn from us.

Before you can see how much progress a student has made, or what level of understanding that student has about what he is doing, you must have some sort of framework or standard against which to judge the work or the output. Routman (1991) writes, "good observation, the most critical component in evaluation, is only as good as the teacher's knowledge base." Teachers see what they believe; in other words, what they believe about learning, errors, and language influence how they view a student's productions. Thus, having a way to "see" what it is you're looking at is of absolute importance.

Galda, Cullinan, and Strickland (1993) write:

> ...early childhood educators long have operated on the premise that children's language and literacy development is interwoven and continuous from infancy...Literacy develops concurrently with oral language. Fluency in oral language is no longer seen as a precursor to literacy, but as a goal to be accomplished with and through literacy as each language process informs and supports all the others.

We agree, but for ease and simplicity we divide our discussion, artificially and cautiously, into a framework for the development of speaking proficiency in another language, and into a framework for the development of literacy. Proficiency, as defined by the California State Department of Education (1983) is "the ability to use language for both basic communicative tasks and academic purposes." Literacy is "the ability and willingness to use reading and writing to construct meaning from printed text, in ways which meet the requirements of a particular social context" (Au 1993).

The importance of context

In the introduction we discussed our four themes (page 4) and asserted that authentic assessment means assessment that occurs within a context. This concept is so important that we have devoted an entire section to discussing it. As Braun (1993) puts it, "Everything hinges on the context." Context, as defined by Gumperz (1966), is "the physical setting, the people within the setting, what the people are doing and saying, and where and when they are doing it. Language is embedded in the flow of daily life."

There are many contexts. Many are embedded within others. Your student must be seen within the larger context of his family and his culture and his language. Reading groups, show-and-tell, centers, and seat work are all contexts within the context of a particular classroom. The classroom operates within the larger context of a particular school, with its individual teachers, principal, and population. The school operates within the larger context of a school district, with its policies and programs for limited- or non-English-speaking students. The school district is embedded within the context of the community—

whether it's a poverty-stricken port-of-entry city struggling with drugs, despair, and severely strained budgets, or a settled middle-class community with pockets of low-income housing, with an attitude toward immigrants that can be summed up as: "If we just ignore them they'll go away, so let's wait a few years before we put money into any programs." The districts are embedded within states and provinces, which have differing policies and laws concerning bilingual education and services for non-English-speaking students and different levels of funding for alternative programs. All these contexts are embedded within a country, such as the United States, with its prevailing attitudes toward bilingual students and its promise of education for all. Each context influences the others, and each has a history, or a set way of doing things, that makes change difficult and slow.

The basic features of language in context

All contexts have certain rules that one must know in order to operate successfully within them. A student's ability to perceive the context, and to function within it, demonstrates language competency.

All language interactions—or *speech events*—have certain features. Years ago, Dell Hymes (1965) put these features into a memorable form:

S — the setting
P — the participants
E — the ends (i.e., what the speakers hope to achieve)
A — the act sequence
K — the key, or tone
I — the instrumentalities (spoken, written, telephone)
N — the norms of the interactions
G — the genre (lecture, joke, round-robin reading)

◆ **Setting.** Where the interaction takes place profoundly affects everything else. The setting can be the classroom, the principal's office, the playground, the reading group. How the speakers interact with one another can change from setting to setting. Students will be more informal and friendly to Mr. McMullin on the basketball court than when he's giving a science lecture.

◆ **Participants.** Who is speaking to whom also affects interactions. A conversation between Felicia and Mr. Chang, the principal, necessitates a certain amount of formality, whereas in a conversation between Felicia and her best friend, Nani, that formality would be inappropriate and unfriendly. Delmar, a native-English speaker, automatically adjusts his speech when he talks to Freddy, who has just arrived from Germany. Il Hwa uses what little English she knows to its maximum effect when trying to make friends.

◆ **Ends.** What the speakers are trying to accomplish by this interaction also influences the conversation. Is Mrs. Law chewing TJ out for missing class, or is she asking how long his grandmother has been ill? Is Dan trying to help Taka learn the rules of basketball, or is he trying to convince his teacher that he had a good reason for being late for class?

◆ **Act sequence.** The rules of procedure are a silent partner to any conversation; no one pays attention unless they go awry. Procedure is determined by our understanding of how an interaction should proceed, from beginning to end. Americans begin conversations with hello and a certain amount of small talk, and a *preclosing* of "well, gotta go," before walking away or "I don't want to run up your bill," before hanging up the phone. Children familiar with school routines know that, for instance, when they enter Mrs. Delp's kindergarten they are to check their desk first, and if there is seat work, they must finish that before doing anything else.

◆ **Key.** This is the *tone* of the interaction. Many teachers, especially ESL teachers, work hard at setting up a comfortable, warm atmosphere where the students feel safe and free from ridicule and pressure. The key of an interaction can be formal or informal. It can be sarcastic or playful. Often the more subtle keys are lost on second-language learners. Saying in a joking voice, "You can't tease a teacher," could lead Chai to never tease again if he misunderstands the tone.

◆ **Instrumentalities.** This is the channel or the medium by which the message is transmitted. Is this interaction written or spoken? Many of our students master oral communication long before they can write, while others write well but are hesitant to speak.

◆ **Norms of the interaction.** These norms are often the most fraught with peril for newcomers. These are the basic underlying, unspoken rules we bring to the conversation, to the classroom, to the school. We make assumptions about how far a person should stand away from us, whether touching the other person is appropriate, how much eye contact indicates shiftiness as opposed to staring. These assumptions are culturally relative—that is, they differ from one culture to another. Studies show North Americans think eighteen inches is the appropriate distance to stand from another; we can be edged down the hall by a bewildered person who wants to move into the closeness of his comfort zone—one that is a lot closer than the North American standard. What we might consider sullenness or an indication of lying by a student's lack of eye contact might simply be his way of showing respect.

◆ **Genre.** This is a class of interactions, such as a sermon, a joke, a lecture, that dictate different kinds of responses. No one expects someone to interrupt a preacher and ask questions in the middle of his sermon. The teller of a joke feels annoyed if someone jumps in with the punch line.

All these language features influence each other by demanding the speaker react to the language context appropriately. And because they are culturally relative, they change according to the context. Understanding these rules is more than "linguistic competence"—knowing the grammar and the words. Together they indicate "communicative competence." This is understanding, within the particular context of a classroom, what the rules are: how to say something, how to understand what was said, when to speak, when to keep one's mouth shut, and how to say what to whom. If the teacher says, "That's not where we put our toys," she's assuming the student knows where they go. If she says, "I'm not going to tell you again," the class knows she's giving a final warning. Each classroom has its own set of rules. In Mr. Trinh's class the children wait their turn politely and raise their hand before speaking. In Mrs. Barker's class they feel free to jump in with their own opinion at any time during the discussion. These rules may be explicitly stated in a list drawn up at the beginning of the year for example, or they can be assumed and inferred as the students become used to the teacher.

Here is an example of a set of classroom rules posted on a wall in an elementary school:

- ◆ Observe your own space.
- ◆ Use an indoor voice.
- ◆ Stay on task.
- ◆ Respect all property.

These rules are probably standard for every classroom. However, the wording assumes a certain amount of cultural background knowledge; even though a fairly proficient newcomer may be able to read the words, he may be mystified as to their meaning. What does "observe your own space" mean anyway? How can you easily explain an "indoor voice" to a non-English speaker who has never experienced a school setting before?

Understanding these implicit governing rules is like wearing comfortable clothes, where a person can operate freely and successfully within a context. When Barb returned to the city where she grew up, she quickly found that the answers to the same old questions, "Where do you go to church?" and "What school did you go to?" were enough to tell her who was who, what to expect, and what to assume about the person to whom she was talking.

Not knowing or not understanding these rules can be a major source of failure for non-English-speaking students, or students from cultures different from the mainstream. Boggs (1985), for instance, found that within the context of the family, overt direct questioning by Hawaiian parents is considered an inquisition, a search for a culprit, and a prelude to punishment; therefore, within the context of the school Hawaiian and part-Hawaiian students would not respond to direct questioning from the teacher. Heath (1983) found that African-American children did not understand indirect questions such as "Is this where we put our toys?" and had a great deal of trouble with the concept of "It's time to put away the games." In their homes they lived in a free flow of time in which an activity was finished when the child tired of it or it had come to a logical end not determined by the clock.

Context and assessment are interrelated

Thus, because whatever we do and say is profoundly influenced by the context we are in and the rules that operate within that context, we cannot separate what is being assessed from the context within which it is spoken, heard, read, or written. Barrs et al. (1989) write, "Children's talk in small groups will be affected by the membership of the group— by personalities that are compatible or not, by relationships between girls and boys; by attitudes to race and culture."

In addition, we cannot use what a student has said in one context to be an accurate indicator of what he is able to do on the whole. Teachers often create a picture of a learner's reading level based on how he performs in round robin or on the seat work he does. But these pictures are incomplete and often inaccurate. We need to look at many different contexts and build a portrait of the student and his capabilities on the basis of how he functions in all.

Lan, for instance, is very shy. She never speaks up in class. She prefers to come to the teacher privately after class or in a quiet moment to ask questions. However, her journal entries about her reading are filled with insights and a depth of understanding that many of the others do not reach. When the class began role playing characters from *To Kill a Mockingbird*, the part of Bob Ewell fell to her. Taking on Bob's persona, she became loud, aggressive, and filled with hatred for Atticus, Tom Robinson, and the Finch children. The transformation was remarkable and a little scary from such a hitherto quiet, unassuming person. The teacher now knows that Lan has understood the character—only too well!

The language framework and traditional testing

In the classroom, we want to know what our students have learned, how much English they have acquired, and how much content they understand. Reviewing the language framework we have just discussed, along with the common procedures for traditional testing practices, it is now easier to see why traditional tests are problematic for non-English-speaking students in one or more ways:

◆ **Setting.** The setting for test-taking may be unfamiliar. Students are often taken to a room away from friends or, perhaps, family. For students whose tests of skills may have taken place within the marketplace ("Did you give that man the right number of fish?") or the field ("Dig the hole and put six seeds in each hole"), the change to a classroom environment for testing makes the entire physical and psychological setting confusing and threatening.

- **Participants.** Within this unfamiliar and unsettling situation, the student interacts only with a stranger, a voice from a tape recorder, or a piece of paper, in a language he has not mastered.

- **Ends.** The students are given tasks whose purpose and meaning are often not clear to them, and, unless there is an interpreter present, that cannot be explained adequately.

- **Act sequence.** In test situations, Westernized students become used to sitting down, pencil ready, waiting for the teacher to say, "Ready, begin," and then proceeding with the test until told to stop. Many students from nontraditional, non-Western societies have not been exposed to this before.

- **Key.** The key is formal, often ritualized. There is little chance for laughter, for trying again.

- **Instrumentalities.** The channel is often limited to one form, such as writing, or reading, or oral production. For students whose progress needs to be demonstrated in an ongoing way, this type of testing is limiting and unnatural. In addition, and perhaps most important, the channel is a different language, one in which the student may have little or no experience. For example, Mary worked in a program whose policy let foreign students attend classes for two years only. They were expected to have acquired enough proficiency to move into the mainstream in that time. Mary worked with many nonliterate students whose progress was almost imperceptible by the standardized tests she had to use from the texts. It took nearly a year of just letting the students absorb the language before they could demonstrate anything on the prefabricated tests. Yet she had to show that these students were learning in order to secure them an additional year in the program. She kept reports, which documented each students's progress in the listening and speaking areas, but it took some lobbying to get the supervisors to agree to the change.

◆ **Norm.** The norm for most tests is "No talking, no looking at your neighbor's papers." This is completely incomprehensible to students who come from cultures where collaboration and sharing are prized and expected. There are also implicit norms, such as, "This is a one-shot measure. If you blow it, that's too bad." The norms do not take into account the fact that Serge might be suffering from recurring malaria, that Bertha had to stay up all night working in a factory because it's pumpkin season and her family needs the money, that Kao is so worried about his father that he can't think straight. Because standardized tests are impersonal and deal with only what the student purportedly can do, they ignore the person and the personality that confronts the test and the testing situation at a particular time.

◆ **Genre.** The genre is usually multiple-choice. As with the setting, it is often unfamiliar to students (as well as a narrow, restrictive method of gaining information).

By understanding and paying attention to the contexts within which each person resides, and the contexts within which we operate as students, teachers, and ordinary citizens, we can understand better how people react as they do, and how these things influence not only who they are, but how each learning situation succeeds or fails.

EMERGENCE

Along with understanding the importance of context in observing the learning processes of our students, we must also understand the continuum of language learning. In the late 1970s and early 1980s, Terrell (1983) developed the Natural Approach to language learning. He defined several stages of developing language skills. These stages are: preproduction, early production, speech emergence, intermediate fluency, and fluency.

Even though some states such as California use Terrell's stages as guidelines for their programs, there are problems with them, particularly the concept of preproduction—the idea that "comprehension precedes production," and that there is a stage where the learner does not comprehend and therefore cannot produce any meaningful strings in writing or in speaking. Recent research has shown that production and performance, in reading, writing, and speaking, often precede comprehension. Children will experiment and play with forms before they understand what they are doing. They will practice before they have been deemed "developmentally ready" for that form. How many children chant the *ABCs* (or swear) before they have a clue what it is they are saying, or memorize long poems without understanding a word? (Witness such songs as "Low in the Gravy Lay Jesus our Savior" or "Strumming on the Old Bad Joe.")

However, we find the concept—that proficiency emerges with exposure and practice over time—attractive for several reasons. One of the most important is that this implies a continuum of learning, not an all-or-nothing focus, with the student being viewed as somehow lacking until he gains proficiency nearly equivalent of a native-English speaker. A student arrives with perhaps little or no English and gains proficiency over time.

Another reason is that in the current literature on literacy the concept of emergence has become an important one.

William Teale (1987) writes that the word *emergent* describes something "in the process of becoming." The idea of a continuum suggests stages that one does not necessarily have to rigidly adhere to but that represents some general milestones along the way. This is useful for looking at not just the speech development, but also the development of literacy and/or proficiency of students learning English as an additional language.

Following Teale, we can demonstrate four reasons the concept of emergence is important and useful:

1. Emergence emphasizes the notion that at whatever point in development we look, students are in the process of becoming literate and proficient in English. It is not reasonable to point to a time when literacy begins, nor is it reasonable to think of a student coming to school either alingual (without a language) or with absolutely no exposure to English. Learners are not transported to the doorstep of school in a vacuum. Newcomers come to school having heard their own language since birth. They arrive at school in North America having seen street signs, billboards, immigration papers, and probably advertisements on television.

2. Emergence emphasizes the continuity of development, from a beginning toward more and more proficiency and mastery.

3. Emergence also suggests discontinuity. Development is taking place and lack of mastery or proficiency is left behind.

4. Emergence suggests that growth occurs without the necessity for an overriding emphasis on formal teaching. The language and the literacy take place within home, school, playground, and work.

Emergence and second-language learners

In addition, with second-language learners, the gathering of knowledge, skills, and proficiency does not happen in isolation but in orchestration. Each depends on the other. The mastery of reading depends on the knowledge of vocabulary and syntax as well as on the skills basic to getting meaning from print.

In figure 4.1, we demonstrate the emergence of oral proficiency and literacy. The terms we suggest are not precise terms, nor are they precise levels—it is not our intent or our place to be precise. We are merely using levels as ways of helping define what teachers are seeing and hearing when they watch and listen to their learners.

Emerging oral proficiency

It is nearly impossible for a student to come to school on the first day without ever having heard a word of English: from the first moment of setting foot in an English-speaking country or community, people are bombarded with the English language. However, the English they know may be so limited that it does not allow them admission into the arena of social life in the school. When the student first arrives he may know no functional English, and be unable to do the simplest activities. From that point on, he moves toward greater and greater command of his new language.

Emergent literacy

Teale (1987) defines emergent literacy as the period "between birth and the time when children write and read in conventional ways, ways

Language Acquisition Development

Theoretical Stages	Characteristics	Behavior
1. Silence	• Understands little or no English. Student "quietly takes it all in." For some this stage may last a few minutes, others a few months.	Does not speak or understand English
2. Nonverbal indications of understanding	• Uses no English except for a word or two • Student will not respond verbally but will respond physically to instructions or requests • Understands only slow simple speech; requires repetitions • Progresses to one word response in English or a response in own language	Understands simple sentences but only uses isolated words or expressions
3. Chunking	• Understands simplified speech with repetitions and rephrasing • Produces some common English words and phrases • Uses unanalyzed chunks of language that perform an important social function: "It's my turn", "What's your name?" "Can I play?" • Understands more than can produce	• Speaks English with difficulty • Converses in English with help • Understands at least parts of the lesson • Follows simple directions
4. Interlanguage	• Understands adult speech but requires repetition and rephrasing • Speech may be hesitant because of rephrasing and groping for words • Uses some complex structures • Overgeneralizes rules of grammar • Has difficulty with choice of verb tense, verb tense consistency, and subject/verb agreement • Vocabulary is adequate to carry on basic conversation; some word usage difficulties • "Interim grammar" one part one language, one part another. "They in school and home's live." "My friend likes the books to read."	Understands, speaks, reads, and writes English with some degree of hesitancy
5. Gaining control in English	• Understands most adult speech except some advanced structures • Speech may be nonnative in evenness. An accent may be present. • Demonstrates a fairly high degree of proficiency • Controls most basic grammatical structures with occasional error in syntax. Some errors in a young learner may be seen as developmental. • Vocabulary is varied	Understands and speaks English well but needs assistance in reading and writing in English to achieve at level appropriate for his or her grade level
6. Fluent Speaker	• Understands everything expected of a native speaker of the same age • Speech is effortless and native-like; however an accent may be present • Expresses ideas creatively having mastered a broad range of syntactic features • Vocabulary is as accurate as a native speaker of the same age • Use different varieties of language depending upon the situation (codeswitching)	Achieves at appropriate level

Fig. 4.1: Language Acquisition Development table

that adults generally would identify as actually being reading and writing. Thus, emergent literacy represents the beginnings of reading and writing for the child." Beginning literacy, continues Teale, is not to be confused with beginning reading, which is closely associated with formal reading instruction in school.

EMERGENT READERS FROM LITERATE BACKGROUNDS

Studies in literacy have most often been done on children who are developing their awareness and mastery of literacy in their first language. Many of these children, especially middle-class mainstream children, come to school with a long history of exposure to print, and there is a gradual emergence of understanding about the concepts of reading and writing. Researchers find that literacy in households mediate nine domains of activity: daily living, entertainment, school, work, religion, interpersonal communication, participating in information networks, storybook time, and literacy for the sake of teaching/ learning literacy. Goodman (1988) writes, "The beginnings of reading and writing occur in individuals when they develop the awareness that written language makes sense."

ESL STUDENTS FROM NONLITERATE BACKGROUNDS

Unfortunately, many of our non- or limited-English-speaking students do not have the luxury of being surrounded by reading and writing. They come to school without what Sulzby calls "the repertoire of knowledge about written language." With no background in print media or awareness that print has meaning, they are suddenly immersed in and expected to be productive in a literate environment.

With these learners we cannot assume such common assertions as "literacy development begins long before children start formal instruction." Many have not learned reading and writing behaviors within the informal settings of home and community (some struggle with literacy into their high school years). Their parents are illiterate; someone must translate for them, pay the bills, write the checks, interpret the laws. Beginning and emergent literacy are often limited to situations that occur strictly within the school: storybook time and learning to read for the sake of learning to read.

Students of all ages entering our schools can fall anywhere on this continuum of literacy development. Teale and Sulzby (1987) write, "although children's learning about literacy can be described in terms of generalized stages, children can pass through these stages in a variety of ways and at different ages." With pre- and nonliterate students, the exposure or lack of exposure to literacy early in life is a key factor of where they enter the continuum, at what age, and how quickly they pass through the stages.

Secondary schools currently being inundated with illiterate and poorly educated students face additional challenges. A fifteen-year-old refugee enrolling in school for the first time in his life is entering at the eleventh hour. He must not only learn English but the basic concepts we take for granted at the high-school level. The curriculum of high school not only demands knowing how to read (notwithstanding knowing how to read in English), but strategies for reading different genres at a fairly sophisticated level. A student must know how to skim; he must have the background knowledge of history, science, and the same North American culture we assume in our mainstream students; he must have years of "practice" not only in learning, but learning how to learn. All these issues must somehow be addressed, and you must have some sense of how to approach this so these students don't just fall through the cracks.

GAINING CONTROL OVER FORMS

Marie Clay (1975) writes, "for children who learn to write at the same time as they learn to read, writing plays a significant part in the early reading progress." There is strong evidence that learning to write helps provide the experience of basic hierarchical relationships between letters, words, and messages; when he's attempting to write, the learner is compelled to pay attention to the significant details of written language. He is learning to "organize his own behavior into an appropriate sequence of actions." As Forester and Reinhard (1989) point out, writing "requires greater attention to letters and their sounds than reading does." Through these comments we can see how critical it is to keep reading and writing together in a literacy program.

What can a student learn about reading and writing by practicing print, and reading his work or having it read to him? A student can learn

- directionality—that print in English goes from left to right, and pages in English are read from top to bottom
- that print carries a message
- that words, not pictures, are read
- what a word is
- what a letter is
- what punctuation does

Levels of literacy production (Writing)

Mastery over the conventions of writing does not take place in a day. There are many models to show the stages of children's literacy development, each with their own labels for levels, and different divisions within the continuum toward mastery. We have adapted several of these, most notably Sulzby (1985), Manning and Manning (1992), and Weaver (1994). This development represents a continuum, and the leaps from one level to the next are never clear-cut.

When we looked at and compared the different texts produced by various levels of readers and writers, it was clear how much reading and being read to influenced the quantity and quality of work produced. Those who had been exposed to books had a much wider range of words and resources at hand than those who hadn't.

DRAWING

Children from literate environments begin drawing very early. It's not long before they can tell you what it is they are trying to draw (even if it doesn't bear any resemblance to the real object). Soon they announce their intention before they begin ("I'm going to draw a cat"). Many second-language learners who do not know how to write yet, or cannot write in English, can demonstrate their understanding of concepts by drawing (figure 4.2).

SCRIBBLING

Many children in literate environments go through a period of what looks like scribbling that gradually evolves into letters and words.

Researchers, examining these marks, find that these early efforts reflect a very clear distinction between drawing and writing, and conclude that the markings are intended to signify meaning. Usually, children can "read" what they wrote, showing that they have begun to understand the difference between pictures and print.

Figure 4.2: This drawing was a response to The Cat in the Hat. *The first grader who produced this loved to listen to the story, and, although she could not write, could demonstrate her understanding by her picture.*

Figure 4.3: This is a letter to God written by a three-year-old English-speaking child: *Dear Jesus, Thank you for taking the spider away. You can come to my house. And you can come to my party with Lala and Robin and Sofie. Amen.* Note that she has a sense of both the standard format of a letter, and of prayers.

Figure 4.4: This drawing was done by a new-to-the-country first-grader. Note the wavy lines he used below the picture and the other non-English-looking script. His drawing shows skill, as well as an astonishing degree of Christian symbolism. The lines drawn below are clearly different. He may have been attempting to depict writing in English and in his own language, Lao.

Students from pre- and nonliterate backgrounds, or even nonprint home environments within Western culture, come to school without that all-important repertoire of knowledge of print. They are not afforded the time for experimentation, and because of the demands of school, most of them probably proceed directly to print.

USING LETTER-LIKE FORMS

Weaver (1994) terms this level "prephonemic," because learners know that letters can "say" something, but haven't yet learned that there is a sound/letter correspondence. Manning and Manning note that a string of letters that represent one word may fill a whole line or even an entire page as the learner writes.

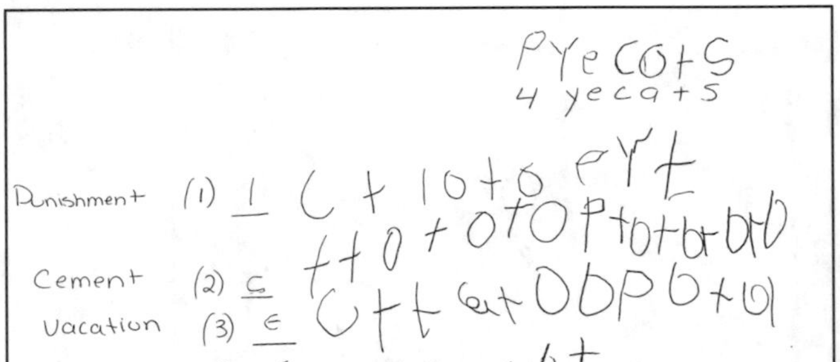

Figure 4.5: Carla, age four, at the prephonemic stage.

Figure 4.6: Choua is making the bridge to phonemic spelling. She has several sight words: he is OK. The rest is indecipherable.

COPYING

It is easy to overlook and minimize the importance of copying. However, a student's practice of forms, and mastery over forms by copying, is a major achievement in his movement toward literacy and proficiency. Clay (1975) continues: "If a child knows how to scan, how to study a word to reproduce it, and how to organize his writing of that word, he has the skills to deal with the detail of print. It is probable that early writing serves to organize the visual analysis of print." You can see real growth when a learner sees words written in uppercase and reproduces them in lowercase. This demonstrates a significant step in understanding.

Figure 4.7: This child recognizes significant features of letters, but has yet to gain control of the formulating of letters. He is not aware of word boundaries.

Figure 4.8: Samantha's kindergarten pretest upon entering school. Most of the letters are upside down.

Figure 4.9: This first grader has more control than the student from figure 4.7 and is aware of punctuation, placing periods after each word.

INVENTED SPELLING

This is also called "phonetic spelling," or better yet, "constructive spelling" (probably for the benefit of doubtful parents and administrators). Researchers and early childhood experts contend this is an important level for learners, and should be encouraged. Weaver points out that there are many advantages to promoting invented spelling:

◆ It affords the student the freedom to explore his knowledge of sound-letter correspondences; that is, "to get on with it" and put his ideas down without worrying about "rightness" or "wrongness." It also allows him to write long texts that, previously, constrained by the need to be exact and the teacher having to spell every word for him, would never have been produced.

For example, in figure 4.10, Katie laboriously sounded out every word in this story about Malificent, after seeing the Disney version of "Sleeping Beauty." It took her a very long time to write, and afterwards she wanted it read to her. Of course, it was almost impossible for anyone else to reconstruct, but she knew what she was saying when she wrote it, and could figure it out and read it because her own internal set of "rules" were consistent.

Figure 4.10:
Katie's story
about Malificent

◆ Students are encouraged to take risks and to construct knowledge for themselves.

For example, Stan was in a class of beginners. One teacher believed that the group was not able to write yet and therefore should not be allowed to try, but the other teacher believed in the students' capabilities and gave them many opportunities. In figure 4.11, Stan was not only demonstrating he knew a good deal of understanding, such as sound/letter correspondence, as well as a number of sight words, but he was learning to apply this knowledge.

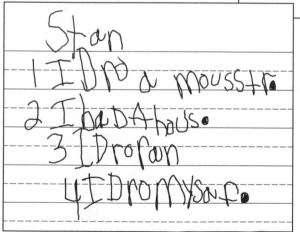

Figure 4.11:
Stan wrote:
I draw a monster.
I had a house.
I draw rain.
I draw myself.

◆ Because they are constructing this knowledge for themselves, these spellers learn and apply phonics rules more readily than those who are simply given spelling lists to memorize. Spontaneously produced texts can reveal a greater understanding than those that were guided by the teacher. For instance, when we look at a list of spelling words from the test devised by the Mannings (see figure 4.12) we get a very clear picture of the learner's understanding of writing, and his representation of spelling patterns and sight words. However, looking at a freely written text (as in figure 4.13), we can see that a learner can reveal a much wider range of understanding.

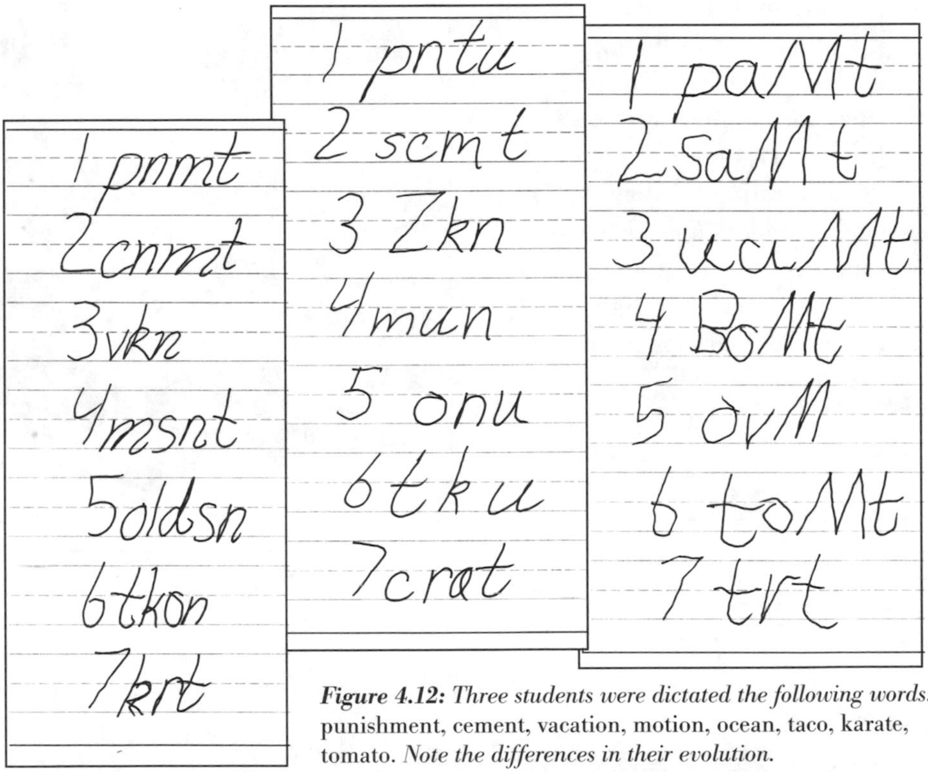

Figure 4.12: *Three students were dictated the following words:* punishment, cement, vacation, motion, ocean, taco, karate, tomato. *Note the differences in their evolution.*

◆ Finally, and this evidence can be used to "sell" administrators and parents to the idea, some research suggests that students who are encouraged to spell constructively do better on standardized spelling and reading tests.

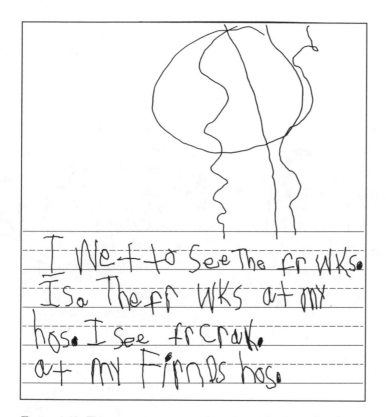

Figure 4.13: *This spontaneous story about fireworks shows that the writer has a number of sight words in his memory and a good command of sound/spelling correspondence. It reads:* I went to see the fireworks. I saw the fireworks at my house. I see firecrackers at my friend's house.

Following are several of the levels within this period of growth. Note that as learners progress, and their experience with the written word grows, they include more and more sight words that they can recognize and produce independently.

◆ **Consonantal.** Writers at this level realize that there are letter-sound correspondences, and use mostly consonants. This starts usually with one letter used to represent the word. As the learner grows in understanding, he moves to initial and final consonants.

Figure 4.14: This beginner only used vowels in a word that consisted of the single vowel a. Her sentences are strikingly consistent in their omission of vowels. When vowels are supplied, her meaning is clear: rainbow /I have a bat / I have a man /

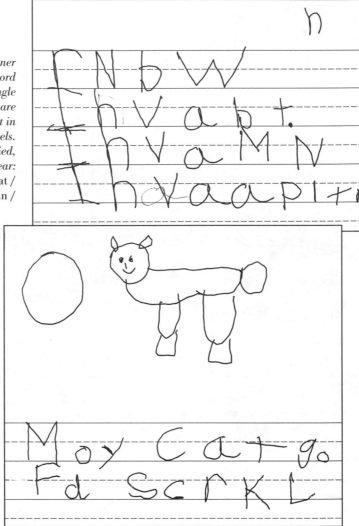

Figure 4.15: This child has more sight words and can supply them, omitting vowels in words not in her sight repertoire. This reads: My cat go find squirrel.

- ◆ **Letter-name.** At this level learners begin to use letters whose name sounds like the sound they are trying to represent, for example, the letter *c* for *see.*

Figure 4.16: This is my snake. I liked him but we had to move to a different house. *This learner is using z for the zzz sound in is, a t for the ending of liked. She was at a level where m and n were confusing, and continually asked "one hump or two?"*

Figure 4.17: *This beginner is also employing the name of the letter to represent the sound, c for see, and c for the s sound in sleep and stair. She has begun to progress beyond simple consonants to represent complete words.*

◆ **Vowel-consonant combinations.** Vowels start to appear in the middle of words. Many of the vowels reflect the letter-name strategy, in which the letter the student uses reflects the name of the letter.

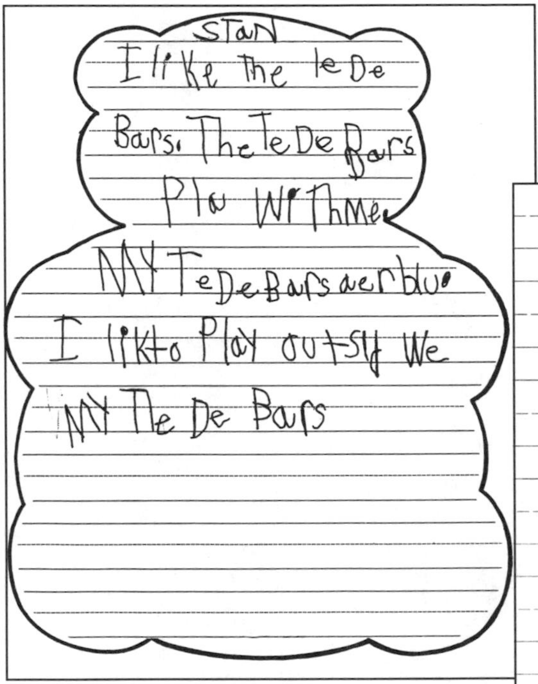

Figure 4.18:
*Here's Stan
again, showing
a lot of vowel
names, such as
the e sound in
teddy, the a in
play, u in blue,
and i in* like
and outside.

> STaN
> I liKe The leDe
> Bars. The TeDe Bars
> Plo Wr Thme.
> MY TeDeBarsaerblu
> I liKto Play outsid We
> MY Tle De Bars

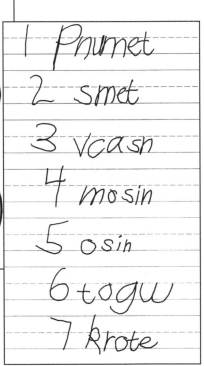

> 1 Pniirnet
> 2 smet
> 3 vcasn
> 4 mosin
> 5 osin
> 6 togw
> 7 krote

Figure 4.19: *Bo is showing an
understanding of the use of vowels
in his words. The dictation was:*
punishment, cement, vacation,
motion, ocean, taco, karate, tomato.

◆ **Words.** This is what Sulzby
calls "full invented spelling"
in which the child indicates
all the sounds represented by
a word. If there are missing
sounds, there is usually an
indication that beginning,
middle, and final sounds
are present.

Figure 4.20:
This reads:
I love you,
I'm sorry.

> I Love YoU I mY
> SiRe

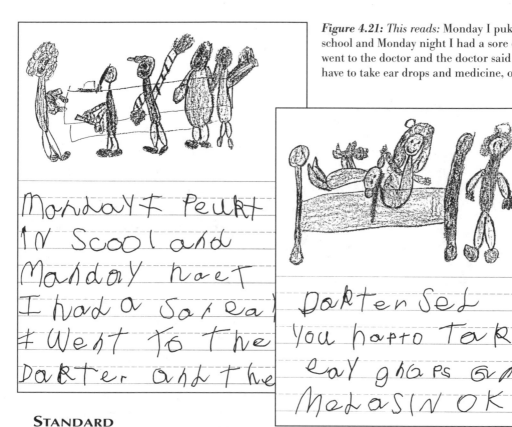

Figure 4.21: This reads: Monday I puked in school and Monday night I had a sore ear. I went to the doctor and the doctor said you have to take ear drops and medicine, ok?

MonДaY Ŧ PeuRŧ
in Scool aИd
MaИdoY Иael
I Иad a Sa ꞁeaꞁ
Ŧ WeИŧ ŧo The
DaRŧer aИd The

DaRter SeL
You haɸʈo TaR
eaY ghaРs оИt
MeLaSiИ OK

STANDARD ENGLISH SPELLING

At this level learners spell most words the conventional way. Forester and Reinhard (1989) remind us that "neat little printers lapse into quite poor performance when shifting

Figure 4.22: Here's a fourth grader who has moved well beyond the basics, and is mastering cursive as well as most of the grammar and spelling of English.

Batman

Batman

My friend likes to play with me.

He is a good friend.

Every day He plays with me.

He is a nice friend.

from copying to composing....When composing, the attention of the writer is focused on the creative task at hand. Neatness of handwriting takes second place."

Levels of literacy development (Reading)

As we mentioned previously, students do not come to school alingual. Unless other factors are operating, their first language is well developed to satisfy all their needs, and now they are setting out to add a second (or a third or fourth). However, this is not always the case with reading and writing. Mainstream middle-class students usually comes from print-rich environments, with a large storehouse of information about print. Many can read; many can write their own name. At the very least, most know that words convey meaning. Not so with many of our refugees. They come in at the most basic level. That first major step toward literacy is the realization that print is meaningful. This may take a year or more. We cannot underestimate the importance of that breakthrough. Neither can we underestimate the time it takes to reach it nor should we start to search for underlying disabilities if it takes longer than we think it should. It can take a long time to reach this level; you can't rush it.

We have formulated these levels of development to help you determine where your student is, so that you can design activities that will enhance the student's strengths and help him continue to build on those strengths. The following levels are very porous and permeable. Emerging readers do not make strict leaps, but can have features of several levels all at once. A beginning awareness learner can also be aware of punctuation. An emergent reader can create long texts using invented spellings when the repertoire of words he can spell on his own is less than ten. Each student is different.

PREAWARENESS

Students

◆ do not know print has meaning. The print is merely squiggles on the page
◆ do not seem to know what books are and what they do
◆ have not held a pen or pencil
◆ cannot look at pictures and see more than simple shades of color

- cannot see drawings of objects and identify them for what they are
- do not know how to handle a book or how to turn pages
- may or may not be able to copy words
- can demonstrate understanding of a story by drawing a picture

Students at this level need to be inundated with print, even though they are not reading yet. It is only by seeing print in use that they can make that qualitative leap to understanding and eventual reading. For example:

> Kao picks up a book and opens it upside down. Then he looks at his neighbor's book and, studying how she is holding it, turns his right side up. Ka Neng is contentedly reading *National Geographic*, not realizing it is upside down until she reaches a picture with people in it. Then she notices, and turns it around.

◆

> Steve is in a group that has been working on colors. The teacher has several colors and the corresponding word for each color on the wall. Steve knows his colors, but when given the word *blue*, he cannot match it with the word on the wall, even though he has been told what the word he is holding says. He has not connected print with meaning yet.

◆

> Eight squirrelly little first-grade boys, whom Carolyn and Shirley call their "challenging group," have been working on school vocabulary such as *book, eraser, pencil, scissors,* and *colors.* They have been matching the word with the picture. Today for the first time they are going to try a writing exercise. They are given a large sheet of paper on which several cloze sentences have been written. They are to fill in each blank with the correct name of the object, draw a picture of, and then color the object (figure 4.23 shows a near-complete exercise).
>
> This turns out to be a revealing exercise. It is the first time that Carolyn and Shirley can see whether the boys are actually making the connection between the object they see and the word pinned above it. Peter, their most verbally proficient boy, is unable to fill in the blank. He can't connect the word with the object, even though they are together on the

wall. In addition, when he receives assistance using a pencil and forming
letters, his writing shows a lack of skill. The letters are large, irregular,
and unevenly spaced.

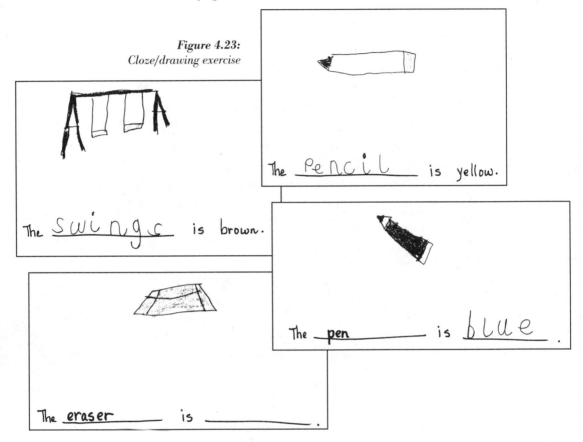

Figure 4.23:
Cloze/drawing exercise

The _PeNciL_ is yellow.

The _swingc_ is brown.

The _pen_ is _blue_.

The _eraser_ is _____.

Students at this level often come from cultures and places in this world
that have no written form of language; they have not connected print
with meaning. This all-important leap in understanding may take
several years, and often teachers get frustrated and begin to look elsewhere for blame when the student does not seem to "get it." It is only
by seeing print *in use* that students can make the qualitative jump to
understanding and eventual reading. Immersion in print means demonstrating to students how to make the connection and giving them
many opportunities to try it out for themselves.

We suggest the following strategies for this level:

♦ Label items in the classroom.
♦ Make lists.
♦ Introduce environmental print in the classroom.
♦ Read to students in their first and second language.
♦ Work with sequencing.
♦ Read predictable books.
♦ Employ the Language Experience Approach (LEA).
♦ Introduce songs, rhymes, and drama.
♦ Provide lots of opportunities to draw and copy, and to practice writing.

Many of the activities and the reading can be done in orchestration. For example, Shirley and Carolyn devised a lesson using *Goldilocks and the Three Bears*. They read the story many times; the boys acted it out; they talked about the words *first, second, last,* as well as *big, bigger, biggest*; they made puppets, and drew the bears' house and its contents on three-part folders. With the puppets and the folders the boys could tell one another the story.

EMERGING AWARENESS
Students

♦ understand print carries a message
♦ can demonstrate understanding of general terms like *read, page, story, book*
♦ engage in "pretend" reading, often using proper intonation
♦ can tell a story from pictures
♦ can read and write their own name
♦ begin to read environmental print
♦ begin to track from left to right
♦ can repeat all or parts of predictable text
♦ begin familiarity with "story grammar" of English-language stories (for example, "once upon a time...")
♦ begin to write words
♦ can copy with relative ease

- are not fully aware of word boundaries
- do not understand the concepts represented by the terms *letter, words, number*

The students at this level have made that all-important first step—connecting print to meaning. "Pretend reading" is another strategy that needs to be welcomed and reinforced. Many believe it is "phony" reading, but it is a time when a beginning reader is internalizing the patterns and the story grammar that form the basis for much that comes later. According to Doake (1988), children who engage in pretend reading "have been able to absorb the meaning of their stories, engage in deep-level processing, and generate meaningful written language on the run. They [are] not simply imitating and remembering but creating and composing their version of the stories using the written dialect and their knowledge of story structure to do so." Eventually the readers will begin to attend to the print on the page as well as the pictures and other cues.

For example:

Alexi proudly "reads" the Brown Bear patterned book that he made in school:

Brown Bear, Brown Bear

What do you see?

I see a...[*He turns the page to look at the next picture*]

...Red bird looking at me.

When asked to track the words he is reading on the page, or to point to individual words, he can't. He had the right intonation and paused in the right places, but he just wasn't at the level where he was attending to the print.

◆

Mary Delie's beginning literacy class, who barely can read their names, can recognize important words in their environment, such as *Cub Foods, KMart, rice.*

Figure 4.24: This first-grader shows beginning control over forms, but erasures demonstrate attention to placement of letters. He is not yet fully aware of the concept of word boundaries.

We suggest the following teaching strategies to enhance this level:

- Do all of above suggested activities for preawareness.
- Use familiar patterned books for modeling.
- Use frame sentences.
- Read, read, read.

EMERGING READING

Students

- can recognize and pick out individual words within a text
- look at the text and words when reading
- can spell a few words on their own, remembering word forms and writing them independently
- understand that the sentence and the picture go together
- are familiar with the "story grammar" of English-language stories
- are developing strategies to predict meaning

- ◆ take information from a variety of sources, such as graphophonic, syntactic, and semantic
- ◆ still read aloud
- ◆ are aware of word boundaries when writing
- ◆ are beginning to understand the conventions of punctuation

Figure 4.25:
A class of first graders read a silly story, and then, using the patterns, wrote their own. This student was very verbally proficient, and was able to invent and illustrate his own story using the model.

It is the middle of January, halfway into the school year. Katie is aware of print, and writes copiously in her journal, but has not seemed to make the connection. She hasn't made the leap to reading yet, and her teacher is beginning to be concerned. Then one day she sits down with a book, says, "I'm going to read this to you," looks at the words, and actually reads the text! It seems just short of miraculous that all of a sudden everything has fallen into place for her, and she can do it.

At this stage the fledgling reader really begins to take off. There is a very large leap between this and the previous stage, one that may take a long time. For older learners this is particularly problematic as many programs give students only a set time to get through; it may take as many as two years just for the student to recognize that print has meaning and make the connection Katie made. These students are bumped from classes and programs by incoming newcomers whose needs seem to be more pressing. But they cannot make the transition to content classes, however, because their skills are just beginning to blossom. At this point, the reader is moving from being a dependent reader toward reading independently. You can observe the learner working with the text, finding clues to predict meaning, sounding out words, succeeding in reading words outside of the story context. In many cases they are "word bound," focusing mainly on phonics skills to get meaning and laboriously sounding out words. They need to be guided to using their predicting skills.

Many teachers are tempted to give emergent readers the old Dick-and-Jane-type books because they have few words. We don't recommend it. An interesting story line is more important than simple words. It may seem counterintuitive to give a student a book like *There's a Nightmare in My Closet* (after all, who needs the sight word *nightmare* or *suppose* at this stage?) That's not the point. Enjoyment of reading is essential. Giving students books they can have fun with, that they want to read over and over, is a big part of the game.

Developing skills are reflected in the student's writing as well. There is evidence of word boundaries, the learner shows some spelling abilities and can use word forms with more accuracy.

Figure 4.26:
This was written
unaided by Maria,
a sixth grader, using
words and frame
sentences she had
previously worked
with, to poke fun
at her brothers.

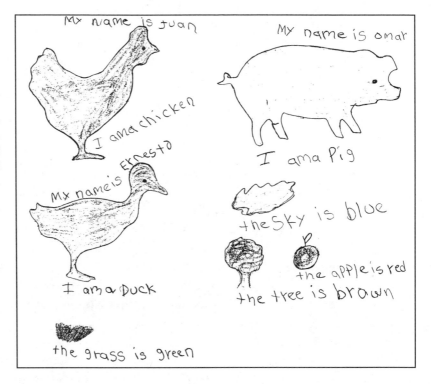

Many students, including older ones such as Lee, are much more proficient orally than they are in writing and reading. In addition, many students from nonliterate backgrounds are skilled artists. In figure 4.27, Lee drew a picture of his home in Laos, and told the teacher about it. The teacher wrote his words down, and they revised it together, producing a clear description of his home.

We suggest the following strategies to enhance this level:

◆ Do all of the activities for preawareness and beginning stages.
◆ Set aside a silent reading time.
◆ Read books to student of a higher reading level than they are capable of on their own. This expands vocabulary and horizons.

My home was in Laos. It was
made of bamboo and grass. It
had a fence around it. We
had a barn with chickens
and six buffalo. We had an
orchard of orange trees.
Sometimes we grew rice. We
grew everything we ate.

Figure 4.27:
Lee's picture
and transcript

A group of beginners were studying "occupations." After much discussion, the children chose an occupation they would like. They were given the sentences:

I am a _____ .

I _____ . This is me working.

John chose to be a doctor. He demonstrated not only his understanding, but his ability to go beyond the basic content by adding his own thoughts. He followed the basic format but added words and structures he knew (figure 4.28, next page).

Figure 4.28:
John's exercise on
"occupations"

I am a Doctor
I look like this.
I wear a uni-
form

I See Sick People
This is me
Working

I work here.
It is a hospital.

GAINING FLUENCY

Students

◆ are confident when reading familiar texts
◆ pay attention to the words on the page
◆ achieve growing independence
◆ begin to read silently
◆ may use invented spelling
◆ can read for a variety of purposes (pleasure, information)
◆ select books that interest them
◆ can retell stories they read in own words
◆ can extract the main idea
◆ use punctuation appropriately

Figure 4.29: Lola, a high-school student, wrote this in response to a lesson on trees. She had some literacy in her first language— the spelling shows influence of this. She demonstrates a clear understanding of the content.

These students are becoming more independent and more confident as their proficiency and knowledge base grow. They need structure, models to base their writing on. This is a period that can show a virtual explosion of errors in writing; the student is "ungluing" from the chalkboard or the book and taking risks by using knowledge of sound/letter correspondence to try spelling on his own. It is always a temptation to correct these errors, but many teachers of whole language don't unless the writing is for publication.

We suggest the following strategies to enhance this level:

◆ Provide structures and models to base writing on.
◆ Have students write responses to reading.
◆ Concentrate more on revision and editing.

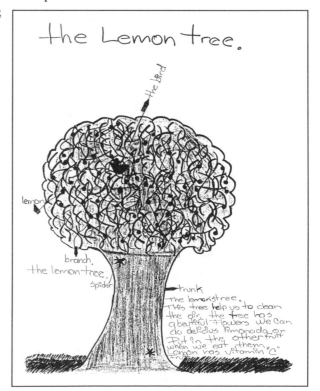

For example: During the few weeks before Christmas, one teacher with a large proportion of non-Western children in her class, spent a good deal of time building vocabulary and building understanding of the Western-style of celebrating the holiday. The students made decorations, wish lists, and read many books, including *The Night Before Christmas.* After discussion, each wrote something about the way their family celebrated Christmas. One boy was afraid to write anything on his own and fussed. So the teacher put a list of suggestions on the chalkboard: Do you have a tree? Do you eat special food? What do you want for Christmas? and so on. Some felt comfortable simply answering the questions, others wrote more.

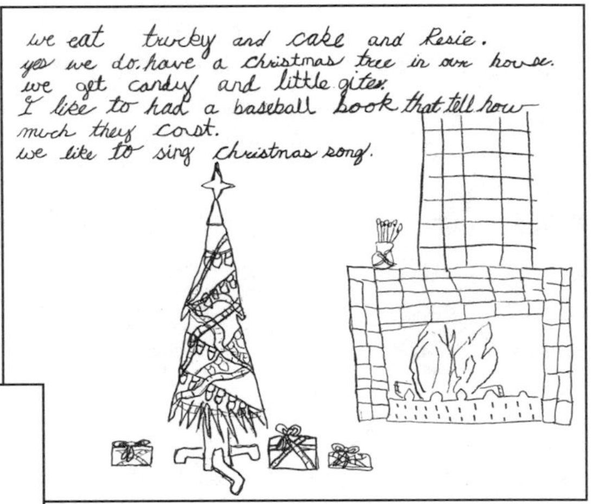

we eat turcky and cake and Resie.
yes we do. have a christmas tree in our house.
we get candy and little gites.
I like to had a baseball book that tell how much they cost.
we like to sing christmas song.

my mom like to go get some christmas toys for all my familys.
my dad Decorations, The window and The thee.
~~Ruddo~~ on TV. I saw ~~Ruddo~~ Rudolph.

I eat was cake and turkey for Christmas.
~~Magyibe~~ Maybe my dad Will buy one for us.

I don't didn't put up stockings

I didn't had a Christmas tree at my hause.

I eat cake, chips, cookies and turkey,

I didn't put up stockings in my house.

I get presents and shoes.

We sing when Jesus is born and we stay to 12:00.

Figure 4.30: These three boys are at the same oral proficiency level, but their writing reveals varying levels of fluency.

INCREASING FLUENCY

Students

♦ can approach unfamiliar texts with a degree of confidence, but still may need support
♦ begin to draw inferences from books
♦ can use directories such as telephone book, table of contents to find information
♦ need support with cultural aspects of texts
♦ can write quite sophisticated stories
♦ pay attention to organization when writing
♦ use context to predict meanings of unknown words
♦ develop personal voice in writing

These students are well launched in reading and are increasingly confident, although they need to return to familiar types of materials to solidify their skills and increase their fluency. They may need support with unfamiliar texts. They know they must apply different styles of reading with different types of text.

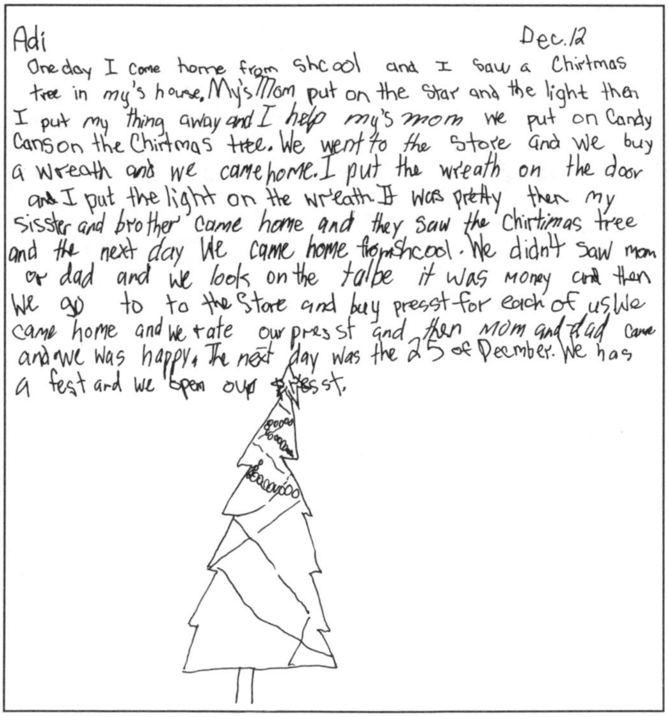

Adi   Dec. 12

One day I come home from shcool and I saw a Chirtmas tree in my's house. My's Mom put on the Star and the light then I put my thing away and I help my's mom we put on Candy Canson the Chirtmas tree. We went to the Store and we buy a Wreath and we came home. I put the wreath on the door and I put the light on the wr'eath. It was pretty then my Sisster and brother came home and they saw the Chirtimas tree and th' next day We came home from shcool. We didn't saw mom or dad and we looks on the talbe it was money and then We go to to the Store and buy presst for each of us. We came home and we rate our presst and then Mom and dad came and we was happy. The next day was the 25 of December. We has a fest and we Spen our presst.

Figure 4.31:
As students increase in their fluency, their ability to write at length about a topic also increases.

- -

Figure 4.32: This example, picked out of the garbage, shows a student playing with the language. When students achieve a certain threshold of proficiency, they can wield the language with a dexterity that lower levels are unable to do. Note the student gave himself 100 percent.

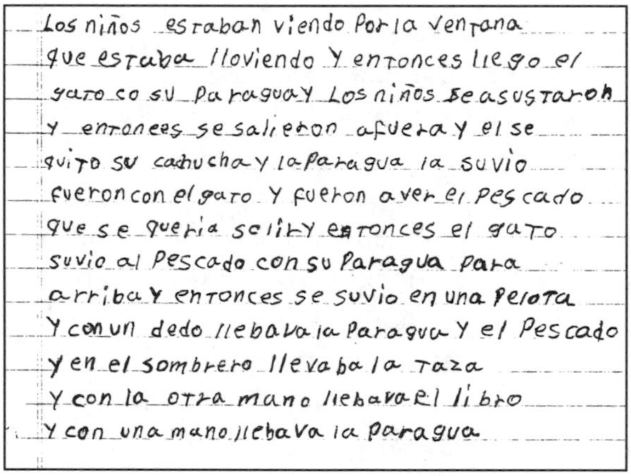

I am bird butt because gam a Bird that have a butt

100%

Los niños estaban viendo por la ventana que estaba lloviendo Y entonces llego el gato co su Paraguay Los niños se asustaron Y entonces se salieron afuera y el se quito su cachucha y la Paragua la suvio fueron con el gato Y fueron a ver el Pescado que se quería salir Y entonces el gato suvio al Pescado con su Paragua para arriba Y entonces se suvio en una Pelota Y con un dedo llebava la Paragua Y el Pescado Y en el sombrero llebava la Taza Y con la otra mano llebava el libro Y con una mano llebava la Paragua

Figure 4.33: This high school student has learned to read and write in his own language, but has not yet learned to read and write in English. There are errors in the Spanish writing, but he has achieved some fluency. This was his retelling of The Cat and the Hat, *which was read to his younger sister during a home tutoring lesson.*

We suggest the following strategies to enhance this level:

- ◆ Provide support for unfamiliar materials or content.
- ◆ Use texts with lower reading levels.
- ◆ Help with abstract conceptual reading.
- ◆ Help with cultural background of reading.
- ◆ Use stories and concepts student learned in first language as take-off point.
- ◆ Work on higher-order skills such as making inferences, comparing, synthesizing, and so on.

For example, Tong's sixth grade class was studying parts of a story: main character, setting, conflict, *denouement*, and so on. To complement and extend this lesson, Mary, Tong's tutor, used fairy tales to illustrate these features for her student. Tong was familiar with the Chinese rendition of "Little Red Riding Hood," "Lon Po Po." After rereading the story in English and discussing these concepts within the framework of that version, they moved on to "Hu Po Po," a Taiwanese variation of the "Lon Po Po" story, and then to a reading of the actual Grimm's version of Red Riding Hood. Then they did a chart of the four versions of the story to study similarities and differences and draw conclusions.

Story Comparison Questions

1. Who are the "good guys" (protagonists) in each story?
Lon Po Po 3 Sisters

Hu Po Po

Little Red Riding Hood - Hunter, LRR H, Granny

Grimm — Hunter, LRRH, Granny

2. Who is the "bad guy" (antagonist) in each story?
Lon Po Po Wolf

Hu Po Po Tiger

Little Red Riding Hood Wolf

Grimm 2 wolves

3. What is the setting in each story?
Lon Po Po In China

Hu Po Po el China

Little Red Riding Hood In Europe

Grimm In Europe

4. Who makes the journey in the story?
Lon Po Po Wolf

Hu Po Po Tiger

Little Red Riding Hood Wolf + LRRH

Grimm 2 wolves

5. What is the danger or conflict in each story?
Lon Po Po He wants eat the children

Hu Po Po He want eat the children

Little Red Riding Hood wolf want to eat the dessert

Grimm wolves want eat the sausages

Figure 4.34: Tong and his tutor discussed many aspects of these various versions. They were able to expand the lesson into the language issues (wolf/wolves, in China/ in Europe, and so on); content (protagonist/ antagonist, conflict/ resolution); and writing (Tong made a chart to illustrate the similarities and differences of all the versions).

ADVANCED FLUENCY

Students

◆ are self-motivated and confident readers in English and/or another language
◆ can process material further and further removed from own experience, and make links to personal experiences
◆ can research topics independently, by formulating topics and questions and finding relevant information
◆ can tackle a wide variety of texts by employing various reading strategies
◆ can make inferences and offer critical opinions or analyses
◆ have sufficient understanding of content vocabulary to read and understand textbooks
◆ can synthesize and expand on information

Figure 4.35, below and opposite: Pages from a retelling by an eighth grader of an old folk legend

As we discuss on page 136, this fluency may or may not be in English. Many of our students come to us from countries with rigorous school systems. Often they can read and write at exceptional levels in their own language. They may have been far ahead of our students in math and science and only their fluency in English is holding them back. Many can read and write in English and know grammar better than we do (often to our embarrassment when they try to engage us in discussion of the finer points of English). Their writing may be hesitant and filled with the grammar that reflects their own system. It could also be vigorous and strong, even though their grasp of English is not complete. They need assignments that challenge them, and that demand a higher level of thinking, analysis, and synthesis that allows them to extend their capacities.

Barb was assigned a higher level of ESL reading and writing. She decided to really push her students. First, she assigned a simple text, *Sarah, Plain and Tall,* on the grounds that the theme of moving to a strange place would be something all students could relate to. Students were required to write responses to the text before they came to class. In groups they worked through questions that required them to go back into the text for answers. Those who understood less than others benefited from the discussions. Questions were literal and simple: "List as many characters as you can." "List in order the events as they occurred." Then the questions moved on to higher level thinking: "Go back to the previous question and star the events that seem important in the evolution of Sarah."[1] The simple prose of the text gave the students confidence and practice in moving through a text without stopping to look up every unknown word.

The class moved on to *To Kill a Mockingbird*. This is a tough text even for many native-English speakers, but Barb chose it because it is a classic American story, one of the greatest pieces of literature produced in America, it has a strong story line and issues students can really grapple with (and she likes it a lot). Barb had to do much intervention in terms of explaining both background and understanding of the text itself. Beginning questions were identical to the "Sarah" questions. Then the class was asked whether they had experienced prejudice in their own country, and if they had lived in Maycomb what they would do for Tom Robinson. Finally, students were randomly assigned parts. They were first instructed to go back to the text and write down as many facts as they could about the character, then as many inferences as they could about the character. As a culminating exercise, other class members brainstormed questions to ask them, and they were interviewed and videotaped as that character.

LITERACY IN THE FIRST LANGUAGE/GAINING FLUENCY IN ENGLISH

Complicating our previous discussion on the levels of literacy development, or perhaps we should say overlaying this template, is the phenomena of students who enter our schools reading in various degrees of fluency in their own language. They may read and write at grade level in the first language, but have not yet achieved proficiency in English to read or write with ease. They're not learning to read over again; therefore, it is inappropriate to teach them as if they were illiterate. Studies show that a person only learns to read once, and the skills gained in the first language transfer as mastery in syntax and vocabulary proceed. As the student gains this control over grammar, vocabulary, and, often enough, the conventions of an alphabetic writing system with all its attendant punctuation and mechanical details, he can demonstrate more and more what he is capable of conceiving, and the gap between his thoughts and his production decreases. Barrs et al. (1989) write:

---

1. These questions were adapted from Petroskey and Bartholomae, *Facts, Artifacts, Counterfacts*, 1986.

> Bilingual children may well be developing as readers and writers in their first languages and, given the opportunity, can use this developing competence in the mainstream classroom...some children may also wish to write at length in their first language without necessarily recasting the writing into English. This kind of activity is valuable in itself, but is also useful as a way of increasing a [student's] awareness of the similarities and differences between different language systems.

It is not uncommon for students to feel the need to write in their own language first. This should be encouraged. It is often easier for them to get their thoughts out in a language they are familiar with than to struggle through the triple whammy of formulating ideas, finding the words in a language they are not proficient in, then transcribing these words onto paper. Writing first in their native tongue gives them a chance to figure out what they want to say before struggling in English. For example, a seventeen-year-old boy who had been placed in the eleventh grade but was reading at a much lower level, wrote first in Spanish:

> La primera vez que yo vine a los Estados Unidos yo fue en Diciembre. Cuando mire lege a la ciudad done vivia mie hermano Estaba enpresionado de lo venino hermoso y organiza de esta pais. Des pues entre a la escuela a aprender Ingles. Lo cual fue muy dificil las primeras semanas en la escuela porque no entendia nada.

He then translated his story into English:

> The first time I come to the United States was in December. When I arrive where my brother was living I was impresionado of the beoric, and organized of this country. After I go to school to learn Inglish, this was very dificult for me the two first weeks, because I don't spoke Inglish.

Many students, during their journey toward proficiency in English use an *interlanguage*. In figure 4.1, page 103, we discussed the concept of interlanguage, an "interim grammar," part one language and part another, in the development of oral language. This phenomenon can also happen with writing. Using the tools they have at the level of mastery they have achieved, students can, for instance, use the spelling and conventions of the first, but the syntax of English. Or they can intersperse their language with vocabulary they haven't learned the English words for yet.

It is critical, also, to support growth in the home language. Even though we may not be able to read it, we can encourage and celebrate the writing. Barrs et al. (1989) concur: "[Students] can be invited to choose to write in their community language(s) or in English...By encouraging bilingual [students] to talk about their writing, the ideas, the content and the way they went about the writing, a teacher who may not understand the language can become involved and give support to their developing biliteracy."

Figure 4.36: This was written by an eighth-grade girl who was an accomplished student in her own language. When writing in English, she would occasionally insert the Chinese character in the middle of the text rather than lose her train of thought by stopping to search for the word she wanted.

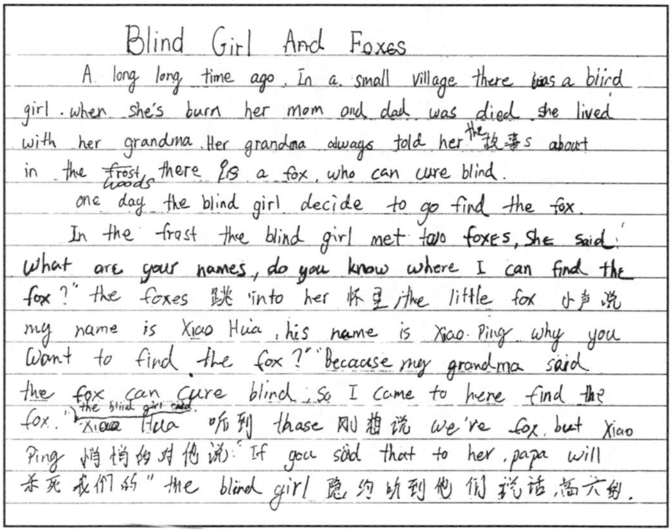
Blind Girl And Foxes

A long long time ago. In a small village there was a bliird girl. when she's burn her mom and dad was died. she lived with her grandma. Her grandma always told her the 故事s about in the frost woods there is a fox, who can cure blind.

one day the blind girl decide to go find the fox.

In the frost the blind girl met two foxes, She said: "What are your names, do you know where I can find the fox?" the foxes 跳 into her 怀里, the little fox 小声说 my name is Xiao Hua, his name is Xiao Ping why you want to find the fox?" "Because my grandma said the fox can cure blind, So I came to here find the fox." the blind girl said. Xiao Hua 听到 those 刚想说 we're fox, but Xiao Ping 悄悄的对他说: "If you said that to her, papa will 杀死我们的" the blind girl 隐约听到他们说话,高兴的.

For example, Song Jo, who came from the rigorous educational system in Korea and was new to the country, completed his report on an animal (figure 4.37). Although the teacher could not read what he had written, it was clear from the amount of writing he did that he knew a great deal about dragons. His tutor confirmed this, relating that he had gone into detail about the mythology of dragons in Korean history and their symbolism. We were dismayed to find out that the teacher had sent the work back to be done over because dragons are not "real" animals. He wrote another one about tigers. The assignment was completed but he did not care about tigers as much, and to Bong Hee, his tutor, the work was inferior to the first report he had written.

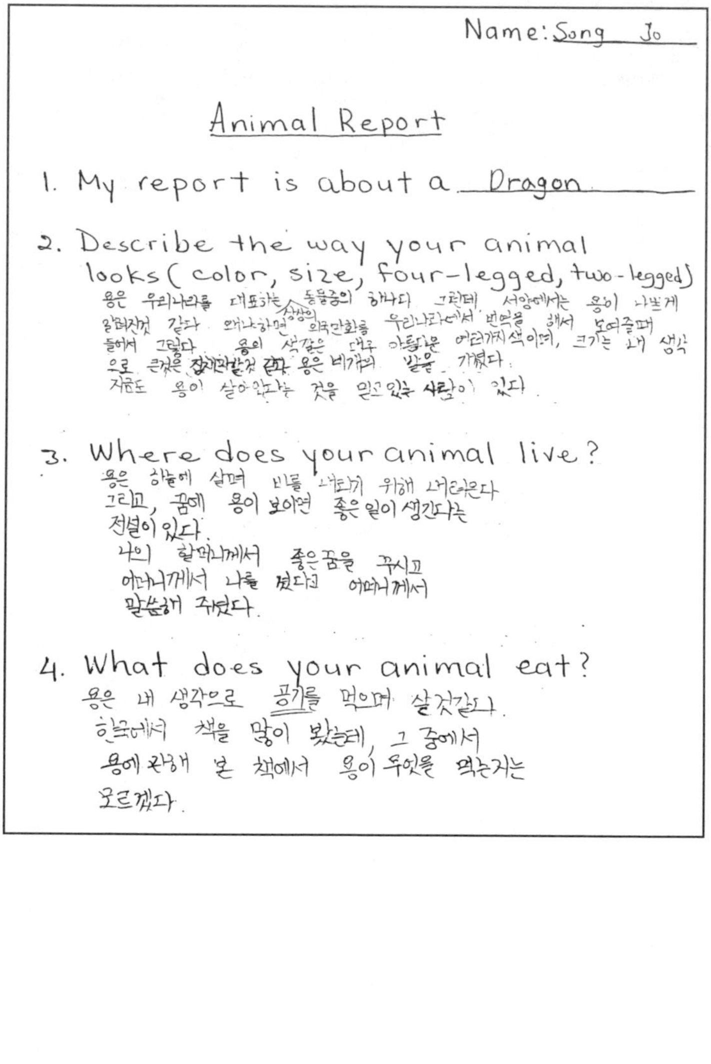

Name: Song Jo

Animal Report

1. My report is about a Dragon

2. Describe the way your animal looks (color, size, four-legged, two-legged)

용은 우리나라를 대표하는 상상의 동물중의 하나다 그런데 서양에서는 용이 나쁘게
알려진것 같다 왜냐하면 외국만화를 우리나라에서 번역을 해서 보여줄때
들어서 그렇다. 용의 색깔은 대부 아름다운 여러가지색이며, 크기는 내 생각
으로 큰것은 집채만할것 같고 용은 네개의 발을 가졌다.
지금도 용이 살아있다는 것을 믿고 있는 사람이 있다.

3. Where does your animal live?

용은 하늘에 살며 비를 내리기 위해 내려온다
그리고, 꿈에 용이 보이면 좋은 일이 생긴다는
전설이 있다.
나의 할머니께서 좋은 꿈을 꾸시고
어머니께서 나를 낳았다고 어머니께서
말씀해 주셨다.

4. What does your animal eat?

용은 내 생각으로 공기를 먹으며 살것같다.
한국에서 책을 많이 봤는데, 그 중에서
용에 관해 본 책에서 용이 무엇을 먹는지는
모르겠다.

Figure 4.37: *Song Jo's animal report*

CONCLUSION

Each student learns differently and struggles with different obstacles. When it comes to evaluating Maria or Yoshi's progress, we need to be able to see the big picture. We need to look at the context they are functioning in and where their skills fall on the language continuum. Understanding these elements opens the door for us to see so much more of our students' abilities. Seeing more factors, in turn, helps focus our planning to facilitate learning for each of our students. As teachers we strive to provide the best environment for learning, and we want to be able to document all the progress that we see happen as accurately as possible. Knowing the broad picture is the starting point.

5

Diving for
Pearls in their Shelves:
HOW AND WHERE TO
FIND INFORMATION

In this chapter we

- discuss the steps you can take to learn about your students
- show where to look to find answers

> The family was camping at Naro Moru, at the base of Mt. Kenya, but for three days the mountain had been hidden, shrouded in mists. Then one evening, just before sunset as they were taking a walk, Barb's father suddenly said, "Look!"
>
> "Ohhh," said her sisters in awe.
>
> She turned and looked but saw nothing out of the ordinary. "What?" "There!"
>
> "Where?"
>
> "There!" He took her face and pointed it in a direction and she looked hard but still couldn't see anything. "The mountain!" he exclaimed.
>
> Then she saw it, the sister mountain of Kilimanjaro, looming over them in the last light of day, so huge it filled the entire horizon. How could she have missed it? It was right there.

This chapter is about looking, about observation. But, like Barb and the mountain, unless you know where to look and what it is that you're looking at, you often don't see it. What is a mountain for some is invisible for those who haven't got the framework for perceiving what their eyes are taking in.

To observe is more than simply to look. It is to *see*, by directing your attention carefully and analytically, and to *perceive*, by understanding what it is you're looking at. When you are observing, you are

on the lookout for significant events, for qualitative leaps in understanding, or even for the almost imperceptible inching forward toward
mastery. Part of our definition of observation includes making judgments about what it is you are seeing, and thus making decisions
about what you will do next.

Besides looking, observing means listening, asking questions, analyzing. It is not a passive activity. In fact, observation could fall under
the heading "snooping." According to Florio-Ruane (1990), eavesdrop-
ping, informal conversations with students, listening for the "why of
things, things people take for granted, those they choose to comment
upon and the themes that recur in their talk," are all legitimate methods for finding what you want to know.

Observation is important because it

◆ is one way to form hypotheses or ideas
◆ is a means of answering specific questions
◆ provides a more realistic picture of behavior or events than do other
  methods of information gathering

DEFINING WHAT YOU WANT TO KNOW

The basic question all teachers ask is: How is this student doing? To
know what we're presenting is reaching the student, what the most
effective reinforcement is, or what area needs to be reviewed, we
must know what our students know. But that question is so broad
and unwieldy as to be unmanageable. We need to define more clearly
what we want to find out. Cambourne and Turbill (1988) have defined
five broad categories of information we need to know about our students.
These are

◆ the **strategies** they use as they read and write and speak
◆ the level of **explicit understanding** they have of the processes they
  can and should use when reading and writing and communicating
◆ their **attitudes** toward reading and writing, conversation, and the
  English language

- their **interests and backgrounds**
- the degree of **control** they display over language in all its forms and the content they are expected to master

Finding the Answers

Finding the answers and collecting information in usable form can be an overwhelming task. You don't want to gather just any information, because then you simply end up with barns full of paper that nobody wants to dig through; you want data that is telling and useful. You must decide where to look and at what. There are many methods, but they fall under three general headings:

- Observing the student working
- Talking with the student
- Sampling student work

As we stated in chapter 1, you need enough information to get a balanced picture of the student. You want to be sure your observations come from a number of contexts. This is important for ESL students, because sampling one area may give an incomplete profile of the student. For example, Il-Hwa, a Korean student, may write very sophisticated and thoughtful prose; her writing samples may demonstrate her competent English abilities. However, Il-Hwa is not able to participate in whole-class discussions because her speaking skills are still limited. She is able to participate on a limited basis in small-group work with her peers because the setting is less formal. Paco, on the other hand, has trouble writing even the most basic sentences; thus you need a method to record the tremendous progress he has made in his speaking skills and his insightful additions to class discussions to balance the weaknesses reflected in his writing samples.

The Quad

Researchers Anthony et al. (1991) have developed a complex framework called "The Quad" (figure 5.1) as a guide for knowing where to look to find answers to that all-important question of how students are doing (we have adapted this for our own use).

Observation of Process	**Observation of Product**
Students immersed in:	Learning logs
Reading	Reading Logs
Writing	Selected pages from:
Speaking	notebooks or journals
Listening	Audio tapes
	Writing folders
	Group work logs
	Projects
Classroom Measures	**Decontextualized Measures**
Text-related activities	Criterion-referenced tests
Teacher-made tests	District exams
Comprehension questions	Provincial or state exams
Homework	

Figure 5.1:
The Quad

Routman (1991) notes that the lower two quadrants consist of the more traditional means of evaluation, often consisting of "summative" types of measures, while the top two are "formative"; these are more dynamic because they are ongoing and can demonstrate cumulative growth.

In addition, we might define these quadrants in terms of *distance*: the physical and temporal distance between the teacher and the learner, between the teacher and the context within which the event took place, and between the actual learning (or nonlearning) that took place, and the measurement of that learning. For instance, when you are observing your class in an activity, you can note who is succeeding and who is floundering, who is working diligently and who is goofing off, and you can intervene at any time. While listening to someone reading you can see what strategies they are using to gain meaning and whether or not these strategies are effective. While students are engaged in writing, you can ask them how it's going, help them find the words they want, and grapple with them to find the best organization. You can listen to their speech and see how they are gaining proficiency through what they say, who they talk to, and how much or how little they can carry on through interaction or a class discussion.

In a testing situation, you often cannot intervene with help, even though you can see a student struggling. In many situations, you do not see or know scores until much later. You are not privy to the method the student used to reach the answer he did—in most cases you can only see if he got it right or not. You have limited insight into all but the student's ability to answer the narrow range of questions of that particular test.

These categories in the Quad are not as clearly delineated as they would seem, simply because what students say about what they have written and read are as important as what they have actually done. We have found that trying to pick apart each of the categories in the Quad might create more confusion. We suggest you not worry a great deal about which category the group project on Native Americans belongs to, but be sure to take the observations you made into consideration. Samples of work can be the subject of conferences and interviews, and written products can be returned to for continued polishing and revision, as we will demonstrate in our discussion below.

We did not attempt to exhaustively answer each category in the Quad, and you should not feel obligated to, either. They are suggestions of where to look for evidence of learning and what to ask your students about their learning. However, with these in mind, we can look at each student and gain insight into his strengths and weaknesses.

OBSERVATION OF PROCESS

Observing learning as it is taking place is part of the central job of each teacher. Processes are the *hows*, *whens*, *wheres*, and *whys* of what happens within the contexts that are a part of every school day, when students are immersed in their tasks of learning. Goodman (1988: 10) points out that "evaluation provides the most significant information if it occurs continuously and simultaneously with the experiences in which the learning is taking place....Teachers who observe the development of language and knowledge in children in different settings become aware of important milestones in children's development that tests cannot reveal."

When you are observing the processes of learning, when students are engaged in meaning making—whether it be reading, writing, working out math problems, conducting experiments, collaborating on a project, or working alone—you are closest to the event, and can respond, react, intervene, and participate in the meaning making. It is here that you can most readily see the learning take place. Observing processes is a natural part of your day.

Speaking and listening

The Primary Language Record (1989) reminds us that there are two main dimensions of talk—social and cognitive—and that talk, above all, is about interaction. "It is to do with interaction between people. It is the principal means of making contact with others, and building relationships. It is also to do with interaction between ideas—[students] hear new ideas, put forward new ideas, and develop new ideas through talking with others." As second-language learners gain experience in English, they grow in their knowledge of the system of English—the grammar and the vocabulary—but they also grow in their ability to use English to gain knowledge in the content areas.

Students come to us already skilled users of the language. They know how to manipulate language for their own purposes: to wheedle the promise of a movie or a treat out of their parents, to make a joke, to weave fantasies or engage in imaginative play, to learn something new and tell others what they have learned. They are simply adding another language system to the skills they have already learned.

Omark (1981) points out that context is particularly important in considering the proficiency of the learner. He writes that a student "may be silent in the classroom, quiet on the playground with new peers, talkative at home, and boisterous on the streets." He goes on to stress the importance of watching the student in more than one setting. In addition, the social relationships of the student affect what the student says. On the playground, for example, relationships based on dominance prevail, and students on the lower end of the hierarchy may be more passive and much quieter. In the classroom, your presence as teacher can have a profound affect on what is said and how much. It is often helpful to have several other adults watching and giving their input on how a particular student is functioning.

For instance, one student was sullen and unresponsive in class, talking in his own language while the teacher was trying to conduct a lesson and refusing to do the work on the grounds that he didn't understand. He only answered in monosyllables to the aide. His mother reported that at home he was disrespectful to the point of being abusive. On the playground, however, he was clearly a leader, bossing a group of smaller boys around, declaring what the play would be for the day, and holding a kingly sway over all activities.

Developing mastery

By watching the processes, you can see most clearly into the five categories Cambourne and Turbill (1990) have defined: strategies, level of explicit understanding, attitudes, interests, and control.

Strategies. These are the means a language user employs to get his point across in a conversational or learning setting. For example, Juan communicates most effectively with his friend Ricardo, whose English is better, and who helps by negotiating a lot of meaning in Spanish. Juan, however, has a very effective strategy for getting help in completing an English sentence with a non-Spanish speaking person. He will mumble through a sentence until he comes to an English word he knows, then mumble some more, and wait for his listener to fill in the gaps. It isn't Spanish, it isn't English. For example:

Juan: Mumblemumblemumble counselor mumblemumblemumble.

Barb: Oh, you need to see the counselor?

Juan [*Relief shows on his face*]: Yes.

Explicit understanding: metacognition. Every user of language has strategies he uses to get his point across. In addition, users are very often aware of the strategies they use, and the choices they have available to them. Even very young children learn that "pwease," a big smile, and large soulful eyes can get them what they want faster than whining, and four-year-olds will try out strategies such as commanding: "You have to buy that for me because I'm the boss"; or bargaining: "If I show you what's in my pocket I don't have to wear my helmet"; or acting like Sam, who said to the checkout clerk at the store, "This isn't really a truck under my shirt, I just ate a lot for lunch." This "knowing about knowing" is called "meta-awareness" or "metacognition." Swartz and Perkins define metacognition as "becoming aware of your thought processes in order to then control them when appropriate" (Barell 1992). Knowing that you have these strategies available to you, you can use them consciously in listening or speaking or reading. Metacognition can be revealed in a student's speech by:

◆ **Experimenting with forms or styles they haven't quite mastered yet.** For example, Valeria is very sociable, and wants to be part of the action at all times. When she first arrived she learned chunks and phrases of language, such as "Can I play?", "It's your turn," and "It's not your turn," that enable her to participate immediately, even though she was unable to articulate the meaning of each word apart from the whole. Later, as her proficiency progressed, she'd pretend she was queen, and say queenly things, such as, "I command you to bring me my pencil."

◆ **Self-correcting oral errors.** Carlos was slowly sorting out tenses. He knew *ed* endings, but was working through irregular verbs. He said, "I buyed...I bought it at K-Mart yesterday."

ATTITUDES. These can be attitudes toward the target language or attitudes about learning language in general. Blia, a sixteen-year-old Hmong girl, came to Mary's ESL class with very little English and class-room experience. She lacked literacy in both Hmong and English. She struggled with her lessons and the going was slow in reading and writing. Yet Blia was making tremendous strides in her speaking abilities. She had already made great friends with many of her teachers at school. The other Hmong students in the class relied on her to help communicate their questions and problems. Blia was a natural nego-tiator and instinctively knew where the gaps were when Mary was having problems getting a lesson across. "Oh, Teacher, they don't look to you now because they feel shy about talking this lesson." Then she would chatter away in Hmong to the other students and eventually they would nod their heads and say, "uh, huh." Blia would then turn to Mary and say, "It's okay. They not be shy tomorrow." When Mary needed to clarify a concept or explain an issue to the rest of the class, she made sure Blia was around. Blia was anxious to get a job to help her family, and she was shameless in letting anyone who could help her know that she was ready to work. She just knew she was able to succeed and she couldn't wait to start.

The student who burst out "English is my enemy forever" had reached such a frustration level that he felt that he was never going to succeed in the language.

INTERESTS AND BACKGROUND. Alva resisted learning. He would do anything to avoid school work. Mary discovered that he loved sports and gambling. Alva knew all the stats on every baseball player on his favorite team, so Mary decided to use this information to her advantage. She used sporting events such as the World Series to create math charts on averages, statistics, and language focus. And when the 1994 Winter Olympics were underway, she seized the opportunity. Mary and Alva made predictions about who would place in the events and which countries had the best shot at the most medals. They developed complicated charts and Alva had to write essays explaining what would happen if this or that athlete were injured or disqualified. Alva was wholly engaged in these activities and developed his language skills by haranguing his teacher over who looked best in this event or who he thought was just a lucky shot.

CONTROL. This refers not only to control over vocabulary and syntax, but also to control over the types of language used in the different domains of life. Learners of a language often acquire the BICS (Basic Interpersonal Communication Skills) first, but take much longer to master the language of school, the kinds of language that one uses in a school situation, and the demands that language makes on its user.

Inna does not speak English to anyone; her teacher believes she knows none at all. But when Donna, her tutor, took her outside to play games in the playground, she found that Inna understood such directions as *stop, go, hop, run, walk, skip.*

Six little boys are sitting in a circle around the teacher who is asking them yes-and-no questions. The teacher, because she is familiar with these boys, can read between the lines of their answers to see what they know:

TEACHER: Does it snow in winter?

CHANG: Yes, we do. (*Chang has been through one winter and although he understands the concept of snow, his control of English grammar is limited, and he often uses formulaic answers.*)

TEACHER: Does she have a hat?

CHOUA: Yes, she doos. (*Choua is showing a good grasp of English and grammatical forms by his answer. He knows that an s ending shows third person singular. He hasn't mastered the finer points of irregular forms and pronunciation.*)

MARK: Yes, she doesn't. (*Mark knows the correct answer, but hasn't learned the difference between* do *and* doesn't, *and gives a formulaic answer.*)

TEACHER: Does he have his shoes on?

ALEM: Yes, he is. (*The answer is no. Alem doesn't have a clue, and simply gives a sentence he's heard before in the course of the lesson.*)

BEN: No, he's doesn't. (*Ben answers this questions correctly, but, like Choua, has yet to refine the nitpicky points of grammar, and adds an s ending to both the pronoun and the verb, showing a good ear for the grammar of English.*)

Understanding how ESL students gain control over their speaking and listening skills will help you see the steps they make towards fluency. Even nonverbal communication demonstrates some level of understanding.

Reading

Students may come to school already knowing how to read in their first language, or they may be illiterate. However, they are already, as we noted before, skilled users of language. They know how to project, to speculate, to predict: skills they need to read fluently. Therefore, in helping them become good readers, we can build on these skills, and evaluate their reading based on what they can say and do while reading.

DEVELOPING MASTERY

Again, we can look at Cambourne and Turbill's five categories to illuminate what a reader is doing:

STRATEGIES. If we define reading as getting meaning from print, then strategies are the methods a reader uses to achieve meaning. Johnston (1992) writes:

> A child reading a book comes across a word he doesn't recognize. Reading suddenly shifts from recognition to reasoning. Some strategy needs to be used to render the word recognizable. Perhaps he will relate it to a different word he does know, or use some of his knowledge of the relationships between letters and sounds. Perhaps he will read on and come back to figure it out, or ask a neighbor.

Good readers have a variety of strategies on hand to use whenever they come to a word they don't recognize or a passage they don't understand.

As teachers, we can note the strategies that students use, and help them learn more or better ones as they become increasingly independent readers. Here, for example are two readers and their strategies:

> Nilakhone, a third grader, has been an accurate oral "reader." She can call out words but can't remember what she has read. Through observation and conversation the teacher discovers that her goal in reading is not necessarily to make sense, but to read "correctly." He works on helping her with this issues by giving her the strategy of continuously asking the question "Does this make sense?" One day, as he watches, he sees her reading a three-paragraph passage. She is just into the third paragraph when she comes to a confusing word. She stops, looks at the words around it, but can't figure it out. She begins reading the entire passage again from the beginning. Her teacher comments this may not be the fastest strategy, but it shows that she is aware she needs to understand the passage. Her comprehension has broken down, and she now has learned several strategies to try to pick up the thread.

◆

> Tonio has very few strategies available to him besides guessing at the word based on the first letter. His most effective strategy to date is to

hesitate at every new word and look up at the teacher with a big pleading smile to try to get her to say the words for him.

EXPLICIT UNDERSTANDING: METATEXTUAL AWARENESS. In addition to having strategies, it is also important for a reader to know which strategy is going to help in any particular situation. For instance, when Tina is confronted by the phrase "the best in the neighborhood" and does not know the word *neighborhood*, she can use any number of strategies (sounding it out, guessing, asking, skipping) to work through it. If she has only one, such as sounding out, she is limited in her abilities to obtain meaning, because the word is particularly unsuited for using phonics to decipher. Explicit understanding of the options she has and knowing which one will work best in any given situation will serve her well. Asking her outright what she thinks she can do when she encounters a word she can't recognize on sight will give you insight into her understanding of what her options are.

ATTITUDES. In addition to the meta-awareness of strategies, several researchers point out that feelings, attitudes, and dispositions also play a critical role in metacognition. Fusco and Fountain (1992) write, "metacognition involves the monitoring and control of attitudes, such as students' beliefs about themselves, the value of persistence, the nature of work, and their personal responsibility in accomplishing a goal." Most readers are very aware of how well or how poorly they read. That the "Robins" consist of the good readers while the "Bluebirds" are the strugglers and stragglers is never—and can never be—a secret from students. Readers can often become disabled simply because they think they are. It is important to be aware of a student's attitudes toward the act of reading and of himself as a reader. The statements "I can't read very well" or "I hate to write" are red flags that need to be taken as seriously as a child stating "I'm a failure" or "I'm a bad boy."

Following is part of a English-speaking student's essay on his struggle to learn to read because it poignantly details the frustrations and feelings of helplessness and worthlessness that came from not being able to read well. Add to this the task of learning to read in a language that is not your first, and you can see how many of our students, struggling below grade level when their intellectual capacities meet or exceed many of our native-English readers, feel about reading:

I was the seventh child of a catholic family. Being the last child in a big family I most of got the reject gene. I also got a brain is one size larger then a peanut unfortunately I was born with a read disability.

As a young lad I notice that I had a problem with my reading. My teachers thought that I would catch on sometime, but I never did. I was alway stuck in the low reading groups and it alway embarrasses me see my friends in the high reading group. I didn't know why it rattl me that my friends didn't care if I was in a low read group. I guess it was those other kids that me fun of me.

Because my reading was so poor I was held back one year. That was hard for me even more seeing my friends in a grade one ahead of me. As we all know kids are the meanest thing around. I was tess by other kids, because I didn't advance into the next grade. This made me close up and not made new friends. I became really shy and it is like that today. I will rather sat alone then to talk to people.

When I finely got into High School I thought that it would be different. I might get awhole of this read problem, but I was wrong. To me High School was a big joke. Not in the way that everyone think of school but in the way that the teachers didn't give a shit about you as a person and a student.

I found my nich. I wanted to do was computer. i wish that read came as easy as computers did. I can sit at a computer and in minutes I can start the program up and running with out the help of the manual. Maybe in the long run computer will get me to read then the teacher couldn't do or I might never get the change to read like the average person.

INTERESTS AND BACKGROUND. The importance of a student's pleasure and interest in topics and authors has been well-documented over the years. Barrs et al. (1989) write, "If children are to develop as readers there must be personal involvement in reading. The pleasures of reading often begin as shared pleasures and arise from reading with an adult. When a child experiences the emotional satisfaction of involvement in story, s/he is likely to want to read more." Thus, encouraging independence and involvement in reading entails encouraging students to choose their own books as often as possible, even if it means reading the same ones over and over again. Interest and involvement with reading can often make the difference in how much a student gets out of a book. Naoki, for instance, is only interested in facts and does not enjoy fiction. While Pam and Lan truly loved *To Kill a Mockingbird* and were moved by the experience of reading it, Naoki was bored to tears and found the reading, discussion, and projects excruciating. Keeping an eye on what the student chooses to read, having students keep a list, and conducting interest inventories are all ways to get a handle on a student's interests.

Background knowledge is also particularly critical in reading for second language learners. Often our students do not have the foundation they need, and that we assume as givens, to understand texts. For instance, an ESL text Barb was using for an intermediate-level class included Shirley Jackson's "The Lottery," one of Barb's favorite stories. The students had no clue what it meant. They did not know what a lottery was, and even after Barb painstakingly explained the concept, the story had little impact. In addition, the text contained a chapter from *Cheaper By the Dozen*, another book Barb had loved as a teenager. The humor went entirely over their heads, and while Barb was chuckling away, they were moping through the story, not enjoying it in the least. The lesson was a dud.

Students from other countries who are placed in content-area classes, such as history, science, or literature, often lack the fundamental concepts to understand the text, even if they can understand the words.

CONTROL. There is no such thing as achieving perfection in reading. Learning to read is a lifelong pursuit. Barb can read difficult linguistics texts with ease, but cannot decipher car repair manuals and is a terrible cook because she can't read recipes—she's always skimming for the main point. There are always new concepts, new ideas, new areas to explore. Learners who come to school with little or no knowledge about print just have further to go. In the next chapter we provide checklists and examples of anecdotes about readers gaining control. You can also see developing control in:

♦ **Growing confidence or independence in choice of texts.** This may involve students grappling with genres and tasks apparently beyond their capabilities.

◆ **Self-correcting (or not self-correcting) of miscues when reading.**
Here is John's reading of a portion of *The Boxcar Children*. The
miscues, in italics, are above the text as it actually appeared. The self-
corrected mistakes are marked with a *C*.

repleed   *Adams*
Come any time, replied Mr. Beach, starting back. The Aldens

say (c)
noticed that Mrs Beach had not said a word.

As the Beach family went into their new house Violet said,

other   *Violet*
"I have an idea." The others looked at her because Violet's ideas

ask   *tried*
were always good. She said, "Mrs Beach will be too tired to get

super (c)   *super* (c)
supper, so let's send their supper over to them."

Reading aloud for the purpose of determining strategies is always followed by a retelling. This portion of a reading is also a critical part of
understanding a reader and his abilities, and his control over the act
of reading. Many readers need to be prompted with questions to help
them both understand the stories they read and retell them. This
process is vital to determining what they know. John, the boy who
read from *The Boxcar Children*, above, was interviewed about his
understanding of the text.

TEACHER: Can you tell me what you remember from that part of
the story?

JOHN: They were meeting at the beach.

TEACHER: What else?

JOHN: Benny and Jessie were staying at home...

TEACHER: What's the excitement in this part?

JOHN: The new neighbor came in.

TEACHER: Where did they come in?

JOHN: To the empty house.

TEACHER: What else happened?

JOHN: Um...Violet asked "Who are the new neighbors?" Um...she ran upstairs into Mr. Andy room.

TEACHER: What did they decide to do?

JOHN: Um, cook supper?

TEACHER: Why?

JOHN: Because, um, the new neighbor didn't have food.

John's retelling confirms that his correction of *supper* for *super* meant that he understood that part; however, his lack of correction of *tried* for *tired* and his subsequent retelling showed that he did not understand why the characters in the story cooked supper for the neighbors. The need for the teacher to continuously question him, and John's short responses, showed that he remembered only basic concepts with few supporting details. John was a very slow, word-for-word reader. A thorough analysis of John's miscues and his retelling revealed that he scored very low in comprehension. He had problems attending to the surrounding context both before and following the words he miscued on. Knowing these things, the teacher was able to plan a program for John that focused on predicting situations and words, using surrounding text to identify words and concepts within a story.

In contrast to John's retelling, Thanousay, another student John's age, read the same text and said

> The part, um, I liked the part is when, um, they making pie, making, um, supper for their next neighbor is they name is Mr. Beach. They got four, four children, think so, and, um, and they didn't know yet when they gonna move in they first time. They um, um, you know, the house near the beach was old, no one had stayed there for long time, no one had moved in, but then a new neighbor had moved to a new, to um, next

door neighborhood so they want to be a friend with them. Benny and they want to give some food to give to them to, um, if they tired, they could eat it.

Thanousay's retelling revealed a much deeper understanding of the story. Thanousay was able to bring out all the main points with supporting details without prompting from the teacher.

OBSERVATION OF PRODUCT

Writing

Observing written work in a variety of forms gives you a chance to see what a student is able to produce and how he has grown and developed over a period of time. In this case collecting and observing go hand in hand. However, the beauty of this quadrant is that you can examine products in quiet reflection outside the classroom, but you also have the opportunity to return to the student with any questions you may have about his production, then observe him as he reflects, responds, and revises. When you are able to look at written products outside the context of the situation in which they were produced, you can identify the control a writer has over both the conventions of writing in any language, and the punctuation, form, style, and cohesion demanded by writing. First we will discuss Cambourne and Turbill's five categories of information in terms of writing, then we will tell where to find evidence of mastery in both reading and writing by looking at written products.

DEVELOPING MASTERY

Learning to write is similar to learning to read. As Barrs et al. (1989) point out, it is "a journey from dependence to independence. Initially a child needs the help and support of another person...support which can be gradually withdrawn and the child takes over more and more of the process." We can also examine the five areas when looking at written products.

STRATEGIES. Strategies in writing are similar to strategies in reading in that the more strategies a writer has available, the more likely the writer is able to solve problems.

Johnston (1992) points out certain constraints on strategy use:

- **The strategies a student has available.** Does a writer who's stuck know that he can find the word in a thesaurus, ask a buddy or a teacher, approximate the word, use an easier word, leave a space and go on, or does he simply bog down waiting for the word to come to him?
- **The knowledge he has relevant to the topic.** Has he been asked to write about a subject he is intimately familiar with (such as the flight from his country) or about something beyond the realm of his experience (such as getting a bill passed through Congress)?
- **The goals he is trying to accomplish.** Is the goal to get every word spelled correctly, to get ideas out, or to develop fluency without worrying about spelling?
- **The situational constraints,** such as deadlines, having an audience, having a dictionary handy, and so on.
- **The student's perceptions of the cause of a problem.**

We can also add another constraint: the language a second-language learner has available to express his meaning adequately. For example, Hide has trouble explaining the theme in *The Glass Menagerie*. He could give plot information, and understands the story, but doesn't have the vocabulary in English to encompass the abstract concepts of the theme.

EXPLICIT UNDERSTANDING. Understanding what is involved in the process of getting thoughts down on paper, of working through drafts, of knowing how to organize, and what needs changing is, like reading, an ever-evolving skill.

Explicit understanding can be revealed by:

- **Self/peer-editing.** Teacher Marlene Hess uses the process approach to writing, in which the students work through several drafts. When the final draft is due, she passes out bottles of correction fluid with the instructions that this is last-chance editing time, and students are given the task of correcting all grammar, punctuation, and spelling so that all papers will come to her perfect, free of error. Armed with their handbooks, students go over their partner's papers with a fine-toothed comb and debate about structure and spelling.

- **Critical appraisals of own work.** Michael, who is active and athletic on the playground, gets frustrated when trying to write and tells his teacher to do it, that he can't. He picks up his pen, makes several scribbles, and gives up. His fine motor skills are very limited at this point.

   Gordon, whose command of spoken English is outstanding and who is deft enough in English to display his wry tongue-in-cheek wit, hands in an essay that is barely a paragraph long, much shorter and less developed than other less-proficient students, and off-topic enough to concern the teacher. Here is a portion:

> Reflecting on my life (which is quite long: oh! I am eighteen years old, an old man) I think that the very first event that has caused the chain of others, without which nothing would have happened to me, is my birth. Unfortunately I don't remember that event. Because of that I cannot tell you in detail how it was. The only thing I can definitely say about it is that it happened approximately at eight o'clock in the evening.

When his teacher confers with him, he hesitates and resists revising, and tells her he thinks it's fine. When it comes time to hand in the final draft, he simply turns in the first draft, having done nothing to it.

   Melanie came to the teacher and said, "I know this isn't finished, but I just tried to get all the ideas I could on paper." When questioned about her beginning, she said, "I read that you should start with one topic and end on the same subject, so I tried to do that, but it doesn't seem right."

   By the fourth grade Lou Lor has improved in her written work from a year before. Her teacher compliments her on her improvement in spelling and verb tenses, something they had worked on together. Her response: "I can't tell if I'm better."

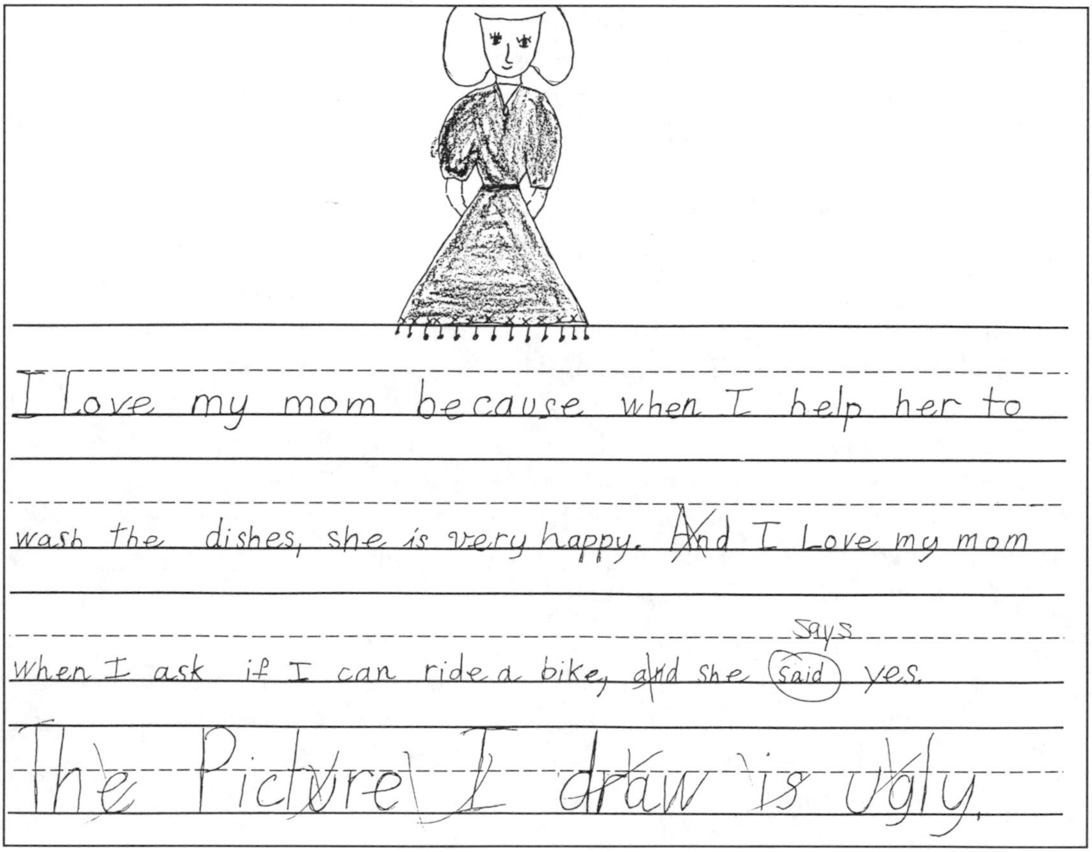

I love my mom because when I help her to

wash the dishes, she is very happy. And I love my mom

says

When I ask if I can ride a bike, and she (said) yes.

The Picture I draw is ugly.

Figure 5.2:
Sandy's analysis
of her own
drawing is very
sad. Rather than
simply crossing
out Sandy's com-
ments, perhaps
the teacher could
have encouraged
her drawing.

ATTITUDES. As with reading, writers can become disabled and helpless simply because they believe they have nothing to say, that they are lousy writers, or because they distrust the teacher. They will not reveal their inadequacies on paper to be bloodied, ridiculed or punished.

Students who know they will be penalized for misspellings, comma splices, or fragments will be cautious writers who will not venture beyond what they know to try anything new.

For instance, Mary recalls a linguistics class in which students were required to write their final paper in Black English vernacular (BEV). The professor found all papers unacceptable and handed them back, then posted the rules for the vernacular on the board with the instructions to rewrite their essays according to these rules. The students complied, but the essays were reduced from in-depth analyses to simple-sentence statements of fact; the students had such difficulty in applying the rules of the dialect, they stuck to the known, unwilling to risk being penalized for mistakes in grammar.

INTERESTS AND BACKGROUND. Writing teachers know that engaging the writer is a very important issue. Often students will produce dull, stilted, uninteresting prose when asked to write on a topic they couldn't care less about, but will produce fresh, vivid images when writing something they care about.

For example, Phoebe generally wrote very structured prose and took few risks with her writing, preferring to stick to safe prose that had few mistakes. She was excited about one particular assignment, however, and wrote:

> If I were a bird I would fly to my lover whenever, and also I can see every-thing beneath of me after sit on the top of the building. And I wish to go in the forest. I will talk with another birds about men in there. because they fly anywhere, maybe they know many things. About honest men, richmen, poormen, children...But especially I wish to know men's mind. We can see everything that we apeard in front of my eyes. But we never see one's mind. It is very difficult that we judge one's mind. Anyhow, birds look like very freely and feel easy to fly But it is only apeared in surface. They feel pain, hunger, loneliness...too. Birds are not necessarily happy. Finally, if I were a bird, that is ony for three days. for three days, I will have many experiences and much emotion. That is enough. And then I will thank what I was born a man to my God.

Phoebe's organization is meandering, and she gets off-topic, but her enthusiasm for the entire idea carries her far beyond what she was previously able to produce.

CONTROL. The following examples of written work, including writing about reading, demonstrate what products can reveal to the teacher. It is a collection of work produced over a period of time to demonstrate growth in conventions, skills, proficiency.

For example, figure 5.3 a–f reveals the explosive growth in Carmela's capabilities over a very short period of time.

Figure 5.3: (a) Carmela copied several patterned sentences when she first started working with her tutor. While all are correct, she is not engaged in the assignment.

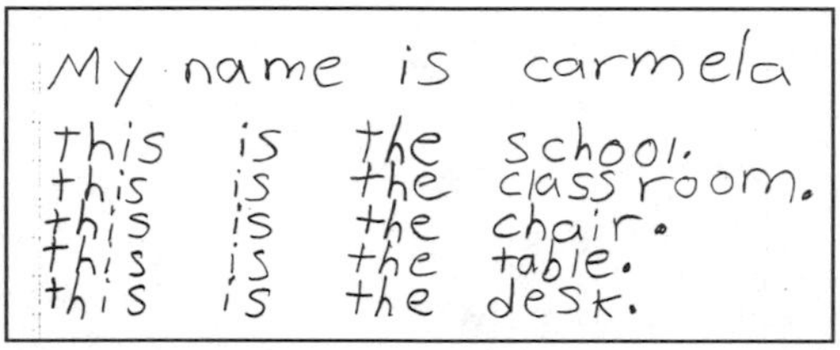

My name is carmela
this is the school.
this is the classroom.
this is the chair.
this is the table.
this is the desk.

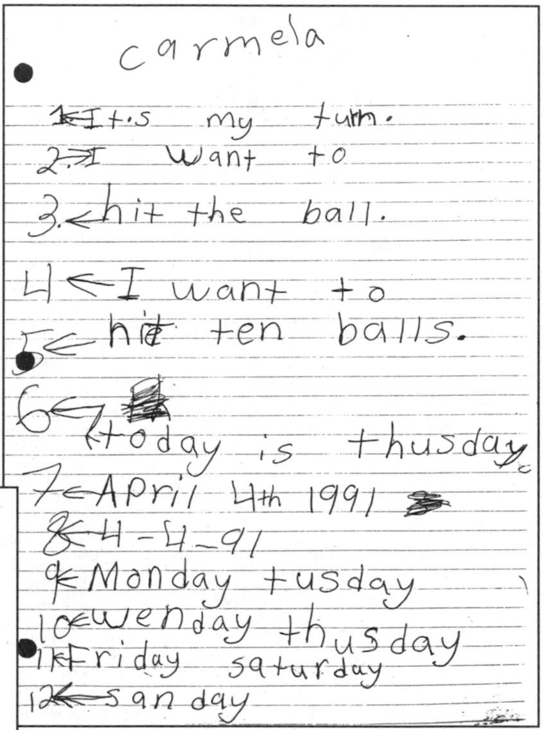

carmela
1← It.s my turn.
2.← I want to
3.← hit the ball.
4 ← I want to
5 ← hit ten balls.
6 ← today is thusday
7 ← April 4th 1991
8 ← 4-4-91
9 ← Monday tusday
10 ← wenday thusday
11 ← friday saturday
12 ← sanday

(b) After several sessions that were excruciating in their silence, Carmela and her brothers and sisters got very excited about learning to play tennis with their tutor. As a group they wrote down some of the vocabulary they had learned, which Carmela copied. She then wrote several sentences on her own, using vocabulary she had learned earlier. The errors demonstrate that she is working from memory using sound-letter principles.

(c) Carmela's "book report" on The Cat in the Hat.

Carmela's artifacts reveal both her interests (tennis) and her strategies: copying, and using her knowledge of English and Spanish to write sentences; her control over forms in the letter; and her increasing control over written English.

(d) *Carmela was supposed to meet her tutor on the playground. She drew a map telling the teacher that she would meet her by the tetherball court.*

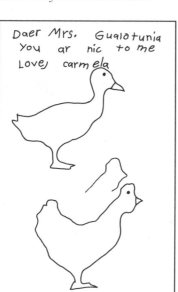

(e) *The tutor read* I Know an Old Lady *to the group. This is Carmela's retelling. She was very excited, and by this time was beginning to take risks with her writing, trying to spell words on her own. Several of her words are in Spanish; others (cow and horse) demonstrate her knowledge of Spanish spelling principles.*

(f) *This letter reveals that Carmela knows a great deal about the standard format for letters. She uses appropriate punctuation. Her spelling is very close to standard.*

As students gain control over written forms, they are able to develop further. The following sections describe various forms of writing that can reveal growth both in reading and writing.

VIEWING THE WRITING PROCESS

Carmela's folder (figure 5.3) was simply a collection of writing produced over time. It is also instructive to collect all work done from
rough draft up
to the finished
product on a
select piece of

MY mother
MY sister
MY brother
MY friend.

mother

my mother and I work

my mother and I cook.

my mother and I wash dishes

Figure 5.4: *This shows the
process Tran went through,
(from top to bottom) choosing
her subject, brainstorming
ideas with drawings, editing
and (far right) rough drafts,
to final copy.*

*MY mother and I wash dishes.
because I love mother and happy. my mother and
I cook. mother and I work.*

writing (figure 5.4). In this way you can see how much a writer knows at the outset, which strategies help him improve, and how much growth he shows during the process. Keeping several, or having students choose a select number for inclusion in their portfolio for grading, is one way to really get a picture of the writer's evolution. Since, as Atwell (1987) points out "writing growth is seldom a linear progress," each piece can demonstrate improvement over the last.

In reviewing and evaluating such artifacts, questions teachers can
ask of these pieces of writing (as suggested by Goodman and Atwell)
are:

Is the writing clear and meaningful?
Is it organized in an appropriate format?
Is the writer able to present information, express a viewpoint,
   or tell a story?
Is the piece interesting to read?
Is there evidence of the writer's voice?
Is there an audience in mind?
Did the writer take risks with his writing?

As we will discuss in chapter 9, collecting and examining these pieces
at the end of the quarter or year reveals the student's growth over time.

JOURNALS

Journals are another good way to note progress. Journals are ideal for
gaining fluency, for practicing getting ideas on paper, for articulating
thoughts and feelings, for exploring language and concepts. Many students resist writing in journals because they feel they have nothing to
write—moreover, they don't know how. They are leery of exposing their
lack of knowledge. They are also afraid they will get nailed for their
errors. (For this reason journals should not be corrected, nor should
they be used to point out grammatical deficiencies.) It takes effort
and commitment to get and keep journals going. Students have to be
encouraged to use journals and should be allowed to copy books,
magazines, and such, until they feel confident enough to express their
own ideas. Dialogue journals help overcome this problem. Having a
real reader who will respond to one's ideas, to the content and not the
form, gives readers confidence that they have something to say that's
worth reading.

Over time, journals can reveal significant growth. For instance, here
are some selections from the journal of TJ, a high-school student, written over the course of two years:

September, Year One

My firsh day come to school comfuse

December, Year One

I like to listen the music because, the music make me fill happy and sad. sometime I go with my family we listen to the radio in the car. It is make my heart blocken. because I love the song.

April, Year One

If I be come the president of U.S.A. I with give people job, education, also I with help the person that don't have money. I want that family go to training job to help there own family.

September, Year Two

The first think I like in school is have lot friend. The second thing I like is do something fun in school. Like rewarding all go to gym and do something that all students do together. I like to do some outside like playing football with teacher and play something that we want to play.

December, Year Two

If I were a president of the United States, I would do some thing good for all the people like to make school for children and make jobs for people. And if people don't have food to eat, I would give money to government to buy food and give to them. Also if I were a president of another country, I were would do the same thing. And I would help people that have no jobs. If I were presendent I would make a no tax because it makes people dislike you all the government. In school the teacher can hit the kids so the kid would not run away from your house or school.

June, Year Two

Yesterday I went to see the Russian dancers at Washington High School. Dancers that I saw yesterday were very good because I get to see something good like jump in the air and spin around for long time with out dizzy. I like when one man and one lady come out with a cow but I like when the cow dring the beer and get drunk he was dancers it was so good. And one more part that I like the most is how they play music because they can play differend kind music. Also I like that two guy that come out with piece straw and play thee music with that straw it was so good and so need to see. Also I like one part that four girl dancers with a candle because when they dancers it was so smooth and soft. Also one girl she scream so loud it all most wake my ear can not hear for 5 second.

That all I can think for now! Thank you for the tacket. I really enjoy the show.

!The End!

READING LOGS

Keeping track of everything students are doing individually can become a severe problem. Having students keep a log of their reading is one of the simplest methods of keeping a record of the student's abilities, interests, and progress. This log is simply a place for the student to list the materials they have read during sustained silent reading. This reading list becomes a

Figure 5.5:
Leah's reading log.
In a conference with her teacher, Leah can bring the log and discuss her progress in terms of specific books read, why she chose those, what she did if the book was too hard, or what trends she notices in her choices. Did she actually finish Little House in the Big Woods? *What does she remember from it? How did she tackle unknown words?*

Date	Level	Page	TITLE
9-18-92	JR	29	The little and the missing cat
10-7-92	E	41	molly's Pilgrim
10-8-92	JR	33	br Beach
11-18-92	JR	29	Fisherman and his Wife
11-18-92	JR	26	Umpelstiltskin
12-10-92	E	45	Little red rade hood
12-999?	E	20	The Imogene Antlers
1-21-93	E	26	The Popcorn Book
1-21-93	JR	32	Play It again Rosie!
1-21-93	JR	214	Goldilocks and the three bear
1-21-93	JR	32	Sweet Hearts for Dolly
1-21-93	JR	39	Toony and the midnight Monster
1-21-93	JR	24	Pictionary
2-4-93	JR	29	Dora Everything It full
2-4-93	C	48	String Bean's trip to the sea
2-4-93	C	1	Jerry Rice
2-4-93	C	1	Joe Montana
2-25-93	JR	64	Frog and Toad together
3-6-93	JR	32	A Toy factory.
3-6-93	JR	47	A Book about Planets and stars
5-6-93	C	238	little house in the Big Woods
5-20-93	E	28	Wynken, Blynken and Nod
5-21-93	E	38	Frog Medicine
5-21-93	E	29	All Tutus should be pink
5-21-93	E	20	I hate English!
5-21-93	C	51	The Trickster

E = Easy C = Challenging JR = Just right

BOOKS I HAVE READ ON MY OWN

Leah Chong   GRADE: 3

profile of the reader. Writes Debra Goodman (1992): "How much reading is she doing? Is he having trouble finding books to read? Is she sampling different genres? What kinds of books is he interested in? What book is she able to read on her own?" One effective method of gaining more information about the choices is to have the student rate each book *C* for challenging, *E* for easy, or *JR* for just right.

This list provides an easy reference for you, for readers and for parents. It gives the student a sense of accomplishment, and parents and other stakeholders a clear representation of what the student is accomplishing.

WRITTEN STORY RETELLINGS AND BOOK REPORTS

Requiring students to do a book report for every book they read, Goodman notes, may discourage them from reporting the full extent of their reading. Thus, a log such as the one illustrated in figure 5.5 results in a minimum of pain. However, you may want to have the students select one book a month to write a report on, share in class, or in some way demonstrate understanding.

Figure 5.6:
Kindergarten book report

Figure 5.6 (previous page) shows a kindergarten child's response to the story *The Princess and the Pea.* She has all the elements of the story in it: the castle, the princess sleeping on top of piles of mattresses, and the pea. She clearly understood and enjoyed the story.

Here is an eighth grader's book report:

> The title of my book is *The Monster in the Third Dresser Drawer.* The author is Janice Lee Smith. The page number is 86 the characters is the monster and Adam Joshua. The setting is when Adam Joshua go to bed. The plot was when Adam Joshua go to bed and the monster come out of the third dresser drawer everyday at night when morning comes the monster go back to the third dresser drawer everynight the monster come out and play with the toys and scary him all the day of the week and for the hole night. At the end of the store Adam Joshua has a baby sister to sleep with.

This student demonstrates a clear understanding of the story. Although there are grammatical errors in the report, it would be pointless and inappropriate to correct them, as this is not the focus of the assignment. If the book report were to be presented to the class, revising, correcting, and polishing would be in order.

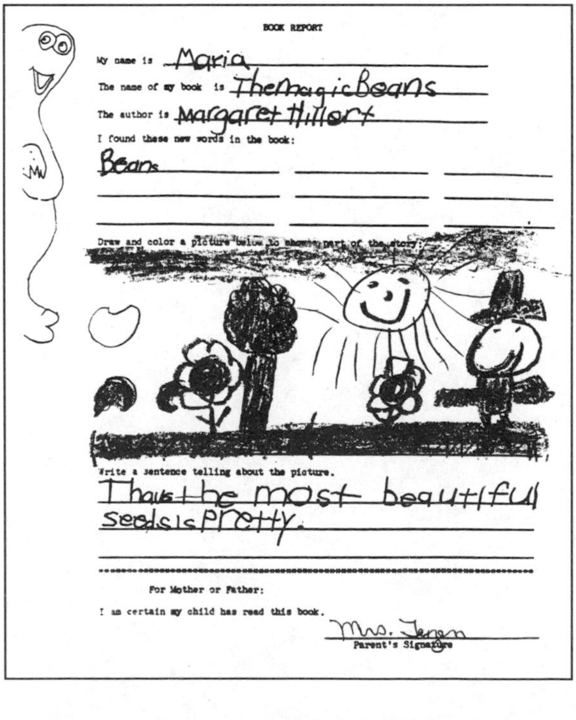

BOOK REPORT

My name is Maria

The name of my book is TheMagicBeans

The author is Margaret Hillert

I found these new words in the book:

Beans

Draw and color a picture below to show a part of the story:

Write a sentence telling about the picture.

Thaus the most beautiful seedsisPretty.

For Mother or Father:

I am certain my child has read this book.

Mrs. Jensen

Parent's Signature

Figure 5.7: A third grader filled out this book report form. It is not clear from what Maria wrote whether she understands this version of Jack and the Beanstalk. *To clarify, her teacher can talk it over with her.*

When judging these book reports, it is not always fruitful to grade each one separately, or even at all. What these are instructive about are the students' understanding of the story, their burgeoning control over both comprehension of texts and ability to articulate what they read. Looking at these over time is more productive that sitting down to give each single report a grade.

RESPONSE JOURNALS

Having students respond to reading is a very important part of their comprehension of the text. Many of our non-English-speaking students—particularly at the high-school level—are shy and quiet, unsure of their language capabilities, and unwilling to talk in class. They are also unfamiliar with many of the cultural references and implicit assumptions made in texts. Thus, they sit in the back of the room and wait for others to expound on what they perceive in the story.

Response journals are a superb way of promoting independent thinking, fluency in writing, and of extracting meaning from texts. Petroskey (1982) writes, "our comprehension of texts, whether literary or not, is more an act of composition (for understanding is composing) than of information retrieval...the best possible representation of our understanding of texts begins with certain kinds of compositions, not multiple choice tests or written free responses."

Thus, reading, responding, and composing are aspects of understanding, and journals are a way in which the reader can express and explain in his own way what he understood from the text. When responses are a part of the reading assignment, then the reader has a chance to explore his own vision of the story or text and articulate it before he has heard what others have to say. These journals, according to Petroskey, can be judged by the usual standards: "adequacy of elaboration, coherence, clarity, and aptness of illustration."

Following are sample thought questions that can be used to elicit and guide responses:

What did you notice while you were reading the text?
What did you think and how do you feel about what you noticed?
What events or ideas from your own life connect to what you read
   in the book?

Such simple questions can elicit sometimes poetic and heart-rending responses from students.

For instance, in response to reading the book *Sarah, Plain and Tall*, one reader wrote:

> What can we expect is in the future? What are we going to do and to have? It is so difficult to give an exact answer because this is life. Sometimes life presents lots of unexpected things and problems. I think that everybody has had some dreams about their future at youth But some did not always come true. I think that Sarah had her own dreams about her future too. But her fate turned on having to leave her home. At first sight it looks like I have the same situation, but that is not correct. And we have different kinds of challenges in our life. It is not easy to get used to a new life. You cannot forget everything from the past. "There are always things to miss, not matter where you are," said Maggie. Sarah has one advantage over me. Any time she might go to see her brother with his wife, her aunts and the sea that she loves so much. But I can't do that, because I and my family and many people from my country are lost everything that we had and mainly we lost our native land.

Another reader wrote,

> I like this lovely story. It let me feel so sweet when I go through it. I find something had missed on the other way. That is I missed how to live with people without trouble. I often gets into trouble with my friends, because I only think about myself. I selden think about what their thinking. Of course I do not take care then. This is why I got a lot of problem in my life. Thank you for this assignment. I very enjoy it.

Another, responding to *To Kill a Mockingbird*, commented:

> We are used to saying "hello" or "hi" to people who we meet on the street. We say "happy birthday" to someone who's having birthday. We can wish to each other a good day, good evening, good luck....But what could we wish people whose life is hanging by a thread? What could we wish a person like Tom Robinson, who has a black skin and who lived at the time of Negro discrimination? Many people like Tom have been penalized for things they didn't do. In my country people are discriminated against

because of their nationality. My mother has been in this situation too. She lost her job because she was Armenian in Azerbaijan. Because of this it's easy for me to understand discrimination.

These were students who struggled through the books, felt they understood little, and missed a great deal of the word-by-word, point-by-point understanding. But their grasp of the stories themselves are solid. In addition, these are the sorts of reactions that one would probably never be privy to if the responses to books were simply elicited from discussions with the entire class or from question/answer quizzes.

TRADITIONAL ASSESSMENT TOOLS

Whether the student produced work in the mainstream or in the ESL class, it is critical to look at his assignments to see if he is:

◆ understanding the content
◆ learning what you want him to learn
◆ learning the ropes of test taking and assignment completion in Western classrooms
◆ achieving as much as he is capable of
◆ missing the mark

Classroom Measures

TESTS

Tests are one hoop all students must jump through. Used at the end of a lesson, they can become "summative" assessments to measure how much the student has learned. Our discussion of the five categories of information (page 142–143) reveals how limited tests are. They rarely reveal strategies, attitudes, interests, or explicit understandings of processes. They mainly reveal control over language and content matter.

As we have stated, it is not a good idea to use tests alone as a way to measure learning or make educational decisions about students—often their performance has nothing to do with their competence in the subject matter. But there are times when it *is* appropriate to use tests. As Genessee and Hamayan (1985) point out, "tests do not allow for much individualization because they consist of one or more standard tasks that all students are expected to respond to in more or less the same way." This factor can be an advantage at times, because it gives you systematic, uniform feedback about the entire class.

Genessee and Hamayan note that it is important to consider how much and what kinds of language skills the student needs to take the test. If the test is on content, to assess how much the student has mastered, then you can select tasks that use relatively little language or allow the student to use either his home language or methods other than language to demonstrate his knowledge. However, if there is "content-obligatory language" involved—language that is so tied to the content that the student can't learn the content without learning the vocabulary too—then you must find ways to integrate the two.

For example, Tong had to take a test for his earth-science class. He could answer most of the questions with words. But for a more complex question, he drew a diagram for his answer.

Science teacher Sandy Johnson uses laboratory tests where her students must identify the picture or the article they are seeing displayed in front of them. They must master the content-obligatory language to pass the test, but are not necessarily required to read extensive text to demonstrate their knowledge. When testing students in her health classes, she has them respond to a question such as "your brother cut his wrist and he's bleeding hard. What do you do?" The student can demonstrate on himself or the dummy what he should do in that situation.

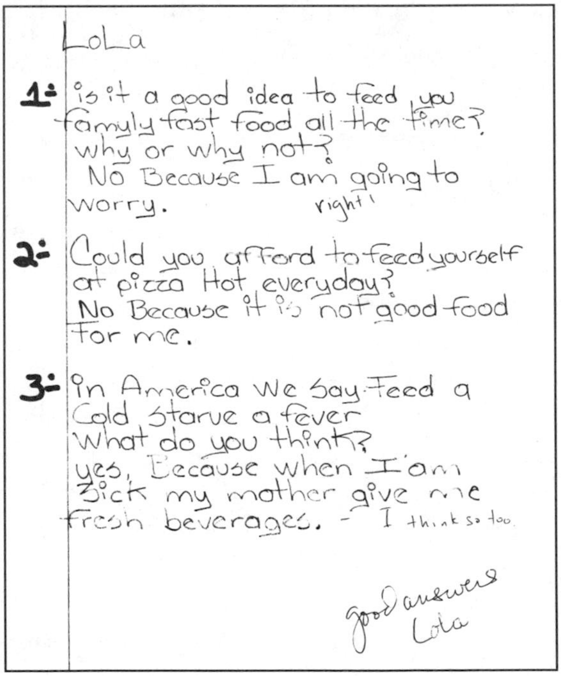

LoLa

1: is it a good idea to feed you famyly fast food all the time? why or why not?
   No Because I am going to worry.   right!

2: Could you afford to feed yourself at pizza Hot everyday?
   No Because it is not good food for me.

3: In America We say Feed a Cold starve a fever What do you think?
   yes, Because when I am sick my mother give me fresh beverages. — I think so too.

good answers
Lola

Figure 5.8:
Lola's homework,
exploring the verb feed

HOMEWORK

A class of very traditional students, who felt that if they were not explicitly taught grammar they weren't learning English, asked for homework. They were given an exercise on one irregular verb per day. The teacher went through the forms and then asked specific questions so that the students not only got to practice the forms, but their writing skills, too (see figure 5.8).

COMPREHENSION QUESTIONS

These are simply checks to see if the student has understood the assignment. They can be as formal as a written quiz or as informal as asking students to write down three things they learned from the lesson. (See examples below from a beginning literacy class's presentations on agriculture).

Figure 5.9: This summary reveals that Flora actually learned a great deal about kiwi fruit. She communicated several important facts. In several cases she was copying, but the facts she chose to copy were correct.

> they eat the rice three
> times a day - breakfast,
> lunch, and dinner.
> In Laos they plant in May
> some baskets and parts
> of houses are made of
> rice plants.
>
> RIA

> Kiwi fruit
> I like the kiwi the
> are important
> was individual
> Grown in California to
> Asia and united states over
> 6 million flats of kiwi fruit
> China Italy
>
> Flora

Figure 5.10: Ria has much stronger skills than Flora, which is revealed by her summary of what she learned from the presentation on rice.

Figure 5.11: Seng is at the lowest level of the class. To fulfill the assignment, he simply copied some lines from the handout, but what he copied reveals that he has no understanding of what he is looking at.

> History of the crop.
> They were first found.

Here are two letters written by high-school students. This assignment asked students to display their understanding of problems of the contemporary farmer by writing a letter to their congressman.

Dear ladies and Gentlmen,

I'm most graceful to write this letter to you at the congressman this time.

I'm very need your help me and my family this year. On these year we don't had enough money to pay my tax. Then we don't have enough money to buy food to my family eat this year. Therefore, please can you low the price to all the farmer. Please can you solve this problem is soon is prosble. Then, please low all of the price to a very low prices, to all the people.

Thank you! very much.

Sincerely

◆

Dear Congressman,

I have problems about my farm this year a lot of insect distral my corn, my corn can't grow every well, so I need help from you, see how much you can help me solve my problem, and how much you can give me the posonous or thing to help my farm, now I am going to poor because I can't buy fertilizer, posonous, seeds clothing, machinery tools or everything to protect my farm from the companies. The companies are sold the thing so expensive, therefore I have no money to buy it and pay for the railroads to go to the store or back home. and I have no enough credit, or loans, borrow money from the banks, the bank charged high rate of interest too. So I hope you would help me for sure this year by regulating the company and giving some loan.

Your farmer

Teachers inexperienced in working with English learners are often overwhelmed by the errors, and concentrate their efforts and their focus on the grammatical problems. It is critical to look past the errors and respond to the content itself. These letters reveal that the students had a great deal of understanding about the issues at hand, of high prices for goods and low returns on the crops they produced. In addition they wrote very compelling letters that also reveal their ability to grapple with audience, purpose, and style.

Decontextualized measures

Standardized tests are, as their name states, given and taken outside of the context of the classroom. They do not, as Anthony (1991) writes, "originate in the instructional context" of our classes, and the content and purposes are removed from our control. Thus, their applicability and appropriateness also lie outside the domain of the classroom.

We discuss standardized testing in chapter 2, and have made our position on them clear. However, they are a fact of life in the careers of most students. Michigan has recently mandated that no student will get out of sixth grade without achieving sixth-grade reading competency. How this edict will affect our ESL students remains to be seen. College entrance exams and the SAT all loom large on the horizon for high-school students who want to go to college. A colleague who teaches ESL for at-risk students at the local college notes that incoming freshmen must take the ACT (American College Testing), whose scores in English are used to place students in writing courses. This test, which only recently has tried to exclude cultural bias, does not even have a writing component and yet is used as a gatekeeper for writing classes.

Whether we like it or not, these tests are going to be a part of the student's academic record.

CONCLUSION

Teachers need to develop a variety of ways in which to view their students' progress. We have a wide range of student behavior to observe and record, and we must have an equally broad range of data collection. Trying to accomplish this assessment feat for thirty or more students is truly a challenge. Be realistic in your attempts. Don't try to change all your assessment methods in one year. This approach to assessment is a process. You can adapt your current techniques as you feel comfortable. We believe you'll find the outcome is worth the effort.

6

The Santa Maria,
the Pimpas, and the Ninny:
CHECKLISTS, ANECDOTES,
AND CONFERENCES

In this chapter we discuss

◆ the three methods of recording observations
◆ the advantages and disadvantages for each method
◆ guidelines for their development

Part of Mary's job at the high school is to provide support for the ESL students she works with. This support can come in the form of clarifying the history packet questions Keko needs to answer, correcting the spelling in Pancho's English assignment, or discussing and challenging the advanced students with their literature assignments.

Kim, one of Mary's brightest students, worked extremely hard on her literature essay. She needed to describe the elements of alienation in F. Scott Fitzgerald's novel, *The Great Gatsby*. She did a magnificent job. She used the right quotes, and she was able to appropriately bring her own experiences of wanting to fit in into the essay. When Mary reviewed Kim's paper, she felt Kim's English teacher would be quite proud, too. Two weeks later, much to Mary's surprise, Kim announced that she was getting a *D* in her English class as a result of getting a *D* on her Great Gatsby essay. Mary was dumbfounded. She met with the teacher, who informed Mary that the problem was not in the paper's content, but that Kim had neglected to turn it in on time. Therefore, her paper was automatically downgraded by 50 percent. Because the paper accounted for two-thirds of the grade in that class, Kim's overall grade was low.

Mary had kept notes and a checklist of papers due when she worked with Kim. These records showed that Kim had the paper done with plenty of time to turn it in. What was more, on reviewing her notes on Kim, Mary was able to see a pattern of self-destructive behavior. The class-room teachers did not have this information. All they knew was that Kim either missed assignments completely or turned them in late. Be-cause of her notes and record keeping, Mary knew something more was going on—Kim had done the work but was sabotaging herself for some reason. With checklists and notes in hand, Mary headed for the counselor's office to get help in dealing with the problem.

HOW TO RECORD YOUR OBSERVATIONS

Observing and gathering the data are two different tasks. Observing, as we have noted, is a natural part of your day.

Collecting is not as easy, because it often has to be done on the run. You don't have the luxury of sitting down and looking at con-crete pieces of evidence. Therefore, the methods of collecting must be simple, efficient, and must not interfere with your first priority: teaching. In a classroom where you have built in opportunities for student interaction and collaboration, however, they can be accom-plished in concert with the methods we discussed in chapter 5: (1) writing down our *observations* of the learner in the form of anecdotes and checklists (process); (2) looking at *samples* of what the learner has produced (product); and (3) through interviews and conferences—*talking to the learner* about what he's doing and what he thinks about what he's doing.

Checklists

Checklists are matrices organized to monitor specific skills, behaviors, attitudes, traits, and accomplishments of individual or all students in the class. They are also record-keeping devices that keep track of who has mastered certain skills and who needs to work on them. Check-lists are compiled from areas you have predetermined you want to assess in a student.

The advantages of checklists are that

- they are a quick and easy way to observe and record skills and behaviors
- they allow you to focus on particulars
- devising one provides a means of thinking through and clarifying what is important about particular processes and products
- they can be useful for summary purposes
- they provide a simple graphic display of what a student knows or has accomplished
- they can demonstrate clearly to stakeholders such as parents and administrators what concepts and/or skills have been learned
- they act as reminder lists for note-taking and observation purposes
- they can show you and your students areas that need working on before it's too late and they fail the test or unit

The disadvantages of checklists are that

- they can be very limiting. Anthony et al. (1991) caution checklists can act as blinders. When you are looking for only certain things, you may miss other significant qualitative leaps in a student that are not as readily apparent.
- they do not provide a rich context for understanding the behaviors. They are simply lists.
- they also "lend themselves to misreading by other people" (Johnston 1992), because scanning quickly for boxes that aren't checked off can result in negative impressions
- they can be time-consuming to construct
- it's difficult to use someone else's if the writer has different agendas or different values. Cambourne and Turbill note that trying to use a checklist someone else has devised can be a frustrating experience, because the original writers may be focusing on things you aren't. Many teachers are happier using ones they have developed themselves.

D. Goodman (1992) notes teachers often

> ...find they can accomplish the same evaluation just as well without a
> checklist. But the lists have served their purpose. They've been a means
> of thinking through what's important about particular processes and
> products....Use them to think through the evaluation purposes they serve.
> Make adaptations that might be necessary for your own situation....Using
> a form without thinking it through or modifying it deprives you of the
> benefit of involving yourself in the process.

Figure 6.1:
Language
function
checklist

LANGUAGE FUNCTION CHECKLIST

Student Name _____ Date _____

Age _____ Grade _____

F	S	N	BEHAVIOR/ABILITY	CONTEXT/COMMENTS
			Demonstrates comprehension nonverbally	
			Uses physical motion to communicate (pushing, pulling, etc.)	
			Listens and attends to the work at hand	
			One-word response	
			Uses English in an informal conversation	
			Makes a request "I want" or "I need…"	
			Talks about himself/herself	
			Participates in formal classroom discussion within small group	
			Understands and answers questions about material presented through discussion	
			Volunteers additional information in the class discussion	
			Asks for additional information privately	
			Asks for additional information within the group	
			Presents a dissenting point of view	
			Uses language to communicate sadness	
			Uses imaginative language, i.e., "If I were a bird, I would fly home to my country."	
			Uses language to be funny	
			Uses language sarcastically	
			Uses language to show anger	
			Uses authoritative language, i.e., "You must…"	
			Uses language to anticipate a future event	
			Communicates using indirect coding, i.e., "You must be tired of correcting all our papers," meaning, "Don't give us so much homework."	
			Other:	

N – Never   S – Seldom   F – Frequently

Checklists are worth the effort to construct, because if properly devised and used, they can yield a great deal of information. For example, Mary devised the checklist shown in figure 6.1 to record a child's oral language mastery.

You can also make checklists for the vocabulary students know upon arrival or have learned during a specified amount of time. Figure 6.2 is an English vocabulary checklist that can be used as a progress indicator.

Figure 6.2:
English vocabulary checklist

STUDENT VOCABULARY CHECKLIST

Teacher _____ Student _____ Grade _____

Have student identify using English vocabulary. Use check marks to note those words the student knows. Leave others blank.

1. Colors
   - ❏ red ❏ blue ❏ green ❏ yellow
   - ❏ orange ❏ black ❏ purple ❏ brown
   - ❏ white

2. Numbers—Kindergarten
   - ❏ 1 ❏ 4 ❏ 7 ❏ 9
   - ❏ 2 ❏ 5 ❏ 8 ❏ 10
   - ❏ 3 ❏ 6

   Grades 1–3, as above plus
   - ❏ 11 ❏ 14 ❏ 17 ❏ 19
   - ❏ 12 ❏ 15 ❏ 18 ❏ 20
   - ❏ 13 ❏ 16

3. Shapes
   - ❏ circle ❏ square ❏ triangle ❏ rectangle

4. Alphabet (present in random order)
   - ❏ A ❏ H ❏ O ❏ U
   - ❏ B ❏ I ❏ P ❏ V
   - ❏ C ❏ J ❏ Q ❏ W
   - ❏ D ❏ K ❏ R ❏ X
   - ❏ E ❏ L ❏ S ❏ Y
   - ❏ F ❏ M ❏ T ❏ Z
   - ❏ G ❏ N

5. Holiday names
   - ❏ Easter ❏ Halloween ❏ Valentine's Day
   - ❏ Christmas ❏ Thanksgiving
   - ❏ New Year's Day

6. Personal information
   - ❏ name ❏ age ❏ address ❏ phone number

7. Body parts
   - ❏ eye ❏ nose ❏ cheek ❏ mouth
   - ❏ neck ❏ chest ❏ shoulder ❏ arm
   - ❏ hand ❏ stomach ❏ leg ❏ knee
   - ❏ foot ❏ finger

8. Spatial orientation
   - ❏ left ❏ right ❏ in front of ❏ out
   - ❏ over ❏ above ❏ beside ❏ behind
   - ❏ in ❏ near ❏ far

Reproducible masters in Appendix B

---

9. School vocabulary
   - ❏ recess ❏ hall ❏ washroom ❏ auditorium
   - ❏ playground ❏ locker ❏ office ❏ lunch
   - ❏ teacher ❏ lunch room ❏ principal ❏ secretary
   - ❏ tardy slip ❏ school ❏ science ❏ phys. ed.
   - ❏ math ❏ school bus ❏ language arts
   - ❏ drinking fountain

10. Classroom words
    - ❏ desk ❏ books ❏ paper ❏ blackboard
    - ❏ crayons ❏ notebook ❏ pencil ❏ glue
    - ❏ chalk ❏ clock ❏ eraser ❏ page
    - ❏ rug ❏ scissors ❏ seat ❏ chair
    - ❏ table ❏ window ❏ wastebasket

11. Clothing
    - ❏ coat ❏ dress ❏ jacket ❏ hat
    - ❏ gym shoes ❏ mittens ❏ pants ❏ shirt
    - ❏ shoes ❏ skirt ❏ socks ❏ sweater

12. Safety terms
    - ❏ stop ❏ go ❏ walk ❏ don't walk

13. Time
    - ❏ morning ❏ noon ❏ night ❏ afternoon
    - ❏ tomorrow ❏ yesterday ❏ year ❏ month
    - ❏ next week

14. Other vocabulary
    - ❏ first ❏ last ❏ big ❏ little
    - ❏ small ❏ smaller

15. Money
    - ❏ penny ❏ nickel ❏ dime ❏ quarter
    - ❏ cent ❏ cost ❏ dollar

16. Transportation
    - ❏ bus ❏ car ❏ truck ❏ plane

17. Everyday directions
    - ❏ wait ❏ sit down ❏ stand up ❏ sit on floor
    - ❏ come here ❏ line up ❏ pick up ❏ open book
    - ❏ touch ❏ cut out ❏ wait ❏ copy
    - ❏ wash your hands ❏ raise your hand

18. Home words
    - ❏ address ❏ brother ❏ sister ❏ father
    - ❏ mother ❏ home ❏ sofa ❏ chair
    - ❏ table ❏ bed

2

There are endless ways to put checklists together to suit your own purposes. Here are some guidelines for developing them:

1. Select the setting in which you want to observe your students:

   - in class
   - playground
   - hallway
   - gym
   - science lab
   - computer lab

   - individually
   - in groups (pairs, small or large groups)
   - with younger students
   - with older students
   - with peers

2. Select the task you want to observe, or the skills you want the student to know:

   - reading
   - talking
   - writing
   - collaborating
   - editing

   - doing experiments
   - computing
   - graphing
   - problem solving
   - socializing

3. Determine the specific areas to include in each checklist.

4. Design the rating scale. Jett-Simpson (1994) advises that instead of simply checking off items in yes/no categories, the best checklists indicate dates and degrees (such as, "degree of independence a child has reached in literacy"):

   - frequently, sometimes, not yet
   - good, okay, not yet
   - yes, no, not observed
   - usually, occasionally, working on
   - not yet, beginning, developing, independent
   - happy, neutral, sad faces (for very young children)

   Or simply leave a space to indicate completion.

5. Leave space for comments

Figure 6.3 is an example of a checklist designed specifically to assess emerging readers.

Figure 6.3:
Checklist for assessing emerging reading

Student Name _____ Date _____

Age _____ Grade _____

CHECKLIST FOR ASSESSING EMERGING READERS	Not yet	Emerg-ing	Yes
Listens to story but is not looking at pages			
Tries to read environmental print			
Demonstrates book-handling knowledge (right side up)			
Watches pictures as story is read aloud.			
Makes up words for picture			
Demonstrates directionality of written language (left to right, page order)			
Pretends to read			
Recognizes some words from a dictated story			
Participates in reading by supplying rhyming words and some predictable text			
Memorizes text and pretends to read story			
Looks at words and tracks words when reading or is being read to from a familiar story			
Recognizes words in a new context			
Reads word-for-word			
Reads familiar stories fluently			
Reads unfamiliar stories haltingly			
Uses context clues, phonic analysis, sentence structure, to read new words and passages			
Reads easy books fluently			
Chooses to read independently			
Reads fluently			

Reproducible master in Appendix B

Checklists can be useful for documenting what a student has learned about writing, skills in particular.

Figure 6.4:
A writing
checklist

WRITING SAMPLE CHECKLIST

SKILL AREAS	DESCRIPTION	LEVEL
Content	❏ theme developed ❏ related ideas and examples supplied	Fluent
	❏ thought development adequate ❏ some unrelated ideas used	Intermediate
	❏ uneven (or no) theme development ❏ many unrelated ideas included ❏ few (or no) examples given ❏ insufficient writing for evaluation	Beginner
Organization	❏ good topic development ❏ opening sentence/or introductory paragraph included ❏ concluding sentence/paragraph included ❏ ideas well organized, clearly stated, and backed-up ❏ transitions included	Fluent
	❏ topic or opening sentence included, but no closing sentence provided ❏ weak organization ❏ inadequate back-up information provided ❏ few transitions included	Intermediate
	❏ no topic sentence development ❏ no opening or closing sentence included ❏ little or no organization ❏ no back-up information provided ❏ no transitions included ❏ ideas confused or unrelated ❏ insufficient writing for evaluation	Beginner
Vocabulary	❏ correct use of word forms (prefixes, suffixes, etc.) and idioms ❏ sophisticated word choice ❏ meaning clear	Fluent
	❏ generally correct use of word forms and idioms ❏ word choice correct ❏ meaning clear	Intermediate
	❏ many errors in word forms and idioms ❏ ineffective word choice ❏ words selected through direct translation ❏ meaning confused or obscured ❏ insufficient writing for evaluation	Beginner
Language skills	❏ correct use of verb tense ❏ good sentence variety and complex construction ❏ good control of agreement, number, word order, parts of speech	Fluent
	❏ most verb tenses correct ❏ simple sentence construction ❏ errors in agreement, number, word order, parts of speech	Intermediate
	❏ frequent errors in tense ❏ forced sentence constructions ❏ many errors in agreement, number, word order, parts of speech ❏ insufficient writing for evaluation	Beginner
Mechanics	❏ few errors made in spelling, punctuation, capitalization	Fluent
	❏ occasional errors in spelling, punctuation, capitalization	Intermediate
	❏ many errors in spelling, punctuation, capitalization ❏ handwriting unclear or illegible ❏ insufficient writing for evaluation	Beginner

Reproducible master in Appendix B

Anecdotes

Anecdotes are focused narratives. They are both a method of watching and a means keeping records of ongoing incidents involving the learner. According to Stern and Cohen (1978), anecdotal records can help you do three things: (1) test hunches about reasons for a student's behavior or learning style; (2) identify what conditions may be reinforcing behavior; and (3) gain feedback about what students have learned from a particular curriculum unit or presentation.

The advantages to anecdotes are that

- they include the context and the richness that checklists lack
- they provide an efficient method of collecting what seems pertinent
- over time they can reveal changes, patterns of behavior, growth, progress, improvement

For example:

Joe, 17, was a student whose social skills were as limited as his English. He sat while waiting to see the counselor, taking the only available chair and leaving his elderly mother to stand. He sat too close to his classmates, and they disliked him intensely. He constantly needed rides because he wouldn't take the bus alone. Once when a teacher was driving him to a doctor (because he seemed to be having a severe anxiety attack), he shouted obscenities out the window at several of his classmates. He sometimes appeared only twice a week for classes and often seemed under the influence of drugs. No amount of counseling seemed to change or improve his attitude, until a chance remark by his mother revealed that the family was in this country so that Joe could escape mandatory military service. After talking with his mother about the conditions of their visas, the counselor was able to reassure Joe that he did not have to return to his country. This improved his attitude and proficiency remarkably.

In response to a request from the counselor, his teacher, Mrs. Jones, kept a log and made the following observations:

February 15, History, first hour.

Joe appeared. He had bathed. He smiled and said hello. He sat at his desk, moving it close to Sonia. When asked to move his seat back, he did.

February 22, History, first hour.

Observed working in pairs on activity on Bronze Age. Found some information in books. First time he revealed he could read or extract information from a text.

February 28, History, first hour.

Joe brought in a book from his country that showed actual artifacts found of Bronze Age tools. He managed to explain some pictures, and beamed when several students asked questions.

The disadvantages of anecdotes, following, have more to do with the logistics and the skill it takes to make them useful than problems with the concept itself:

- It takes persistence and practice to make them concise enough so that you don't get bogged down trying to write them for every student.
- It takes practice to include information that will be telling and revealing to you or another stakeholder days or weeks after the event happened.
- It takes thought in order to see and perceive what behaviors are salient to what is happening in the student.
- You have to organize your classroom so that you have time to stand back and watch and record while students are working independently.
- Trying to do them for every student can be overwhelming if you don't make the process efficient.
- They tend to lose their practicality at the secondary level. If you are like Barb Ducharme, teaching Spanish at two schools to three hundred junior-high students, finding time to fit them into your day can be prohibitive. However, you can pick and choose who to do narratives on. As Mrs. Jones did with Joe, you can focus on the ones who seem particularly in need of focused attention because they are disruptive, don't seem to be getting it, or are otherwise not functioning at expected levels.

Following are the guidelines for writing anecdotes:

- Write down an anecdote about your observation as soon as possible after it occurs.
- Describe an event as specifically as possible.
- Identify the basic action and what was said, and include the response or reactions of other people in the situation.

- Include setting, time of day, and context within which the event or interaction took place.
- Give general descriptions of what everyone involved was doing.
- Report rather than evaluate. Instead of saying, "He was obnoxious," write, "When I came to help him with his math, he said, 'I'll wait for Mr. Chou. He knows what he's doing.'"

One method of recording that seems to work for many teachers is to divide a large sheet of paper into small squares, affix this to a clipboard, and jot comments about individuals. This also works with a sheet of sticky address labels, one label for each student (Post-it notes are a useful alternative). Record the main points of the anecdote on the label or Post-it note for transcription into a more permanent record at a later time.

ANECDOTES ABOUT READING

Anecdotes about the process of reading can demonstrate over time how a reader has progressed. The following transcript shows a tutor's notes about a thirteen-year-old who was reading at a second-grade level:

Student Name: Choua

October 6

Material: *The Alphabet Book*

Read aloud a Richard Scarry book to Choua. Choua enjoyed listening to the story, and smiled and laughed at Scarry's humorous pictures. We discussed various animals. When asked "Which ones have you seen?" she was able to answer with farm animal names such as *chickens, cows, horses,* as well as *mice, dogs, cats.* "Which ones have you seen here in America?" "Do animals really wear clothes?" Choua laughed and said no very loudly. Her spoken vocabulary is good, and she can understand much better than she can read.

October 8

Material: *Birds Fly, Bears Don't*

Choua read a story from her basal reader out loud. She read as fast as she could and as quietly as possible. When asked to retell the story, she couldn't. I read her each paragraph at a normal pace, pausing to explain words or point to pictures to help her understand. When the story was finished, Choua was able to answer questions and retell story.

October 18

Material: *Birds Fly, Bears Don't*

I read a story aloud and Choua chimed in on words she knew. When, again, she read on her own, she rushed through without pausing and had a hard time retelling what she had read.

October 21

Material: *Clifford at the Circus*

Choua encountered some new words like *didn't, wasn't,* and *I'm* that were hard for her to understand or sound out. Her strategy for the contractions was to ignore the meaning. I suspect this is because she doesn't know why they were there or what they mean. After we discussed that a contraction is really two words put together and specifically which words were put together, she began saying the endings and understood them.

November 22

Material: *Birds Fly, Bears Don't*

I'm noticing a large difference in her reading. She has slowed down quite a bit. We still have to go over it together after she reads, to make sure she understands it. Today she read one paragraph, then I read another. I've found that this works better than having her read a whole page, because she will remember more, and give herself more time.

November 27

Material: *The Foot Book*

Choua read aloud today. She read very easily.

December 10

Material: *Birds Fly, Bear's Don't*

Choua read from *Bird's Fly, Bear's Don't*. She likes to read all of the pages now, so I don't trade with her. She is getting better at understanding, but still often speeds through, slurring the words she doesn't know.

ANECDOTES ABOUT WRITING

Steve was a small boy enrolled in an extended-day kindergarten. He had been born in the United States to preliterate parents, into a home with no books, pencils, or crayons . He seemed to make no connection between print and meaning, and showed no interest in pencil-and-paper tasks. In February, the teacher noticed he was beginning to get interested in reading. These are her notes:

February 12
The children were cutting out and coloring valentines. Steve picked out a red crayon and, holding the crayon clumsily, laboriously colored a heart.

February 21
Steve has continued to show interest in coloring. Today he drew, for the first time, a face that looked like a face, with eyes and a mouth.

March 3
Steve held the pen correctly for the first time.

March 8
Steve wrote his name.

March 10
Steve likes to make shapes with pipe cleaners. He then asks what that letter is and what animal begins with that sound.

April 3
Steve goes to the wall where there are simple faces showing all the emotions, looks at one carefully, and returns to his desk to draw it from memory. It is very accurate.

Figure 6.5: *An early drawing of Steve's. Squiggles at top and middle right are the combination of "letters" he consistently uses to represent his name, even though the s is the only letter present in his name.*

Interviews and conferences

Besides watching students and looking at their work, a third critical way of learning about your students is simply to sit down, talk, and listen to them. Florio-Ruane (1990) advises that interviews should never be the sole source of information because people—especially second-language learners—can't or won't always tell you all they know. If you can find answers to questions by a method other than an interview, do so; save the interview for finding out thoughts, feelings, memories, values—things you can't ordinarily see or pick up by listening and casual conversation. Kay Burke (1993) suggests using interviews and conferences with groups or individuals, to collect feedback and reactions to the following:

◆ books
◆ their own work (projects, research papers, scientific experiments, pieces of writing)
◆ films or videos
◆ field trips
◆ assemblies or guest speakers

Interviews can also be conducted with individuals

◆ to check for fluency and grammar
◆ to review portfolios
◆ to discuss grades

Conferences can be either short and informal, carried on throughout the day or the class period as you move around the classroom, or more formal, in which a set time is allotted for the student to meet with you with a specific agenda or set of questions.

Interviewing and conferring are more than simply sitting down and talking with a student. As Johnston (1992) points out, "if an interview is to provide useful information, it is important for the student to do most of the talking. This seems reasonably obvious, but in my experience teachers...often have the greatest difficulty keeping quiet....In general the more you listen, the more you learn (and often the more the student learns about himself). If the dialogue sounds stilted, like a test, then it probably *was* a test, and any information gained will be about as useful as if it had been gathered on a test." His advice is to "strive for opening the mind and closing the mouth."

Some advantages of interviews are that

◆ you can gather information that sometimes you cannot find any other way
◆ ESL students in particular are often more verbal when speaking than they are when writing. With a sympathetic and helpful audience they can reveal what they know better than with paper and pencil.
◆ they can give you insight into the student's awareness of their strategies and why they do things as they do. (For instance, Annie was writing and illustrating a report on Paul Bunyan, but abandoned it midway. When asked why, her answer was simple: she couldn't draw an ox.)
◆ you can see where comprehension of a question breaks down as it happens and intervene, rather than simply looking at a blank answer on a questionnaire

Some of the disadvantages are that

◆ the logistics of finding time to sit down and talk with each student can be tough, particularly at the secondary level, and especially if you have thirty others who have a tendency to horse around when you're not looking
◆ unless students are comfortable and trained in the process, they may dismiss it or clam up
◆ students may often feed you what they think you want, rather than give honest answers, or they may read into a question something other than what you intended

Following are guidelines for interviews and conferences:

◆ Select a time when other students are occupied and don't need your attention.
◆ Establish rules with the classroom so that quiet discussions can take place. If students are constantly interrupting, then you can-

not devote your attention to the student you are with; your thoughts, your attention and the interview will be disrupted and disjointed.

◆ Don't ask questions to which you already know the answer or questions that are available from tests or your grade book.

◆ Strive to "balance the power differences" between you and the student, so that you are not the knower or the keeper of all knowledge. Let the student be the expert.

◆ Keep it short.

WRITING CONFERENCES

Written work is essentially a product, but you can gain insight into the writer's control mainly by questioning him. Williams (1989) calls writing conferences "the single most effective tool you can use" to improve writing, in both native and nonnative speakers. There are two kinds of conferences: those that take place while the writing goes on, and conferences for revision purposes. Williams also notes that two factors are crucial to making writing conferences successful. First, students have to do most of the talking: "If you find yourself saying more than your students, chances are you're beginning to appropriate the text. Remember that it's their writing, not yours, and the more they talk about it, the better they will understand it. Second, work on no more than two points at a time...select the most important points and work on those."

For in-progress conferences, Nancie Atwell (1987) suggests circulating quietly among writers at work, asking them how it's going, giving feedback, and listening. Here she advises to keep conferences short, not more than a minute or two. Ask writers to tell you about their piece. Longer conferences, trouble-shooting entire pieces at a time, will lead to students becoming dependent on you to solve their problems rather than learning to solve them on their own. Following are some suggestions for writer's conferences:

◆ Begin by telling writers a major strength of their paper. Focus on the positive: "I can tell you did a lot of research already"; "You have a good strong thesis statement."

- Don't tell writers what to do. It's their piece of work. This is the hardest part—many writers want you to tell them. If they knew what to do, they would do it. Barb recently found herself simply writing the thesis statements for the students themselves based on the ideas they were trying to articulate simply because they did not know how—not a good solution.
- Build on what they have done, finding good things to commend; do not dampen their enthusiasm or crush already shaky writers' egos by finding fault.
- Resist making vague judgments such as "it's good." Give specific feedbacks on parts that were particularly effective. For instance, when Freddy writes, "It was like standing under a waterfall," point out that the image really helped you see what he was trying to convey.
- Read as a reader, not as judge, jury, and executioner. Read as someone who is genuinely interested and wants to know more.

Reid (1993) suggests asking questions such as

How did you choose this topic?
What is this paper about?
Who is your intended audience?
What are you going to do next?
If you were to add information here, how would you do it?
How do you feel about the paper so far?
What do you like best about the paper?

These questions put the focus on the writer and place the responsibility for making decisions back in his hands. She cautions that students who are in most need of help are often the least successful at getting it, because they are unable to take charge and negotiate meaning. In addition, we have noted that many students from more traditional countries feel that this is your job as "master"; teaching is synonymous with telling them what to do. Training beginning authors, especially ESL students, not only to think for themselves but to have the confidence to take authorial control, takes a great deal of time and effort.

CONCLUSION

There are many ways to record what and how well a student is doing. However, the old checks or letter grades are not very revealing, especially in the upper grades when you have many classes and students.

One of the most important facets of the three methods we have discussed is the process of deciding what to look for and what is important to find out. The clarity of values and priorities these activities demand are as worthwhile for you as the teacher as the checklists, anecdotes, or interviews themselves.

7

Flying Without an Earplan:
STORIES FROM THE TRENCHES

This chapter is a collection of anecdotes from teachers and aides who work with ESL students. These stories deal with students of differing backgrounds, ages, and challenges.

In this chapter we discuss

♦ the experiences of four teachers who went the extra mile to find out what it would take to help their students achieve success

Following are four stories of students in different situations, and the teachers who resolved to find out what they knew, what they liked, and how to make their learning successful. We chose these stories because they reflect the challenges many of our readers face: difficult placement situations, struggles to reach the students, lack of training, and time limitations. We hope the successes reflected in these stories inspire those who struggle with the daily challenges presented by ESL students.

DAN'S STORY: ALICE
BACKGROUND

THE TEACHER: Dan, ESL teacher (used as pull-out and push-in classroom support)

THE STUDENT: Alice
Age: 12
Nationality: Iraqi (Kurd)

Home language: Kurdish
Grade placement: Fifth grade, ESL pull-out
Competency in English: Very limited, some basic words, limited
    comprehension
Educational background: No previous schooling

THE STORY

Alice was twelve years old and repeating fifth grade. Her classroom
teacher was concerned because Alice was not making progress; she was
very shy, reluctant to speak English, and didn't seem to care about her
work or her surroundings. She would be going on to the middle school
next year, and everybody was worried that she would not be ready.
Alice went to her younger sister Layla's second-grade class for reading
instruction. Between the reading instruction, ESL, tutoring, special
programs, and so on, Alice spent barely two hours a day in her
regular classroom.

Dan was new to the school so not familiar with Alice's history. He
set out to find out about her. This is what he learned:

Alice was the second-oldest daughter of eight children. Her father
was killed when she was very small. Her mother remarried a man who
was later killed by a shell just outside their tent in the refugee camp.
Her mother again remarried and is pregnant with her ninth child.
Alice and her oldest sister are in charge of cooking, shopping, and
cleaning for the entire family.

The mainstream teacher, Mrs. Eaton, said that Alice did very little
work in class and seemed lost. During writing, she just sat. Her skills
were too low for her to work independently, her fear of making mistakes was too great, and she was too shy to ask for help. When the
teacher had time to work with her, Alice could usually begin a project
but would seldom finish.

Dan went to visit the second-grade classroom where, each day, Alice
attended reading group. Here, Alice met with the second-grade parent
aide. Dan observed very closely and noticed that the children took
turns reading aloud from their basal reader while the aide prompted
and corrected them. She seemed to correct them soon and often; they
knew that if they hesitated long enough, she would say the hard words
for them. Then they worked on their workbooks and she fed answers

to them. Many of the words in the stories were impossible to explain, so she simply told them the answer. Dan also noticed that Alice was much taller than the second graders, and whenever they stood, she spent a lot of time either hunched over, stooping, or actually kneeling so she didn't tower above the others.

Dan went to observe the class when an art specialist was visiting. The children were working with clay. Alice's eyes constantly darted to what her classmates were doing so that she could copy, rather than try to listen and comprehend on her own. She was also quick to notice the teacher's gestures and copy what she was doing. Her vocabulary was not developed enough to understand verbal instructions given to the class, but when the art teacher came to her desk to help her individually, she seemed to understand everything that was said to her. During the course of the art lesson, Alice constantly reprimanded herself when she made a mistake, seeming embarrassed—even when no one was ridiculing her. She spoke very little during this time. Her only words in English during the activity were *yes, no, how* or *what.*

There was no one in the school system who knew Kurdish, but her previous teacher, Mrs. Orloff, had a soft spot in her heart for Alice, and Alice liked and trusted her. Mrs. Orloff took time to sit down with Alice and Dan. From the interview, the two teachers learned that Alice's mother often spoke about going back to the home country. Thus the family was constantly in a state of anxious flux, anticipating a return, even though it was probably an impossibility.

They also discovered that Alice preferred speaking Kurdish over English. As her English was still halting, and she was the only one in her grade who spoke Kurdish, she felt alienated and alone. Her uncles, who didn't speak English, made fun of her when she tried to do so. She was afraid that when she went back to Iraq everybody was going to laugh at her because she spoke English.

Her embarrassment extended to speaking English in public. She told Mrs. Orloff a story about how, when she ordered a hamburger in English, the waiter didn't understand her at all. He brought her the wrong item. Even though she told the story in an amusing way, Alice was deeply disappointed and hurt by the incident.

Finally she admitted that she was ashamed of going to the second-grade class with her younger sister.

THE ISSUES AND RESPONSE

Dan was facing several issues:

◆ how to help Alice work independently so that the teacher did not have to be at her side at all times
◆ how to increase Alice's reading and writing ability
◆ how to lower Alice's anxiety level and raise her self-esteem

The first thing he decided to do, with the support of Mrs. Eaton, was to stop sending Alice to the second-grade classroom. The damage that arrangement had done to her spirit and self-confidence were too great to merit the advantages of working with those at her reading level. They dispensed with the workbooks, and moved Alice back into her class for most of the content part of the day.

Then he enlisted the help of a parent tutor who began to work with Alice. Under Dan's direction, they chose books that interested Alice. They got two copies and the tutor began by reading aloud, with Alice following along. Gradually, as time went on, Alice began to chime in when she knew the words. Then they began reading every other paragraph to each other, and finally every other page.

Dan decided that to help Alice and other students in similar situations work independently, he would give them enough structure and organization so that, on their own, they could write a story and not be lost for ideas. During the pull-out time, Dan used simple repetitive stories in which the students read the book, took its structure, and then, using the basic form, wrote their own stories. This was very difficult at first, but after many hints, Alice came up with the idea of a flower bud. Then they brainstormed about things the flower would eat. During writer's workshop, Alice relied heavily on the book itself for reference but came up with the story shown in figure 7.1.

Then Dan moved Alice and the students on to more independence. The students needed to know basic story structure so they would have a scaffold on which to hang their own ideas. They used *The Three Little Pigs*. First they read the story and did a story map, then wrote "The Three Little Ducks" (see figure 7.2).

From there Alice was able to move toward independence and confidence. By the end of the year she was writing much more freely, with a good grasp of vocabulary and syntax.

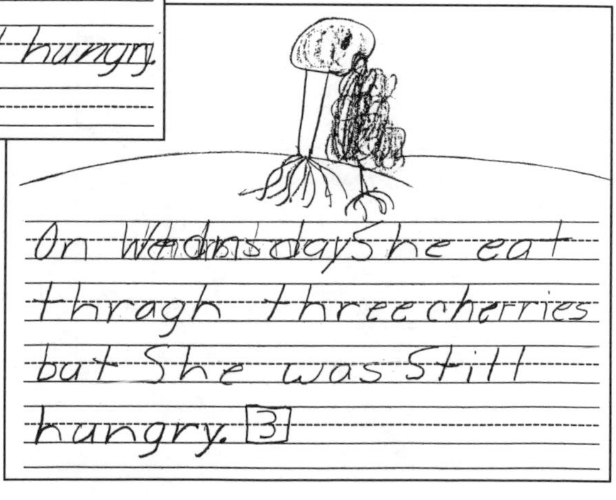

One upan a time
There was a Very
hungry flower bud.
On Sunday She eat
through One banana
but She was Still

Figure 7.1:
Excerpt from Alice's
flowerbud story,
based on The Very
Hungry Caterpillar

hungry.[1] On Tuesday
She eat through
two carrot but
She was still hungry.
[2]

On Wednsday She eat
thragh three cherries
but She was Still
hungry. [3]

Figure 7.2:
Excerpt from Alice's story of "The Three Little Ducks"

ANDREA'S STORY: HUNG

BACKGROUND

THE TEACHER:
Andrea, hired as an ESL support tutor, with no ESL training.

THE STUDENT: Hung
Age: 17
Nationality: Vietnamese
Home language: Vietnamese
Grade placement: Senior in high school
Competency in English: Spoke fairly well, but due to poor
    pronunciation was frequently not understood
Educational background: Extremely limited

THE STORY

Hung was a senior in high school. His school had no program for ESL
students; the number of immigrants was so low that the district largely
ignored them. His high school engaged a tutor, Andrea, to help him
with his studies. Andrea tried to meet with his various teachers to see
how he was doing; she found that they had all given up on him. With
his minimal literacy and lack of background, he was so far behind that
they felt he was never going to catch up. He—and his teachers—were
pretty much marking time until he reached eighteen. Though well-
meaning, they didn't know how to help him. They were grateful to
have him off their hands, which only made them feel guilty. Left to
her own devices, Andrea had to decide what to do with him.

Hung brought his geography and science assignments to class. He
had difficulty following directions and understanding even basic sentences. There were huge gaps in his comprehension. Andrea believed
that he was lacking even more in his reading skills than his teacher
realized.

She noted that teachers got frustrated and gave up on Hung because,
no matter how hard they tried to get a point across, or how many ways
they went over material, he would shake his head and say, "I don't
know, teacher." They had begun to believe he just said that because
he didn't want to try.

Hung brought a Language Master (a small machine with pronunciation tapes) to his tutoring session. At his teacher's request, he and Andrea worked on pronunciation. Andrea felt not only that he didn't need this, but it wasn't helping him. He had trouble with *sh, th, d, b,* and *l* sounds. The more they worked on them, the worse his pronunciation got. He could not hear the "correct" pronunciation of the words, and therefore could not formulate the sounds. Frustrated, seeing little use in continuing, they abandoned the exercise. Several days later his English teacher informed Andrea, in front of Hung, that he would be going to the community college next semester where "he will hopefully be able to get more help." She added that his pronunciation had gotten worse and that she just couldn't understand him. Andrea could see the hurt in Hung's eyes.

Andrea asked Hung several times about his life in Vietnam, but he didn't want to talk about it. Finally she asked his older sister about him. The sister told her that his mother and sisters had come to America twelve years before. Hung and his father had stayed in a refugee camp until a year and a half ago, which explained why his sister was so much further ahead academically. His father told Andrea later that the village they were living in was attacked with a chemical bomb. His sister was severely disabled because of it. The family thought that Hung was affected as well, and this may have been why he was slow.

THE ISSUES AND RESPONSE

Andrea was facing several issues:

- how to help Hung improve his reading and writing skills
- how to help him improve his oral speaking skills and pronunciation
- how to fill in the gaps of his background knowledge
- how to help him learn academic content-area skills
- how to put together a program for him in the vacuum created by the teachers who had given up

Hung had seen some cartoons on TV with one of his friends. He started telling the story, and together he and Andrea enjoyed making up a complete story.

Hung: And son...son...uh...sea...sea.

Andrea: Did the son fall in the sea?

Hung: Yes, but he didn't die. Finally he arrive America.

Andrea: How could he arrive in the U.S.?

Hung: Wood! (*He gestures*)

Andrea: Did he find a piece of wood? He drifted on a piece of wood to the U.S. Is that right?

Hung: Yes, uh...did you say drift?

Andrea: Yes, I said drift. Drift means...uh...float.

Hung: He can meet his family. Happy end!

Andrea: I like a happy ending.

Hung: Me too.

From that incident, Andrea discovered that Hung liked movies. She capitalized on his interest by having him recreate the plot and retell the story. With help, such as in the example above, he could do so. She would write it down for him, and have him read it.

She learned that the family had a small garden plot outside their apartment and that Hung liked to grow things. He told her about his home and their life in the mountains. Andrea discovered that he knew a great deal about rice farming.

Finally she had hit upon something that this young man really could succeed at. She took him to the library, drove him out to the rice fields and to the county's Agriculture Extension office (agriculture is an important facet of the California curriculum). Using videos about agriculture, they discussed how farming differed in his country from California.

Andrea developed a long-term project on rice. She came up with a series of research questions that Hung had to answer. Together they went to the library and learned about how to use the encyclopedia and the computer catalog. They pored over books, and Hung slowly and painfully put together a treatise on rice. Then he drew diagrams.

Andrea took him to the computer lab and showed him how to use the word-processing program. It took him several days to type his information in. Then they read aloud, again and again, what he had written. Finally, many weeks after they started, in a culminating activity, Hung presented his project to his senior science class. He received a standing ovation.

Figure 7.3: *Hung's completed project on rice*

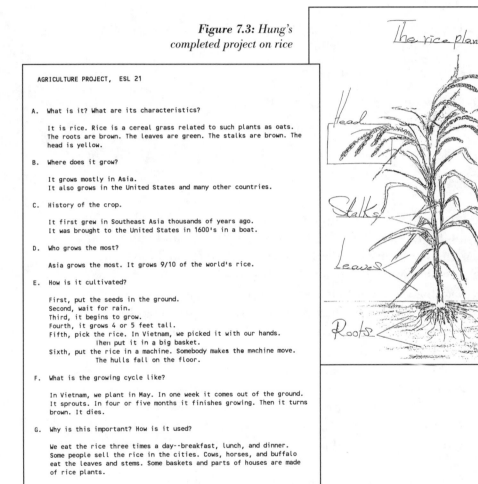

AGRICULTURE PROJECT,   ESL 21

A. What is it? What are its characteristics?

    It is rice. Rice is a cereal grass related to such plants as oats.
    The roots are brown. The leaves are green. The stalks are brown. The
    head is yellow.

B. Where does it grow?

    It grows mostly in Asia.
    It also grows in the United States and many other countries.

C. History of the crop.

    It first grew in Southeast Asia thousands of years ago.
    It was brought to the United States in 1600's in a boat.

D. Who grows the most?

    Asia grows the most. It grows 9/10 of the world's rice.

E. How is it cultivated?

    First, put the seeds in the ground.
    Second, wait for rain.
    Third, it begins to grow.
    Fourth, it grows 4 or 5 feet tall.
    Fifth, pick the rice. In Vietnam, we picked it with our hands.
        Then put it in a big basket.
    Sixth, put the rice in a machine. Somebody makes the machine move.
        The hulls fall on the floor.

F. What is the growing cycle like?

    In Vietnam, we plant in May. In one week it comes out of the ground.
    It sprouts. In four or five months it finishes growing. Then it turns
    brown. It dies.

G. Why is this important? How is it used?

    We eat the rice three times a day--breakfast, lunch, and dinner.
    Some people sell the rice in the cities. Cows, horses, and buffalo
    eat the leaves and stems. Some baskets and parts of houses are made
    of rice plants.

DOLORES'S STORY: RICARDO

BACKGROUND

THE TEACHER: Dolores, classroom aide, speaks some Spanish and takes responsibility for Ricardo

THE STUDENT: Ricardo
Age: 7
Nationality: Mexican
Home language: Spanish
Grade placement: Second grade
Competency in English: Limited
Educational background: Attended several bilingual programs, repeated first grade, and had done well in the bilingual second grade he had attended previously

THE STORY

Ricardo was a second-grader who had been in several bilingual programs. He had repeated first grade, and had done well in the bilingual second grade he was enrolled in. He arrived in late November at a small school that had no bilingual options. The second-grade teacher, Mrs. Ringer, was against having Ricardo placed in her class. She already had two Spanish-speaking children who were fluent in English. Mrs. Ringer had a reputation for referring to Special Education anyone who wasn't working at grade level; the minute they started lagging behind she sent them for special testing and got them transferred out as soon as possible. Mary Beth, the principal, usually placed all the other non-English-speaking children in other classrooms. In this case, however, she felt that being with Esgar and César in Mrs. Ringer's class would make Ricardo feel more comfortable. Dolores, the aide, had a working knowledge of Spanish and assumed the primary responsibility for seeing that he made a smooth transition.

THE ISSUES AND RESPONSE

Dolores faced several issues:

◆ how Ricardo was going to be able to function, since bilingual education was not an option
◆ what strategies Ricardo used when reading

- what sorts of things he succeeded at that she could capitalize on
- what kinds of translated materials she could use to help Ricardo in his native language

Dolores was concerned that because there was no Spanish bilingual program, Ricardo might fall behind quickly. At first he told her in Spanish that he didn't know any English. However, on the playground, she noticed him talking to his new friends in English. When she asked Ricardo in Spanish how old he was, he told her in English, "Seven." When he was talking about his little brother in hesitant Spanish, she asked his brother's age. He answered in English, "He's two."

During the third week, Dolores was working with a group of students on a review of addition and subtraction facts. Until then, Ricardo had been usually quiet and shy. However, with the other students, he was very lively and kept yelling out "nine!" as the answer to every question. He wanted to do everything in English and spent a great deal of time giggling and laughing with the other children.

The next week, during reading, Ricardo took great pleasure in saying dirty words in Spanish that Mrs. Ringer was unfamiliar with. However, Dolores knew what they were and asked him to stop. He took his vocabulary out to the playground where he made himself the center of attention by calling the other children dirty names in Spanish and making crude gestures; he called Crystal a pistol; she ran complaining to Mrs. Ringer.

From these incidents Dolores learned that Ricardo was a very outgoing little boy who used his bilingualism to his advantage. He was motivated to make friends and had unique strategies for getting attention. Socially, he had adapted very well.

Dolores turned to the issue of reading. She borrowed some basal readers and small stories in Spanish from another teacher.

First they worked on letter recognition. Ricardo had trouble identifying ten letters: *n, p, s, r, q, b, d, e, g, t.* Then they read a story from the reader. The sounds the story focused on were basic vowel sounds and a few consonants: *os, as, es, us, is* and *so, sa, se, su, si.* Ricardo had trouble distinguishing the *os* from the *so.* He also had trouble distinguishing between *oso* and *osa;* he said *oso* for both. Some of the sentences in the story, about some bears in the circus, didn't make sense to him. For example, in the sentence "So So es un oso," he didn't understand that *So So* was the name of the *oso*.

Dolores also discovered that Ricardo did not sound out words well. He had a tendency to say the first syllable and guess at the ending, using a familiar word. He would see *ni* and say *niño*.

She had Ricardo read a story entitled *La Miel* to her. He had already read it but got mixed up on a few words. He substituted *brincan* for *saltan* (both essentially mean "to leap" or "to jump"). However, he predicted the correct outcome of the story, using different words. He had more trouble with the book *La Casa Vieja* because it was new to him. This time he looked at the first two letters of the words, then at the picture, and predicted what he thought the words would be. He understood the story line well when talking about it afterwards.

From these incidents Dolores ascertained that Ricardo had mainly been taught by phonics methods, but they had not worked effectively for him. She also learned that he knew print had meaning. He had a good grasp of story grammar and had proceeded beyond pretend reading to looking at the words, sentences, and pictures in an effort to make meaning. He had learned several useful strategies.

Dolores decided that even though Spanish was phonetically regular, and that some teachers argued it was easier to learn to read in for that reason, she would focus on reading in English. She still encouraged reading in Spanish and supplemented his reading with as many Spanish materials as possible.

After reading *Ralph and the Motorcycle*, Esgar, César, and Ricardo drew pictures of their favorite parts of the story and told Dolores about their drawings. On a card, Dolores wrote what they had told her in sentences; the boys then copied these onto their papers. Esgar and César were very confident with their English sentences, so Dolores wrote down what they said. Ricardo wanted help articulating his ideas but insisted that the sentences be in English.

During tutoring time, Dolores read stories in Spanish to Ricardo, and they would do Language Experience stories in whatever language he chose. For instance, Ricardo listened to a story about a duck. Here is his dictation, in English:

The Duck and The Chick

The duck came out of the egg. Next say the chick, "Me too." The duck go walk. Next say the chick, "Me too." The duck go to the swim. Next say the chick, "Me too." The chick cannot swim. The duck go to another swim. Say the chick, "Not me!"

For several months Ricardo relied a great deal on his friend Esgar to negotiate the meaning of activities in both English and Spanish. In class he usually copied Esgar's written work. Then one day in February he began the assignment himself and chose a topic separate from Esgar's.

Dolores also observed Ricardo in other classroom contexts. She found that he loved math. She called his old school and got a copy of his Spanish math book so that he could continue at his current level. One day he proceeded to do three pages out of his math book without assistance. He was able to sing along with the butterfly song, the caterpillar song, and the praying mantis song (while working on double-digit addition and subtraction), songs that the students were singing as they worked on drawing insects. He was doing his math in Spanish, but when he came to a word problem that was in English, and was given the choice between having it read to him in either language, he chose English.

Dolores called his mother to ask for help on the home front. His mother could not read, but Ricardo had an older sister who agreed to read aloud to him in Spanish every night. They also worked out a plan for homework. Ricardo then took his spelling words home to study. The next day he got 100 percent on his paper; the following week he got another 100 percent. He smiled for an hour. One week later, he got another 100 percent. Mrs. Ringer commented to Dolores that he was progressing in his other subjects as well. Dolores, in an aside to Mary Beth, said it was a revelation to Mrs. Ringer that lack of proficiency in English didn't mean deficiency elsewhere.

MARY'S STORY: TONG

BACKGROUND

THE TEACHER: Mary, ESL pull-out teacher

THE STUDENT: Tong
Age: 11
Nationality: Taiwanese
Home language: Chinese
Grade placement: Sixth grade
Competency in English: Limited; some comprehension, some verbal
    skills, some reading and writing
Educational background: Attended school in Taiwan through
    fifth grade; excellent reading, writing, and math skills in
    primary language

THE STORY

Tong was a sixth grader when Mary was hired to work with him. His
parents had sent Tong and his two sisters from Taiwan to the United
States to stay with their aunt and uncle. The children would have a
chance to master English so they could continue their education at a
university in the United States. Mary was hired to help Tong for social
studies and science. He had tested NEP.

When Mary arrived at class that first day, his teacher pointed out
a lanky boy with shiny black hair, gold wire-rimmed glasses, and a
contagious smile. Since school had been in session for a month, Tong
seemed familiar and comfortable with his surroundings. Mary could
see that he got along well with his peers; they liked him and helped
him when he needed it. Tong kidded around with the boys seated in
his group, mischievously flicked their hats to the floor when they
weren't looking, and laughed at their surprise. He had little problem
in conversations with the kids around him, but Mary could see that
the discussion on the ancient Greeks and their forms of government
was completely over his head—the technical vocabulary and the background information were beyond him. Tong valiantly tried to follow in
his text for several minutes but was soon lost. He was not able to keep
up with the outline the teacher put on the board; he was just marking

time until the end of the period. His teacher felt that Tong would be better off if he were pulled out for both his social studies and science class periods.

Mary remembers those first few pull-out sessions as painful for Tong and herself. He didn't want to talk to her at all. He answered almost anything she said with "Yes," "No," or "I don't know." She was persistent. After a few days Tong got over his shyness; Mary discovered that Tong was quick, bright, and had a wonderful sense of humor. She saw that he understood quite a bit more English than he let on. Tong's strategy for speaking was to get the listener to fill in any words or gaps he had in his vocabulary. When he was animated it was easy to carry on a conversation, but when he was withdrawn or uninterested, it was like pulling teeth. Their classes usually ranged between both extremes (which could be quite draining on some days).

Tong's classroom teacher gave Mary outlines for the science objectives until Christmas and a sixth-grade autobiography project. The autobiography assignment was divided into sections that began with the student's birth, childhood, and favorite things, and progressed to the family, home, friends, and the future. The teacher wanted to give Tong the time he needed to complete the project, so she said he could do the items in any order he wanted or could skip any that were too difficult.

The first topic, "The Day I was Born," asked the students to write an essay covering the following information: Date of birth, place of birth, the town where you were born, the trip to the hospital, what was going on in the world, who was president, styles, music, and any other interesting information you can find out from your parents.

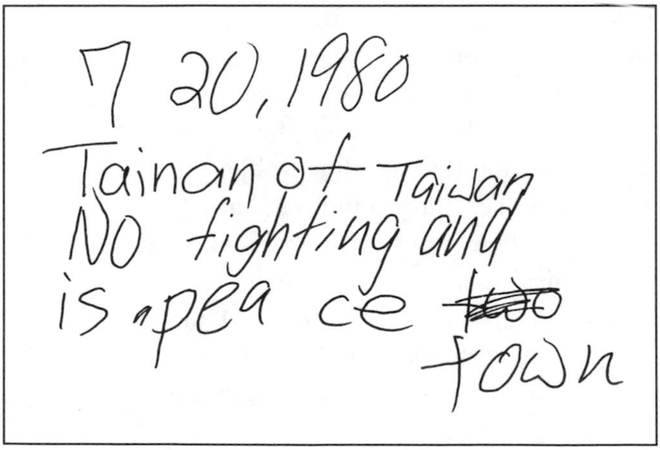
7 20, 1980
Tainan of Taiwan
No fighting and
is peace ~~two~~ town

Figure 7.4: *Tong's first attempt at "The Day I Was Born" assignment*

Tong handed Mary his first draft.

Mary learned much from Tong's first attempt (figure 7.4). He can use English script, he uses capitals, and he was able to get the gist of the assignment. She also could see writing at length about complicated topics was beyond Tong just yet. She knew her first steps with Tong would have to be dealing with the here and now.

He could answer the date, place, and what was going on (*is peace town*). Beyond that, he did not have the tools to do this assignment without help. Mary asked Tong's sister to explain the assignment to him in Chinese; Mary then rewrote the topics as questions. He did better with this format, but clearly, the objective of this assignment was beyond his capabilities. Mary decided to try a different writing assignment with Tong and let this one go for a few months.

While Tong could not complete the first autobiography assignment, Mary could see that he was capable of some things. He could print and write in English, he had a decent vocabulary for a beginner, and he understood enough about the assignment to attempt to answer the questions.

As they worked together on class assignments, Mary took an informal assessment of Tong's reading skills. When Tong worked on his science papers, she observed that he was very good at skimming for the answer. Tong was motivated to fill in the blanks and get the page done so he wouldn't have to do it for homework. Mary was amazed at how fast and accurately he could skim. As she assessed Tong's oral reading abilities, she saw the same savvy strategies he used for speaking. He would start to read a passage and get stuck on an unfamiliar word. He would usually do one of two things: mumble the pronunciation or just skip the word. In either case he hoped Mary wasn't paying much attention. Depending upon the context, the situation, and just how blatant he was being, Mary would correct him or let it go.

THE ISSUES AND RESPONSE

Mary faced these issues:

◆ how to improve Tong's language skills
◆ how to cover as much content as possible and keep it meaningful
◆ how to increase Tong's work independence so he could work unaided in the classroom and at home
◆ how to increase Tong's English self-confidence so he could function on the level of his peers in the classroom
◆ when to place Tong back into the classroom

Within the next few weeks, Mary learned that Tong could give a detailed description of a subject. He could work hard on a project and accomplish the goal, as he did in an essay describing his school in Taiwan. In figure 7.5 you can see that Tong could organize and develop the theme of the school routine in Taiwan and used details to make his point. His sentence structures were basic but effective. He understood sentence boundaries. He used an exclamation point. Tong understood paragraphs although he did not indent them—he broke each section with a blank line. His spelling was surprisingly good for a recent English speaker. Mary's next step would be to repeat this writing process with his autobiography assignments.

Figure 7.5

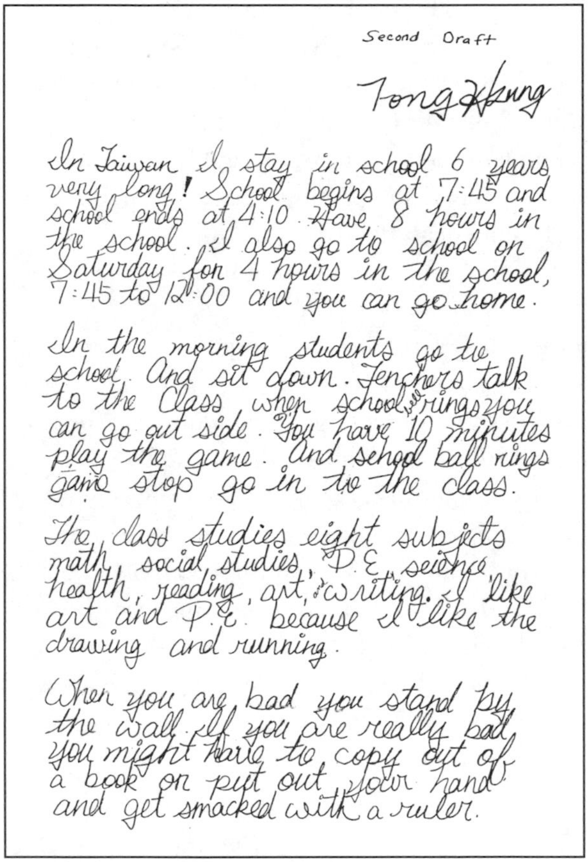

Second Draft

Tong Hung

In Taiwan I stay in school 6 years very long! School begins at 7:45 and school ends at 4:10. Have 8 hours in the school. I also go to school on Saturday for 4 hours in the school, 7:45 to 12:00 and you can go home.

In the morning students go to school. And sit down. Tenchers talk to the Class when school bell rings you can go out side. You have 10 minutes play the game. And school bell rings game stop go in to the class.

The class studies eight subjects math, social studies, P.E seince, health, reading, art, writing. I like art and P.E. because I like the drawing and running.

When you are bad you stand by the wall. If you are really bad you might have to copy out of a book or put out your hand and get smacked with a ruler.

By Christmas, Tong could do quite a bit. He was making progress on his autobiography project. He and Mary attacked one topic every other week when he did not have any other work that needed to be finished. At first he was overwhelmed and hated the first draft of writing; he did not have the competence to say what he meant and got frustrated. Mary didn't push too many of the assignments because she thought he would do better as time went on. Mary and Tong stuck to the easier topics and worked on homework or targeted skills. Figures 7.6 and 7.7 are from the autobiography assignment. They are the descriptions Tong wrote of himself. He did not develop these in much detail, but trying to describe who you are in a new language is difficult. Tong poured more of his effort into the visual self-portrait, but the personal description and the personality description, although brief, were also significant. He did both as homework without help. He correctly used self-descriptive vocabulary he learned from his sessions with Mary. He correctly used commas and periods and apostrophes in both possessive and contractive form.

Nov. 19, 1992
Tong Hsung

When I look in the mirror, I see a boy. The boy looks like average, thin, and young. The boy is twelve years old. The boy has black hair, black eyes, face like monkey and the boy has glasses. The boy's name is Tong Hsung.

Figure 7.6: Tong actually did very well on this assignment despite the short length. He wrote these at home with no help from Mary and managed to communicate what he is like, even with limited English skills.

Dec 2, 1992
TONG HSUNG

I'm very funny because I like joking with people. Sometimes I do a lot of crazy things, like I put my dog in the swimming pool. People think I'm a hardworking boy, but I'm very, very, lazy boy. But sometimes I'm very intelligent I don't know why. I think I'm a very cheerful boy.

By March, Mary could see a tremendous difference in Tong's abilities. He could write much more easily and could tackle larger assignments with less anxiety. At the same time he was more fidgety and harder to engage than before. Mary asked, "Are you squirrelly like this at home?" He shook his head and answered, "No, I don't do squirrel at home. My uncle don't like squirrel."

At the end of the month Mary came down with pneumonia and was out of work for about six weeks. This meant that Tong had to stay in regular science and social studies classes. The teacher was surprised at how well he did. When Mary returned, they decided that Tong would stay for science and would work with Mary for the remaining period. He was doing great and was proud of the fact that he had made such strides.

By the end of the year, Tong could handle most school work himself. He finished his autobiography, completing the first topic of the assignment that he was not able to do at the beginning of the year. He wrote his description of the day he was born (figure 7.7). Mary could see now he had the confidence to answer the questions that were possible and add information that was pertinent to his situation. Instead of discussing fashion and music, Tong focused on what he *could* describe: his country. By this time he was also able to use the English alphabet to write the names of Taiwan's president and vice president. He could give more information about his family members and the name of the hospital where he was born. Mary felt his approach to this assignment showed some real growth. Tong did not have a mother or father here to consult about the events of his birth; his sisters were too young to remember much; he did not have reference materials to use for fashion and popular songs. That made this topic extremely challenging for him. He came up with the solution by himself. Mary was proud of his progress because he had the confidence and understanding of the assignment to write about what he knew. He had come a long way from the beginning of the year. He was proud of his autobiography.

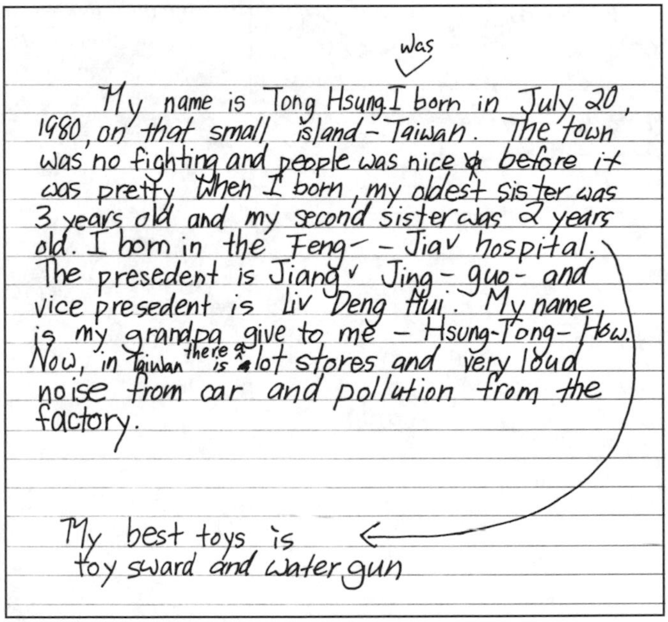

My name is Tong Hsung. I was born in July 20, 1980, on that small island - Taiwan. The town was no fighting and people was nice before it was pretty. When I born, my oldest sister was 3 years old and my second sister was 2 years old. I born in the Feng - Jia hospital. The presedent is Jiang Jing - guo - and vice presedent is Liv Deng Hui. My name is my grandpa give to me - Hsung-Tong-How. Now, in Taiwan there is a lot stores and very loud noise from car and pollution from the factory.

My best toys is toy sward and water gun

***Figure 7.7:** Tong completed his assignment on "The Day I Was Born," which demonstrates real control.*

Tong was getting ready to go on a sixth-grade science trip to the Pacific coast; he was trying to learn everything he needed to pass the written test before the end of the year. By this time his oral reading had improved to the point that when he was stuck on a word, he would say "No, don't tell me." He would then attempt to figure it out on his own. His work time with Mary was productive as long as they were working on homework or tests that he could see the necessity of passing. He was ready for immersion at this point and he needed to be graded on the work he accomplished. Mary felt that his seventh-grade year would be a challenge for him, but one that he could meet.

CONCLUSION

There are never any cut-and-dried answers on how to work with ESL students. One precarious aspect of working with them is that you deal with so many variables: educational background, literacy in the home language, level of English acquisition, learning styles, and so on. These variables make the ongoing assessment process so important. You need to know what the student can do now so you can decide what to do next. At times you look at your student's work, behavior, and the overall classroom context and try to understand just where he or she is on the learning continuum. To be honest, the answers aren't always clear. There are times you have to take an educated guess at what you think the student needs next, step back and observe how that works, and then go from there. The formula that works for one student is not necessarily a template for all other students; each student's learning process is unique. However, the insights you gain from observing your student, in combination with what you know about the language-learning continuum, will help when you struggle with another student's learning continuum. Teacher and students become empowered. You are able to do your job and teach, and your students find that they do not have to flounder because of limited English ability.

The Final Nail
in the Coffee:
GRADES

This chapter is about methods of reporting student progress to the stakeholders involved.

In this chapter we discuss

- who the stakeholders are
- the thorny issue of grading ESL students
- the question of setting standards

José and Anna are concerned and conscientious parents who want their daughter Luisa to succeed in school. With their limited English, they help her with her schoolwork every day as best they can. Luisa's report card (figure 8.1) was a blow to them. Luisa feels discouraged.

Luisa's parents had a lot of questions: How did her teacher Mr. Mansfield decide on these grades? What criteria did he use? Is Luisa

---

GRADES 4 - 5 - 6 REPORT CARD

Dear Parents,

This report is a record of your child's achievement in basic skills, study habits, and citizenship. Close contact between parents and the schools is important to provide the best learning opportunities for your child.

We encourage you to meet with the teacher, visit classrooms, and participate in school activities.

Teacher's comments: *Luisa is doing well, but is capable of much more. I enjoy having her in class and I look for more of her best work this next quarter.*

Pupil *Luisa Fernandez* Grade *4* School Year _____
School *Cedar Valley* Teacher *Mr. Mansfield*

REPORT PERIOD		FIRST
SUBJECTS	GRADE	BELOW GRADE LEVEL
READING	C	
with understanding		
uses skills accurately		
LANGUAGE *written*	C	
SPELLING weekly lesson *Compacts*	C+	
OTHER SUBJECTS *Tuesday homework*	5	
ARITHMETIC	D+	
fundamentals		
reasoning		
HISTORY	C	
GEOGRAPHY	S	
SCIENCE	C+	
HEALTH	S	
FOREIGN LANGUAGE		

SUBJECTS REPORT PERIOD	FIRST
PHYSICAL EDUCATION	S
HANDWRITING	S
ART	S
MUSIC vocal	S
instrumental	
CITIZENSHIP	
obeys school rules	B
courteous/considerate of others	B
respects property of others	B
assumes responsibility	B
STUDY HABITS	S
listens and follows direction	✓
does neat and careful work	S
completes work on time	✓
uses time and materials wisely	
ATTENDANCE RECORD	
Days present	43
Days absent	0

KEY: A: Superior   B: Good   C: Average
D: Passing   F: Failure   ✓: Needs improvement

S: Satisfactory   U: Unsatisfactory

Figure 8.1: Luisa's report card

being compared to her other English-speaking classmates? What does a *C* in reading actually mean? What does she need to learn to improve in arithmetic? He writes she's doing well but is capable of much more: in geography? English? Where? What exactly does "doing well" or "much more" mean?

◆

Harris was one of the loves of Barb's life. He was loud, he was obnoxious, he would boom, "I hate this!" in the middle of an assignment. Harris spoke Hawaiian pidgin as his first dialect, had no ESL program available to him, and English as a Second Dialect (ESD) had not been invented yet. He was tracked in a low-achieving seventh-grade class of nonstandard English speakers, with a number of NEP students who received no special help. The books they used were twenty years out of print; there were no pencils and few other materials. Harris didn't hand in his assignments, so the grade book had large gaps that caused his average to spiral downward. But when he was engaged, such as when the class made a newspaper, he worked harder than anyone—helping Hung Than, just off the boat from Vietnam; planning the layout; bullying the others in his group to finish. He even cut other classes to sit in on Barb's two and three times a day, crawling in through the window in the back of the room. Giving him a *D* based on what he had turned in was such a hardship that Barb gave him a *C* based on his effort. And she wished there was a place on the report card where she could let others know what a great kid he was and give recognition to what such an ornery, irrepressible, likable boy was really capable of doing, instead of pushing him further down the road to failure or second-class citizenship.

The typical report card, writes Shedlin (1988), "has become increasingly narrow in focus, it uses quantitative terminology and data almost exclusively to describe the quality of a student's work—little more than a recording of grades, scores and attendance." These report cards are what Wolf et al. (1991) call "punitive," the source of dread for many, and, for others, a deterrent for taking challenging courses. To have your entire effort summed up in a neat row of letters can be a dismal, defeating experience for many. As Covey (1989) writes, "People are not graded against their potential or against the full use of their present capacity. They are graded in relation to other people. And grades are carriers of social value; they open doors of opportunity or they close them. Competition, not cooperation, lies at the core of the educational process. Cooperation, in fact, is usually associated with cheating." Report cards focus not on what a student can do or has learned, but on how he competes. Both Luisa and Harris came up short.

Reporting methods and grades, such as the ones Luisa and Harris were subjected to, need to be revised to give a better view of the whole student, without the negative effects.

For the Harrises and the Luisas of the world, we need to try.

THE STAKEHOLDERS AND WHAT THEY NEED TO KNOW

Luisa's and Harris's report cards are standard for the district, but they are too vague to be of help to the primary stakeholders in their lives. Who, then, has a stake in Luisa and Harris's learning?

- ◆ their parents
- ◆ administrators
- ◆ teachers (mainstream, next year's)
- ◆ ESL teachers or aides
- ◆ Luisa and Harris

Each stakeholder wants—and has a right—to know what Luisa and Harris are doing and how well they are doing. What each wants to know, however, might be different:

- ◆ **Parents** want to know what and how Luisa and Harris are doing so they can help them and encourage them, and begin intervention if things are going wrong.
- ◆ **Administrators** (including principals, board members, legislators, state and provincial department of education staff members, and superintendents) concerned with accountability and programs, want data so they can plan and budget for resources. Administrators make important instructional and policy decisions based on information about student achievement. Anthony et al. (1991) write, "Administrators are called upon to formulate, implement, and guide broad policy.

They make far-reaching decisions. With regard to language instruction, administrators need to know in general terms whether present programs are working satisfactorily. If not, they must ask what changes should be made." Because they need to see things in broad terms, bound as they are to representing large numbers of people, they are often obliged to use standardized and decontextualized measures that do not take into account individual teachers and students.

◆ **Teachers** want to know so they can plan instruction. Next year's teachers want to know what Luisa has accomplished and how well so they can meet her at her level. Counsellors want to know how Harris has done so they can make a reasonable academic plan for him. Mainstream teachers want to know what ESL teachers have covered in their lessons, and vice versa.

◆ **Luisa and Harris** want to know so they can feel good about themselves, be sure of what they've accomplished and what they need to work on, and have a concrete record of what they have mastered so that when they go on, they can demonstrate what skills they have.

These groups are what Stiggins (1991) calls the users of data. He states that users must understand "the decisions they make, how those decisions relate to effective teaching and learning, and what kinds of data can inform their decision making." But Stiggins continues that if the decisions they make "are made well, students benefit. If they are made poorly, students suffer. But those decisions can only be as sound as the data on which they are based." Thus it is in everyone's best interest to provide good data upon which administrators can make these important decisions. Stakeholders also need to understand the four key attributes we discussed in chapters 1 and 2: a clear target, appropriate samples, known sources of interference, and usable results. In this chapter we will discuss grading. In the following chapter we will discuss how to help supplement whatever reporting method you are using to reflect the capabilities and knowledge of students.

GRADING ISSUES FOR ESL

Winograd (1991) states that one of the major issues facing teachers is that of setting standards of student performance. What is an *A?* Many schools don't grade ESL students. However, in most schools grades are a reality, and sooner or later ESL students are going to be subject to them. (Even in this book about alternative assessment we felt we had to address the issue because it won't go away.) We can put off grading while students are in the lower levels, but in high school and upper levels, student mastery and achievement eventually need to be aligned with the rest of the system. Shedlin (1988) writes:

> ...while there is an occasional movement away from an emphasis on grades, the truth of the matter is that grades are still seen as a fairly accurate measure of a student's accomplishments by most of the educational establishment. Many schools still use grade-point average as one factor in determining placement purposes; it is the single most important criteria in determining class rank.

There is a time and a place for summative assessment. Grades and report cards are what Newman (1992) calls, "institutional record keeping." The big problem: how do we decide on grades? The monkey on the back of every teacher is how to give grades that are fair. And the problem is, the better we know students and the more we care about them, the harder it is to be objective and—in many cases— cold-blooded about giving grades.

This is because grades are muddy issues. They are summative, and cannot concretely demonstrate progress or effort. Often nongrading issues get mixed in with grades. For instance, Mary remembers failing a test which ruined her grade-point average so that she couldn't go on the field trip for honors students during her senior year in high school. The teacher asked questions such as, "What was the color of the book?" "Who was the author?" "When was it written?" rather than the pertinent content questions which Mary had studied so faithfully. Many teachers lower grades because students have been absent for more than their allotted misses. Giving a lower grade for such a reason disregards a student's competency or ability. So is docking them for handing in an assignment late. Teachers apply these strictures to grading because they often feel they have no other method of imposing consequences for laziness or class-cutting.

Hills (1991) and other scholars have come out strongly against this practice. Hills writes, "If we start with the assumption that grades should be meaningful and that they should communicate meaningfully the academic achievement of individual students in the content explicitly being taught, then...grades should *not* be used for disciplinary purposes. If a grade is altered as a way of inflicting punishment, it no longer accurately reflects academic achievement, and its proper meaning is destroyed." As well, he goes on to state, this is probably illegal.

The other extreme often occurs, too. As in Harris's case (page 220), a teacher's feelings for a student, and the clear understanding that a student knows and can do a lot better than his grade point average shows, gets in the way. So does the contention that he tried really hard and should be rewarded. (This is why we are moving toward clear-cut demonstrations of what students can do as opposed to what a grade reflects.)

There is little, however, to guide us. "Think about it," writes Pat Belanoff (1991). "Have you ever noticed that you can find lots of articles on assessment and evaluation, but how many articles have you seen published on grading—on the actual giving of grades? Not very many. Most of us would just rather not talk about it at all; it's the dirty thing we have to do in our own offices."

It's true. We had to search hard for literature on grading, on something to tell us how to cope with this issue or provide us with real advice. Most of the discussion was centered on grade bashing and what Smith calls the "disabling consequences" of grades.

Barb remembers those painful consequences of grading in her own life: when she got an *A*- on a project and was asked why she didn't get an *A*. "I don't know," she would say helplessly, not understanding at that age just how subjective grades could be. In tenth grade, she failed her geometry final. That huge *F* and the final grade of *D* in geometry somehow obliterated and rendered irrelevant all the *A*s and *B*s she received in her other courses, and she has only taken one math class since, in college—bonehead math for the math-impaired.

Activists such as Frank Smith advocate eradicating grading and
evaluation altogether. Smith (1988) writes, "Grades are the sole reason
that most school activities are undertaken, requiring or enticing students
to engage in tasks they would never otherwise go near. And grades
degrade undertakings that could otherwise be worthwhile in their
own right."

Eradicating grades is a worthy goal, but their existence is a reality.
At this point schools are not about to abandon them altogether, and
they are something that our ESL students are subject to. What then,
are we to do?

Questions to consider

For Barb, one of the great things about teaching ESL was not having
to give grades. It was great just to be able to see students' progress
without the pressure and the hassle of trying to pin a grade on the
work. As a junior professor teaching both lower-level composition and
upper-level linguistics courses, after the luxury of years of not having
to give grades at all, Barb was extremely uncomfortable with the idea.
She would read a stack of papers and think, "Well, this one is pretty
good"; then, "Well, that's better than the first." Then she'd read one
that didn't quite follow the assignment but was so fresh and vivid she
didn't know what to do. She'd observe student presentations, and
watch some that were great, others that were well presented but thin
on theory, others totally borrowed with little thought from the pre-
senter. What was an *A*? How was it better than a *B*? In graduate school
a *C* had been an unacceptable grade. So what did that make a *D*, and
who deserved one? After her first lecture course, the chairman of the
department came to her and said she had given too many high grades.
After some hesitation, she explained that several of the students had
not done well on the tests, so she had given them extra-credit assignments to make up for their low grades and bring up their averages.
She had given everybody a chance to do extra credit work. He seemed
dumbfounded, and told her that not many teachers would be willing
to spend the time to do that. No more was said about the high scores.

Even more problematic for her was the issue of grading ESL students.
When she taught beginning literacy, there was a huge range in both
proficiency in English and experience with schooling. Several students

were much more proficient and competent as readers and writers, as well as more studious than others who had barely begun to read and write. The semester before, she had taught intermediate composition. Was an *A* in beginning literacy the equivalent of an *A* in composition? Were these *A*s the same as an *A* in a mainstream course?

Take for instance, Kao's essay, laboriously typed into the computer:

My top mountain

Black mountain is a taller and famous mountain.

Near my village when I was a childhood everyone spend one week in the summer to climb on the top and stayed. At there they were have many kind of bird their are singing very different sound. When I hear that bird singing my hart got lonely and I missing the honey girl looked down there are many villages the wind brow up all leaves dried below me. Upper there are green leaves on me. It was only the dirt road their haven't car haven't traffic they are some rode the horses very often all people took walk by foot.

I love that mountain very much.

This was the most Kao had ever produced, and was truly his best effort. There is so much good in this piece of writing: Kao has managed to capture his feelings for that particular spot, he includes descriptive details, and shows why it means a great deal to him. And yet, for the average English-speaking tenth grader, or even eighth grader, this would not be acceptable because it is not the quality or quantity one should be able to expect from a fifteen-year-old. Should Kao be graded against the standard for a tenth grader, which he was, or as a tenth-grade beginner doing his best in an ESL class?

We have attempted to lay out some questions you need to consider and answer for yourself concerning this important issue:

What standards are you using to make judgments?
What criteria will you use in assessing and grading students' work?
If you use portfolios how will you calculate traditional grades
(*A,B,C...*) based on those students' portfolios?
How will you deal with issues of subjectivity in grading?

Will you continue to use tests as a major source of grades or will
you include samples of students' work in the decisions?
If you do use alternative assessment procedures will they supplement or replace tests?

We cannot give answers to these questions. However, we can at least
open the discussion (or Pandora's box) so that you make your way
toward finding answers for yourself.

Setting standards

Irmscher (1978) writes, "Evaluation implies values, but many teachers
evaluate without defining them or just feel frustrated they can't quan-
tify the values they hold. Without clearly defined values, it is impossible
to make consistent judgments and discriminations. What most charac-
teristically happens when...teachers read student papers, or for that
matter, when students read each others papers...is that they find fault.
Comment emphasizes what is wrong and not what is right major concern focuses on the limitations of the prose; the strengths are taken
for granted."

As Irmscher points out, even with the troublesome issue of grades
the focus can be on what has been done right, with an emphasis toward
improvement, not punishment. We recommend examining Irmscher's
evaluation scale (see Appendix A, page 281). For Barb, it helped clarify
what to consider an *A*, and what made a *B* different than a *C*. Even
though this scale was developed strictly for compositions, it has much
to offer in terms of focusing on what is important.

Irmscher used a five-part numbering system used by the College
Entrance Examination Board to develop his scale:

A – demonstrates unusual competence
B – demonstrates competence
C – suggests competence
D – suggests incompetence
F – demonstrates incompetence

In regard to non-English or nonstandard dialect speakers, Irmscher writes:

> The writing of these students can be atypical in many ways. In content, it may be mature and perceptive, although lacking in formal control. In language it may be vigorous, although lacking in consistency of tone and usage. In style, it may be moving, although fragmentary and error-ridden. Often the psychological barriers to writing are so strong that special emphasis must be given to encouragement, whenever and wherever possible.

The idea of a student demonstrating competence in any given subject is a fruitful way to perceive the issue of grades. Grades can and should be a positive force in a student's progress. Competence can be demonstrated in spite of lack of proficiency, if one can look through and beyond the errors to the essence of what's important, and focus on the learning that is taking place.

This means, as Rhodes and Shanklin (1992) point out, reexamining the concept of the bell curve, "because a normal curve, after all, operates under the assumption that some students cannot learn what we teach. Of course, it's usually the same students who are at the bottom of the bell curve; they learn to expect that they cannot improve their grades because someone has to be at the bottom." Teruko writes of the use of the bell curve in her own country:

> At elementary schools and junior high schools our evaluations (I mean grades) is very strict. In some schools, only 7 percent of students can get A, 27 percent can get B, 32 percent can get C, 27 percent can get D and 7 percent can get F. Even though teachers don't want to give F to anybody, he must give it to someone, exactly 7 percent of the students. How much students make efforts doesn't count: for example, if a first exam is 30 percent, and a second exam is 90 percent, the student can get C. The teacher doesn't see his effort and progress. They can't give him a B.

This philosophy denies the fact that all students can demonstrate competence and can improve. It is, as Bloom et al. (1981) write, "the distribution most appropriate to chance and random activity. Education is a purposeful activity, and we seek to have the students learn what we have to teach. If we are effective, the distribution of achievement should be very different from the normal curve. In fact, we may even insist that our efforts are unsuccessful to the extent that the distribution of achievement approximates the normal distribution."

Rhodes and Shanklin suggest, "instead of grading a student in comparison to other students, we can grade against a set of criteria, or against a student's own past performance and what we know we can expect next developmentally."

An *A* can be an *A* for any class. For instance, an *A* might demonstrate superior ability to identify and assess important ideas in text, in history, or demonstrate superior ability to understand and solve algebra problems. Suggesting or demonstrating incompetence can transcend language.

What can a student demonstrate in spite of an incomplete handle on the language? A student can demonstrate

- his or her depth and breadth of understanding of the content
- the amount of grappling he has done with the ideas
- her control over subject matter if not language
- an awareness of the parameters and the subtleties of the topic at hand
- an ability to organize
- the competence with which one wields not just the language but the understanding of the issues

For example, figure 8.2 (next page) shows Lan's response to *To Kill a Mockingbird*. While her grammar has errors, the depth of her understanding of the essence of what Harper Lee was trying to convey was beyond what most teachers could hope for.

In *The More-Than-Just-Surviving Handbook* we discussed criteria for grading tests:

Did she understand the question?
Did she answer the question?
How well did she develop her thoughts?
How thoroughly did she present her case?
Is she performing to the best of her ability given her stage of
    language competency, or is she just goofing off?

Figure 8.2:
Lan's response
to the book
To Kill a
Mockingbird.

> ⟨Reflections⟩ ⟨To Kill a Mockingbird⟩
>
> 1. This book teach me a lot.
>
> First, humanbeing like to make society, and then they are interested in each other, especially in small society, but sometimes they talk about others, and make rumour and finally have prejudice. It's so hurt others, but they never realized that.
>
> Second, humanbeing make a class in society and then look down people whom they feel better than. If I have much money or better education, or upper class, I look down others, and want to get along with same class or upper one.
>
> Third, people who is only one animal has racial problem. colors are no matter. Black, Yellow and White are equal. But there is still problem as you see.
>
> Last, people kill others without any sadness or guilty. It's so scare.
>
> I thought these things after I read this book. People have a prejudice about Boo. Boo had to stay at home for a long time. There were not exactly rumour. It was hurt Boo. His life was gone by neighborhood. Also, People look down Bob. Because, he was uneducated, and lower class, and live beside dum and Black people. Eventhough he was White, he was looked down by other White people. So, he hated Black people who were lower than him, and lived beside him. Tom was also victim by society. Eventhough Atticus tried to depend him, he had to go to the jail. Because he was Black. And he was killed by others who didn't have any guilty.

For instance, a seventh-grade beginning literacy class read a Hmong folk tale about the first farmer. One of the questions was: "How long did the farmer wait? Why?" Here are some of the answers given:

Seven. Because he lazy.

Seven. So the corn could grow big.

Seven. He waits so many day because he want to get rest and sleep.

Seven. He's lazy and want the weeds grow bigger. So he doesn't have to come alot of days.

Seven. Because he wait until the corn grew and ready for eat then he only take them home and one thing he was lazy man.

Each student had the correct answer. However, in class they had discussed the fact that the farmer was lazy. The additional inference, that he wanted to wait for the weeds to grow higher so that he didn't have to come as often or work as hard, was made on their own, and revealed an added depth of understanding by several of the students. The teacher awarded two points for each correct answer. She might have chosen to give extra credit for the inferences, but did not.

This was her choice as a teacher whose values, standards, and philosophy may differ from yours or ours. This is nothing to be alarmed about or seek to change. We cannot set the standards for every teacher or every course. Standards, and grading, reflect the values, philosophies, as well as the tastes of each teacher. Teachers have different things they consider important, including individual objectives and priorities. We cannot and should not establish absolute standards. According to Belanoff (1991), the inability of teachers to agree on grading systems and standards is "a sign of strength, of the life and vitality of words and the exchange of words [because] texts reflect life and the multitude of tastes and standards in real life."

Rhodes and Shanklin suggest a number of guidelines to keep in mind when you must turn in grades for reporting to the stakeholders:

- Grade selected student work, work that is selected because it is the student's best work or because it is most representative of the student's reading and writing. Grade a minimum amount of work.
- Grade what you consider important for students to be learning. If learning to make reading an integral part of their lives is important, find a way to grade it.
- Grade both process and product in student work. Students frequently make progress in the processes of reading and writing before the learning shows up in their products.
- Carefully define and communicate to students what you will grade in their work. This is important in teaching, not just in evaluation.
- Involve students in the grading process. If we want to develop students' ability to critique their own work, we must provide opportunities for them to learn how to do so.

◆ Remember that the fundamental goal of grading reading and writing should be to improve reading and writing. Critique your current grading practices—and those you develop in the future—with this goal in mind.

However, grades must also reflect the standards of the institution. There are many mitigating factors that are, and must be, taken into account when grading.

A student who challenged Barb intellectually most was Bob Doupnik, a retired career military man, who, in an upper level linguistics course, suggested the following hierarchical view of grading. It has some very interesting ideas to consider:

1. **Purpose of the work**
2. **Execution of the work (or document)**
   a) **grasp of the idea being expressed**
   b) **flow of supporting information, management of the idea**
   c) **resolution of the idea**
3. **Mechanics of the delivery**
   a) **choice of supporting vocabulary**
   b) **packaging of word groups**
4. **Fundamental language skills**
   a) **sentence structure and punctuation**
   b) **appropriate word structure**
   c) **spelling**
   d) **penmanship and neatness**
5. **Standards of the institution employing the grader**
6. **Demonstrated effort of the student**
7. **Extenuation and mitigation**
   a) **age and linguistic background of the student**
   b) **time available to finish the project**
   c) **mental and physical state of the student**
   d) **cultural and social standards of the student**

What Bob did was acknowledge all the things that we, as teachers, take into account when grading a student's work. Whether we like it or not, when a student becomes a person, and not a number, who he is and what his emotional, intellectual, cultural, ethnic, and moral makeup consist of influence the grade we give him. Is it not reasonable that we admit it does? Now the question each one must address for himself is can we and should we?

In figures 8.3, 8.4, and 8.5 we present some test answers, without giving our own commentary. It is worth considering how you would grade these particular answers.

Figure 8.3: This was a test given in sheltered high school social studies class. How would you rate these students' answers to the questions?

> 3. If you were Jewish and forced to wear the symbol, would you wear it? Yes or No. Explain why you said yes or no.
> I can still be part of my religion but had not to wear the star; I just didn't let anybody know. Beside the German put me in concentration camp if they see me wear the star where I don't want to be.
>
> 4. What is a concentration camp? Give me an example of something that happened there.
> Concentration Camp - Place where the German put Jewish in. There the people were served little and bad food. they had to work and the German had the Jewish woman - take their child and go to shower room.
>
> 5. Write a conversation that Anne and her Daddy would have.
> Anne: Can I bring my cat with me?
> MR. Frank: No, we did had food to the cat and they only so much stuff that we had to bring with us.
> Anne: I guess you right daddy.
> MR. Frank: Is that ok with you that we couldn't bring the cat with us?
> Anne: yes, but I'll miss the cat!
> MR. Frank: I know, that just the way thing work out — Sorry.
> Anne: It OK. Thank daddy.

> 3. If you were Jewish and forced to wear the symbol, would you wear it? Yes or No. Explain why you said yes or no.
> yes becuas I not wear than got kill. Than I have to wear.
>
> 4. What is a concentration camp? Give me an example of something that happened there.
> The Hitler don't like Jewish people.
> They no pilwal on the bed than they have every thing are dirty in the concentration camp.
>
> 5. Write a conversation that Anne and her Daddy would have.
> Anne: Daddy do you has a book for me to read? yes I has one.
> do you like it?
> Anne: yes I very like
> Daddy: ok you can take it

> 3. If you were Jewish and forced to wear the symbol, would you wear it? Yes or No. Explain why you said yes or no.
> because I am very belive my god so I wold like to wear it. If I dont want Mr. Hitler see I can put the symbol inside the shirt.
>
> 4. What is a concentration camp? Give me an example of something that happened there.
> The concentration camp is Mr. Hitler take the jewish people come to stay in this camp. the jewish in this camp this hurries and get sick in the camp.
>
> 5. Write a conversation that Anne and her Daddy would have.
> Anne = Daddy can you tell me something?
> Daddy = yes, what is your Question Anne
> Anne = Why Mr. Hitler hate jewish people?
> Daddy = because he is belive another god but is not jewish just why he hate jewish people.

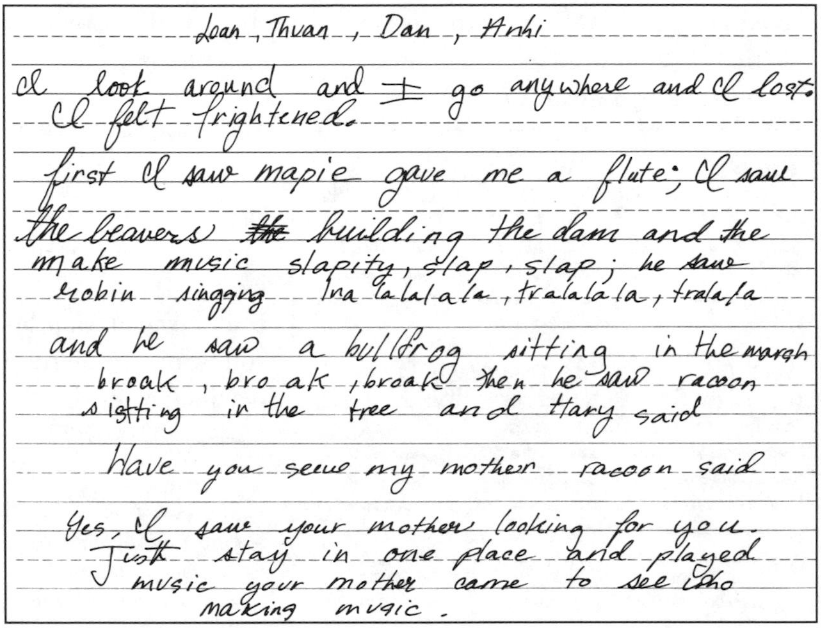

Figure 8.4:
Here is how one group of fifth graders retold in writing a story they had just heard. They included all salient points of the story. Is this an A?

> Joan, Thuan, Dan, Anhi
>
> I look around and I go anywhere and I lost. I felt frightened.
>
> first I saw mapie gave me a flute; I saw the beavers building the dam and the make music slapity, slap, slap; he saw robin singging Ina lalalala, tralalala, tralala and he saw a bullfrog sitting in the marsh broak, broak, broak then he saw racoon sitting in the tree and Hary said
>
> Have you seue my mother racoon said
>
> Yes, I saw your mother looking for you. Just stay in one place and played music your mother came to see who making music.

MODIFYING GRADES

No one has yet resolved whether grades can or should be modified in the regular classroom for ESL students. If you do decide grades should be modified, which students do you modify the grades for, just the beginners, beginners and intermediates, or all? If you modify for beginners, where is the cut-off point?

Strickland (1990) writes that modified grading systems should maintain as many characteristics of the regular grading system as possible. This returns us to the concept of "base-line competencies." She states that the same grading indicators, such as *A, B, C*, should be used whenever possible to ensure continuity instead of moving to a different system, such as check, check-plus, check-minus.

Modifying may include

◆ adjusting the time available for completion of tests and assignments. For many ESL students, reading the test and understanding the questions can take up to half the class period. They run out of time to answer.

- ◆ administering tests orally rather than in written form
- ◆ using an interpreter during testing
- ◆ modifying the format of test from narrative to short answer
- ◆ altering course requirements to focus on those that are most important, with less critical requirements omitted
- ◆ additional reports that interpret that grade

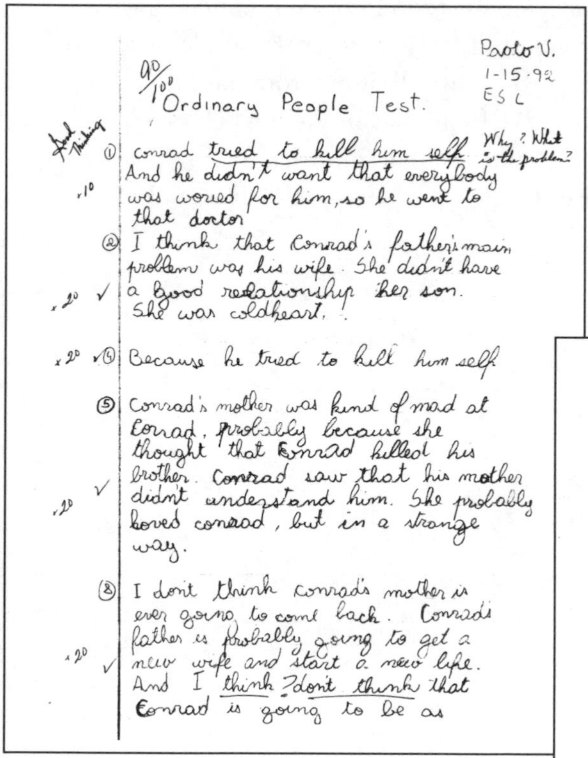

Figure 8.5: *This exercise was given to a high-school ESL class. The teacher gave Paolo (left) a grade of 90 percent and Serafine a grade of 100 percent. Do you agree? What were her standards or her criteria for grading?*

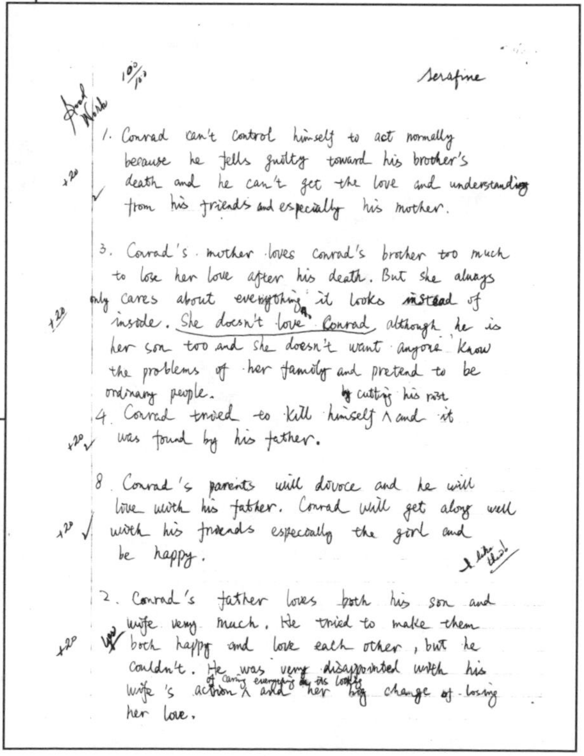

CONCLUSION

This chapter was so problematic we almost chucked it, but grading is an issue that won't go away, so we faced it as we've tried to do all other issues. We feel that Rhodes and Shanklin give the best advice when it comes to grading: establish criteria determined by what it is your students at that particular age, level of proficiency, and literacy are capable of doing and producing. We must grade to their competence within the demands and the content of the course or the grade level. If they meet or exceed the standards within that environment, then they receive an *A* for that course. We hope that in the next chapter, presenting real products to stakeholders and demonstrating real progress is one way to demonstrate what our students really can do given a chance.

Lunching Several Measures:
PRESENTING THE INFORMATION
TO STAKEHOLDERS

This chapter is about

- systematizing information about students
- presenting the data in usable form
- holding conferences

There are two steps to reporting to the major stakeholders in the school system: putting the information into usable form, and presenting it. We will first discuss how to put the information together, then we will talk about conveying that information in spoken form.

SYSTEMATIZING INFORMATION

Mindamon, a small Midwestern town, opened its school doors the first day of school to find forty-seven Laotian and Hmong students ready to enroll. The system had never experienced the challenge of non-English-speaking children before, and the appearance of these students sent everyone into a panic. Somehow, students were tested and placed, and gradually the flurry died down. However, no one had any idea what to do as far as grading and record keeping. It was clear that the old standard report cards wouldn't work, and that files needed additional information in them. They decided to investigate alternative methods of reporting and began a slow overhaul of their system.

The reporting system objectives

Designing a system to report the appropriate information to each stake-holder can be overwhelming from the outset. Peter Winograd (1994), discussing the challenges of developing accurate alternative assess-ment, states that "changes in assessment involve challenge. These are 'problems worth solving' because addressing them successfully will help us realize the full promise of alternative assessment." How can we fashion a reporting system that can give each of these stakeholders a clear picture of how a student is doing? What should a reporting system do?

Assessment—and its counterpart, reporting—should

- ◆ recognize, acknowledge, and give credit by differing methods (such as report cards, grades, and so on) for what students have achieved and experienced in a variety of different contexts
- ◆ increase pupils' awareness of their strengths and weaknesses, and provide encouragement and opportunities to enhance motivation and personal development
- ◆ help schools support and encourage the development of students' diverse talents and skills
- ◆ provide a summary document of a student's qualities and achieve-ments that can be used by others (1984, *Report on the Records of Achievement*)

This is a tall order, and will not be achieved overnight, nor without struggle. But we must begin somewhere.

FIVE STEPS IN COMPILING INFORMATION

Begin by keeping records that contain valuable and useful informa-tion that will tell not just you, but others, where your students are on the learning continuum and what they have accomplished, so that intelligent decisions about what to do next can be made. There are five important steps in the process of compiling information:

1. **Establish a "system."** Mindamon made a file for each student. This was a critical first step. They had a place to start, a place to put the data they were going to accumulate, and the process of creating a system got them thinking of the students whose work would go into these folders.

At this stage these were not portfolios, which are selected collections of student work that are specifically chosen as assessment samples. These folders were merely files designed to hold relevant information about a student.

2. **Decide who the audiences are for these files.** This was a critical decision. The Mindamon school district had to decide: Was the file for the mainstream teacher to monitor progress? Was it for the part-time ESL teacher? Was it for the administration? Was it for next year's teacher? Who was going to have access to the file? How much was going to stay in the room? How much was going home? How much was the student going to carry on to the next year?

Different audiences need different information. Winograd (1994) points out that assessment can be tailored to its stakeholders by recognizing that assessment data serves different audiences with differing agendas. With more specific information available, the stakeholders can make their decisions based on the accumulated data they need: administrators can determine if programs are successful or other forms of support are indicated; teachers can better shape their teaching; parents can gain specific insight into their children's progress as learners; and students can focus on where they have succeeded and what areas need attention.

Mindamon decided to create three subfolders for each student: the mainstream teacher's folder, the ESL teacher's folder, and the cumulative folder. When they had decided which stakeholders to present data to, they could continue the process through the next steps and then decide what would go into each teacher's folder.

The folders kept by the teachers represent the first level of work, a collection of documents of ongoing projects. The next step, the portfolio, represents selections from the two working folders.

3. **Define the purposes of the folder.** Winograd (1994) refers to this step as "selecting and developing assessment techniques and tasks." He states that beyond identifying the stakeholders, it is equally important to collect the data that best reflects the "goals to be evaluated." In other words, collect the student work that best illustrates the type of instruction and learning taking place. You must decide whether the

anecdotes, writing samples, reading records, checklists, and so on, will demonstrate competency for a particular audience. This step goes hand-in-hand with step two, defining the audiences. It is of utmost priority to shape the data and keep this folder from being simply a pile of papers that has no form or meaning to anyone. These purposes, therefore, must be clearly defined. For ESL students, for example, the teachers at Mindamon felt it was important that data

- demonstrate growth over time
- demonstrate mastery of skills
- demonstrate mastery of content
- provide an authentic and concrete picture of the student's capabilities to the stakeholders
- help students become self-reflective
- provide concrete support for bringing about change
- shift the focus from negative, "missing-the-mark" indicators to those of positive achievement

4. **Decide in which areas to show progress and mastery.** The ESL teacher and classroom teachers in Mindamon needed to decide which areas of the Quad (page 143) to concentrate on. They felt it was better to start slowly and build as they got accustomed to this kind of collecting and reporting.

Following is a sample table of contents for a complete student file:

- cover sheet
- content lists
- reading and writing inventories
- student reading and writing surveys
- student work samples
- list of books read
- tests
- videotape
- student attendance record/personal data
- standardized test scores
- individual diagnostic report
- checklists of skills learned
- student progress reports: objectives taught/met

- areas needing work
- student profiles from previous grades
- placement notices
- objectives checklist
- dated entry record of parent contact
- parent-teacher conference reports
- self-evaluation

The teachers at Mindamon chose to include the following in each of the three subfolders:

- *The mainstream teacher's folder.* In this folder, the teacher kept work done in the mainstream classroom, charting progress in reading, writing, and language arts, and in content areas. The elementary and secondary language-arts teachers decided to begin by collecting

  - a reading log
  - four writing samples, one from each quarter of the school year
  - a running record
  - a record of a student conference

- *The ESL teacher's folder.* In this folder, the ESL teacher kept work done in ESL, charting progress in English proficiency. The ESL teacher decided to collect

  - checklists of vocabulary learned
  - samples of writing
  - work samples from the themes covered

- *The cumulative folder.* This folder contained both the information the school keeps in its cumulative record and a student portfolio. The portfolio, put together at the end of the year by the mainstream and ESL teachers, demonstrates mastery, and shows what the student accomplished during that year so that the next year's teacher knows where to begin. The cumulative folder stays with the school or is sent on if the student moves. In the cumulative folder, they collected

  - regular data such as previous grades
  - standardized placement test scores

herself. It is important that the teacher find positive things to say. In the above example, her teacher has also let Anna's parents know specifically in what areas she needs to work harder and how they can help her at home.

Many schools use narratives exclusively. To be useful and effective—especially when they are the only means of reporting—they must be

- specific
- concise
- geared to the audiences reading them
- useful to the reader (give a clear idea as to what to do next with the student)
- indicative of the student's strengths and weaknesses

Davies and Politano (1994) suggest ways for making reports specific and effective:

- Have a collection of evidence upon which to base your observations.

- Support what you say with samples of classroom activity. For example: *Tien is making real strides with her listening and speaking skills. She is beginning to raise her hand to ask a question during group discussion.*

- Include quotations from students' work. For example: *Chun is making good progress in his language skills. He can write his assignments on his own more and more. I notice when he gets stuck trying to find a word for what he wants to say, he finds a phrase that is close to what he wants out of the books and inserts it into the text. Even if the syntax is awkward, he can get his point across. For example, on the erosion assignment, Chun wrote, "Wind is one of main force erosion. It move only [highlighted words are copied from the text] **small rock particles. Abrasion and deflation help wind erode the land.** Also help erode mountain too."*

- Use quotations from students. For example: *Maria is much more relaxed in her conversation this year. She has all but mastered conversational English, even to the point of using the popular slang of her peers who use the phrase "I'm all" (the word all functioning as a verb) tacked onto another phrase. For example, "Barb told me this homework was easy, but I'm all, sure it was a piece of cake." As*

Maria explained her disagreement with her brother, she said, "Tonio is so lazy he won't do anything, and I'm all, 'what do you want, I can't do everything for you.' "

The following narrative was on the right track but didn't give enough information:

Tou is very ambitious to do and complete just about anything. He doesn't have a problem being creative at all. His striving for perfection, such as in spelling, sometimes keeps him from advancing. Over all he's doing well, but sometimes lacks certain cultural knowledge due to his own culture.

This narrative could have been improved by citing examples of Tou's creativity. In addition, providing examples of cultural knowledge that he needs to have could have pointed both his mainstream teacher and his parents to try to help him fill in the gaps.

The following one is better, but still misses the mark:

Diana has a developing number base. She can tell if numbers are greater or less, that numbers have a sequence, and that there is an order when writing them. She continues to recognize patterns not only with numbers and objects but also in her reading. Diana is a slow math worker. We have worked on solving one- and two-digit addition/subtraction problems. Diana understands the process and uses manipulatives to help solve the problem. Subtraction is much harder for Diana to understand and we are practicing only one-digit problems with that.

This report was frustrating for Diana's mother, because it just didn't seem specific enough. The entire tone of the report card seemed as if the teacher was really reaching for something nice to say about Diana. In addition, it didn't tell Diana's mother whether or not Diana was working at the level she should for a first grader. At that time, Diana complained that she hated school and continually tried to invent reasons to stay home. Because Diana had always loved to go to school, this set off alarm bells for Diana's mother. So she did what good teachers do: she watched, listened, asked questions. She learned that Diana was so slow completing her work that she never finished in time to get free time, which the other children teased her about.

This was such a source of anguish for her that she didn't want to go to school. In addition, at home, Diana would cry when she tried to do work sheets. Her mother discovered that when trying to add and subtract she knew how to add one, zero, and the same digit to itself. Beyond that she had to count on her fingers. Subtraction was extra hard. Once when trying to figure out five take away four, she counted out five fingers on one hand, four on the other, counted down four and came up with the answer of five. It was clear she was not grasping the basic principles.

Diana's mother returned to the teacher and told her what she noticed. Knowing what Diana did and didn't understand helped both Diana's mother and her teacher determine how to help her both in school and at home.

The following narrative provides concise, specific information:

Ahmer is improving in math. He has shown that he is very capable in adding two-, three-, and four-digit numbers. He handles regrouping well. He can carry and borrow in addition and subtraction. For the math assignments, Ahmer worked independently. During any problem solving Ahmer worked with a partner or small group. I am beginning to use story problems in class, and in this area, Ahmer is having a difficult time. I feel he does not understand the language of the problem and thus has a hard time with the problem solving itself. This type of problem also shows up in science and in social studies. Ahmer does well in classroom discussions, but when it comes to reading independently, doing Idea Maps or similar activities, he struggles. He did not do well on the science test, and for future tests his ESL teacher will have him take it with her so he will be evaluated on his content knowledge, not his language ability.

Ahmer is a likable little boy who gets along well with his fellow students. He is artistic and is a reliable and hardworking student. Ahmer is a nice child and tries very hard to work to the best of his ability.

Until real change takes place, as it is beginning to in Europe and Australia, it is unrealistic to expect narratives to play more than a small role in the reporting systems of upper grades. When you have 135 or more students in seven classes, keeping on top of the logistics of teaching, marking papers, and making lesson plans, to be saddled with narratives could be the proverbial last straw. However, as discussed in chapter 8, grading is one of the most aggravating aspects of teaching. How many times have we looked at that *C-* or *D+* and thought, "There's so much more to this kid. How can I convey it in more than a letter grade that's just going to defeat him?" A couple of simple sentences would go a long way toward remedying that situation.

Used in conjunction with checklists, portfolios, and videotapes, narratives can be invaluable to each of the various interested parties.

Checklists

We discussed checklists in chapter 6. However, we want to emphasize the usefulness of checklists for reporting both formative and summative data. Figure 9.9, which appears on page 262, is a good example of such a checklist. However they are used, checklists must reflect your philosophy and your beliefs about what is important.

Rubrics, such as those in figure 9.1, can also be considered checklists.

Sheltered Science	
Written Lab Work	
Answers questions with numbers only	
Answers with phrases and short sentences	
Gives clear details in answers	
Group Experiments	
Participates in experiments in groups but only as support	
Participates in group experiment as equal member	
Carries leadership role in experiment	
Class Participation	
Does not ask or answer oral questions, but reflects understanding through written work	
Answers review questions when asked	
Volunteers answers and asks more insightful questions	

Figure 9.1:
Rubric for
sheltered science
class

Portfolios

Portfolios have been rather loosely defined lately, and it's tempting to think of them as any collection of student work. However, Paulson et al. (1992), in defining a portfolio, write that beyond being "a purposeful collection of student work that exhibits the student's efforts, progress, and achievement in one of more areas...the collection must include student participation in selecting contents, the criteria for selection, the criteria for judging merit, and evidence of student reflection."

Collections of work can become portfolios with the addition of one ingredient: student input. The key difference between a portfolio and a folder is the *student participation*. Students play an active role in creating, maintaining, and evaluating their portfolios. Ellen Kallio, a fourth-grade teacher, notes:

> ...the real value as I see it is the ownership role that it puts the students in. They can take initiative in their own interest, have some control over how they are seen, and be able to make decisions that affect them. In addition to this, a portfolio can reveal a student's growth and strengths in a way that standardized testing cannot. It can present a more complete and tangible picture of student's academic and creative abilities. The use of portfolios represents a philosophy that demands that educators view assessment as an integral part of instruction; that they provide a process for teachers and students to use to guide learning.

According to Lauren and Resnic (1991), portfolios initiate a "thinking curriculum by stirring up a decision-making process." They oblige you to decide

- what's important
- how this will affect your teaching
- how your teaching can affect your students' work
- how students perceive what they're doing and learning

Several cautions to portfolio assessment have been mentioned: long-term credibility, time factors, teacher training. Administrators have been resistant to using them. In addition, in places where they have been mandated and put into place before teachers were ready and able to implement them, portfolios have already met a backlash of criticism, and the entire idea is teetering. In addition, portfolios are not neat. They require tolerance of bulky folders full of writing and works-in-progress—collections full of "young effort." Portfolios like other innovations, do not provide the complete answer, but they are a step toward authentic assessment.

The advantages, according to Valencia et al. (1990), are myriad. Done well, they can capture all the elements of alternative assessment that we have been discussing in this book. Portfolio assessment

◆ captures and capitalizes on the best each student has to offer, rather than on errors

◆ is an ongoing part of instruction. Teachers don't have to take time away from instruction, nor students from learning, for assessment to take place.

◆ informs instruction. The *process* of learning is as important to record as the *outcome* of learning (the product). Teachers learn from portfolio assessment not only *what* to teach, but also *how* and *when* to teach it (Teale 1990).

◆ is multidimensional, including cognitive, affective, and social processes

◆ provides for active, collaborative reflection by both teacher and student

◆ is authentic. Children are assessed while they are actually involved in literacy learning.

As with all other departures from tradition, it is easy to jump in and get in over one's head, only to be overwhelmed and flounder back to the safer waters of the known: report cards. We again advise you to go very slowly. It seems unwise to abandon other forms of grading and reporting for an idea that has still not been tested over the long term and has yet to be accepted by the primary stakeholders. It makes so much more sense to start small and work up, adding pieces as you and your students get used to the idea. For a good example of one school's evolution in the use of portfolios, read Lamme and Hysmith (1991).

Portfolios can be used for both in-class assessment or for the larger picture—the cumulative folder assessment. They can be as varied as the classes and teachers wish, because the concept is so adaptable. We believe portfolios are of real importance in documenting the growth of ESL students.

Because folders are messy and bulky, they can become unmanageable. It makes perfect sense to include students in selecting the work samples that go from the working folders into the portfolios, and eventually, into the cumulative files. Tierney (1991) writes, "Whenever students feel involved in activity, they usually invest greater energies in doing that task well. It is not unreasonable, therefore, to give students the major responsibility of compiling and evaluating their own work."

Students can do this by

- selecting their work and justifying their choice
- filling out checklists (see chapter 6)
- reviewing their files, analyzing them, and making comments on the contents

This is another way for students to improve self-reflection and gain insight into their own learning strategies. One criticism of portfolios, or student-selected collections, is students often use inappropriate criteria to choose their work, such as "I liked this." This is not necessarily a legitimate criticism. Even though a student may not select work the teacher feels best reveals his strengths or abilities, students must begin the reflective process somewhere, then set on the road toward better selection through the use of specific criteria and guidance.

For example, Barb, experimenting with portfolios, devised selection guidelines for her upper-level class. She designed a checklist of all the assignments students had completed that term, then adapted questions students were required to answer in selecting the works they wanted to be graded on:

1. Fill out the assignment checklist. Check all that you have completed. The entire set of assignments is to be handed in, numbered, with page numbers on the checklist beside each item.

2. Rate your writing. Which was best? Which was worst? How did you decide?

3. Make your own portfolio of works. Include the ones you would like to be graded on. Fill out the self-evaluation sheet on your portfolio.

Graves (1992) points out that "the portfolio movement has uncovered just how much help students need in order to learn how to evaluate their own work." He goes on to state that writers often know when their writing is good, but it's hard for them to know why. We cannot expect them to know how to do this on their first try. This is especially true for many foreign students from traditional cultures who are simply recipients of the knowledge bestowed upon them by the master, and do not take an active part in their own learning. The questions on the self-evaluation form referred to in point 3, above, require much thought and reflection, and, with their responses, are an essential component of the portfolio. Figure 9.2 shows how one student responded.

Portfolio Self-Evaluation

Name *Ana*

1. What does your portfolio reveal about you as a reader?
   autobiography

2. What does your portfolio reveal about you as a writer?
   student

3. What does your portfolio suggest your strengths are?
   enough

4. What does your portfolio suggest about how you have changed?
   I do better English

5. What do you think people will learn about you from your portfolio?
   other people's experience

6. Select what you think is your best piece of writing from your portfolio.

   a. How does this piece compare with other items you've written this semester?
   autobiography. I like it. It is short but I am satisfy this piece.

   b. How does this piece reflect your strengths in writing?
   Not long, but I am satisfy it.

   c. How does this piece reflect any difficulties you are having in writing?
   No, I could write easily, it doesn't mean be lazy.

   d. Why did you choose this selection as best? What were your criteria?
   After I finished to write, I was satisfy.

   e. In reflecting on this piece of writing, what do you think you would do differently if you were writing it again?
   No

7. How has your English improved over the past semester?
   I notice I learned many vocabulary

8. How can you document that improvement in your portfolio?
   I return to think mine. I made clear what I did it.

Figure 9.2:
Portfolio self-evaluation form

Having had little experience articulating what was good and why it was good, this student struggled and came up with vague, inadequate answers. Perhaps the questions were too ambitious for beginners, and Barb should have built up to them slowly. However, because students have difficulty on the first try, or teachers fumble around trying to come up with the right questions and procedures, doesn't mean the idea is not worth merit and should be abandoned. Students need to be trained to look at their writing or their content work and judge for themselves what they have accomplished.

Following and at right are examples of different self-evaluation formats used for different purposes. Figure 9.3 shows the work of some NES fourth graders in an English school in Paris who did a simple evaluation of their year. Figure 9.4 is an example from a student who evaluated the final draft of a writing assignment by using the writing checklist found in chapter 6 (figure 6.4). In this case, how-

Figure 9.3: Simple self-evaluations from two fourth-grade students

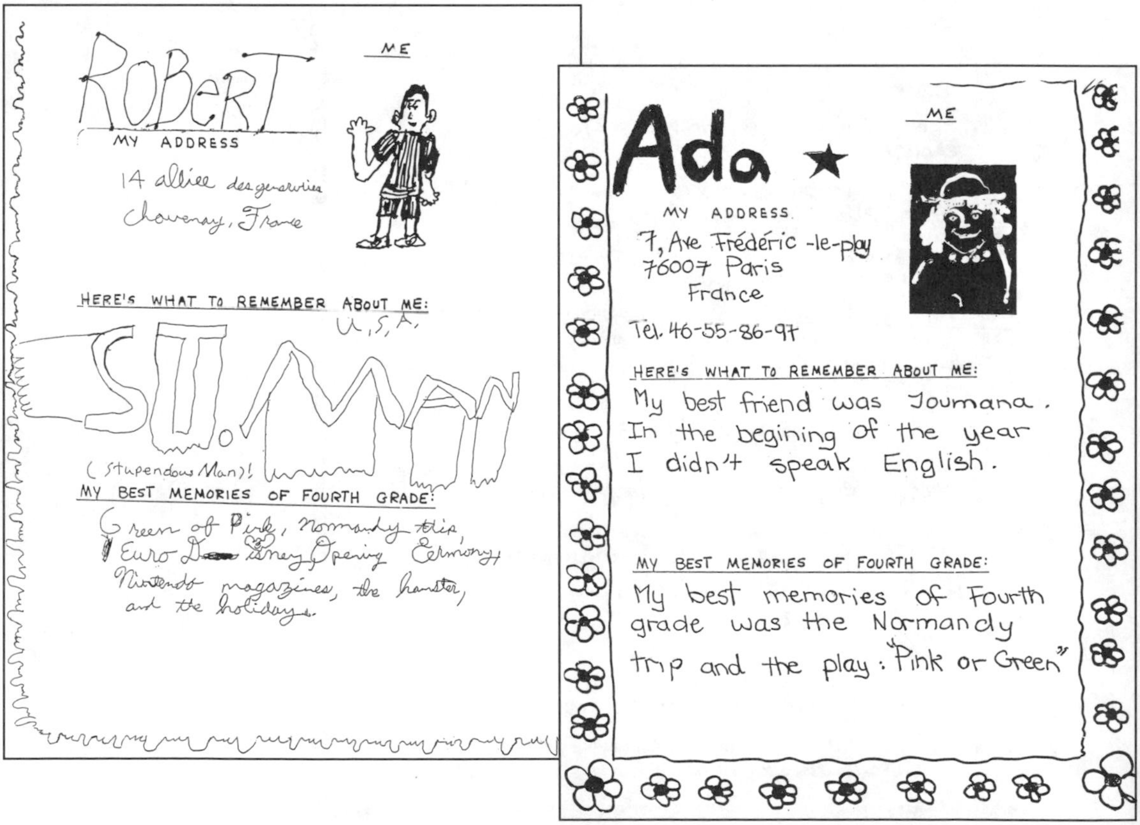

ever, he evaluated his own work according to the categories outlined, and assigned letter grades to each. Figure 9.5, page 254 is one student's evaluation of a group presentation in which he took part.

In the past in Banvinai camp, all of the Hmong people had a hard life there. They didn't have enough food or money to buy things. Everyone was poor and did not have enough education for the students. Many of people didn't have money to pay to the teacher.

   About the hard life in Thailand it was very hard, everyone was poor and had no money to pay for everything. But in the United States it is better. The government still gives food stamps or money to the poor people, so everyone doesn't worry about that. But some of the Americans don't understand about how hard it is for the refugee from Lao. They don't like us.

   In the United States it is good to learn more English because the federal and state Government can help every student. If you go to college they still help with money for you until you get the degree.The education in the United States is better than Thailand.

   However I hope the future of my life and everyone would be a good life in this country.
Everyone is free. Our life is like in the heaven.
I also like my school and my job that is regular work for me. It's hard for me to do my regular teachers to help me. So I hope my new life will be come true.

                    Amen.

Figure 9.4:
Writing sample and self-evaluation using writing checklist, from a high-school student

WRITING SAMPLE CHECKLIST

SKILL AREAS	DESCRIPTION	LEVEL
Content	❑ theme developed ❑ related ideas and examples supplied	Fluent
(A)	❑ thought development adequate ❑ some unrelated ideas used	Intermediate
	❑ uneven (or no) theme development ❑ many unrelated ideas included ❑ few (or no) examples given ❑ insufficient writing for evaluation	Beginner
Organization	❑ good topic development ❑ opening sentence/or introductory paragraph included ❑ concluding sentence/paragraph included ❑ ideas well organized, clearly stated, and backed-up ❑ transitions included	Fluent
(B)	❑ topic or opening sentence included, but no closing sentence provided ❑ weak organization ❑ inadequate back-up information provided ❑ few transitions included	Intermediate
	❑ no topic sentence development ❑ no opening or closing sentence included ❑ little or no organization ❑ no back-up information provided ❑ no transitions included ❑ ideas confused or unrelated ❑ insufficient writing for evaluation	Beginner
Vocabulary	❑ correct use of word forms (prefixes, suffixes, etc.) and idioms ❑ sophisticated word choice ❑ meaning clear	Fluent
(B)	❑ generally correct use of word forms and idioms ❑ word choice correct ❑ meaning clear	Intermediate
	❑ many errors in word forms and idioms ❑ ineffective word choice ❑ words selected through direct translation ❑ meaning confused or obscured ❑ insufficient writing for evaluation	Beginner
Language skills	❑ correct use of verb tense ❑ good sentence variety and complex construction ❑ good control of agreement, number, word order, parts of speech	Fluent
	❑ most verb tenses correct ❑ simple sentence construction ❑ errors in agreement, number, word order, parts of speech	Intermediate
(C)	❑ frequent errors in tense ❑ forced sentence constructions ❑ many errors in agreement, number, word order, parts of speech ❑ insufficient writing for evaluation	Beginner
Mechanics (A)	❑ few errors made in spelling, punctuation, capitalization	Fluent
	❑ occasional errors in spelling, punctuation, capitalization	Intermediate
	❑ many errors in spelling, punctuation, capitalization ❑ handwriting unclear or illegible ❑ insufficient writing for evaluation	Beginner

started. This gives you a chance to know your student somewhat, but not long enough to have formed set opinions. Early on, a parent's insight can help you learn a great deal about your student.

BEFORE THE CONFERENCE: GETTING TO KNOW THE PARENTS

Establishing communication from the outset is essential. One way of getting to know parents and their children is by asking them about their child. You might try sending home a questionnaire asking questions such as

> What are your child's interests?
> What are your child's strengths?
> What do you feel are your child's weaknesses?
> Are there any things about your child that concern you?
> Is there anything you would like us to know about your child?

Admittedly, getting these questions to (and returned by) non-English-speaking parents can present problems, but translating them and having them answered by whatever means necessary are worth the effort. Parents know more about their child than anyone else and can offer insights that you may not have. You want to do this early, before you have had a chance to form hard and fast judgments about a child.

Following this initial contact, you can set up a three-way conference to include teachers, parents, and the child.

TEN STEPS TO HOLDING AN ESL CONFERENCE

1. **Be prepared.** There are several important things to do when preparing for a conference with a parent and student:

   ◆ Find an interpreter
   ◆ Compile the portfolio. Make sure it's updated, and shows examples of the student's mastery and strengths as well as weaknesses, chosen with this conference in mind.
   ◆ Invite the student. It is not appropriate to use the student as your interpreter if you have serious problems to discuss. This puts the student in an extremely awkward, if not anxiety-ridden, position.

He may not relay the information between the two of you accurately, and this can only lead to more problems.

◆ **Have a plan.**

This means have specific questions to ask, specific issues to focus on, specific recommendations for the parent and student to follow through on. Filling out the conference record illustrated in figure 9.6 allows you to think through what you will say to the parents. The form also obliges you to think positively about the student, rather than focusing simply on needs.

ESL Conference Record/Notes

Student _____ Date _____

Teacher _____

Parents or Guardians _____

Others in attendance _____

Reasons for conference:
Overall classroom performance:

Areas of strength in language acquisitions:	Areas needing improvement in language skills:
Areas of strength in content:	Areas needing improvement in content:

Recommendations and goals:

Student will:	Teacher will:	Parent will:

Comments:

Figure 9.6:
ESL Conference Record/Notes form can be used prior to the conference, to organize thoughts, and during the conference, to record notes and establish direction and goals.

2. **Allow time for parents to review the work** in the portfolio, and to explore the room together with their child.

3. **Keep it simple.** Parents may not have any experience with schools. Don't use overly technical words they may not understand.

4. **Respect their culture, heritage, and language.** They may feel threatened because they are not literate in their own language. They may have vastly different perceptions of a teacher's role.

5. **Keep a record of the conference,** and make sure all relevant issues are addressed.

6. **If you use an interpreter, look at the parents while you are talking, give time for translation, and keep your attention on the interaction,** even if you don't understand what is being said.

7. **Discuss both strengths and weaknesses.**

8. **If the student is not working at grade level, be sure that is explained.**

9. **If there is a problem, tell the parent, but offer a solution.** It's difficult for some parents to help their children with school work.

10. **Set goals together.** Map out a plan with each party having specific goals to accomplish.

TWO CONFERENCES

Here are two conferences, chosen because they weren't run-of-the-mill and because the parents' needs and wishes had a profound effect on the outcome and change of goals for both children.

ABIR

When Abir arrived from Egypt, no school records were sent, so her new school simply placed her in the eighth grade. She did poorly on initial assessment, placing NEP. She did little in school, never turned in homework, rarely completed any work. In ESL she didn't fare much better. She always smiled and whispered, but her answer was usually, "I don't know." She was overweight and wore clothes that the other students found loud and clashing. The boys quickly discovered they could goad her into violent outbursts. She would scream, slam locker doors, and chase them when they provoked her. She was absent at least twice a week. She had arrived in October, six weeks into the term. By the end of the second quarter, she had been absent nearly half the time. However, repeated phone calls to her house were never answered.

Finally, her father was reached. He agreed to come in for a conference. The teachers had little or no written work to show him. At this

---

ESL Conference Record/Notes

Student __Abir__   Date _____

Teacher __Mrs. Crockett__

Parents or Guardians __Father__

Others in attendance __Team Teachers Mrs. Morley and Mr. Dyer__

Reasons for conference:
Abir's attendance has been very low. Has made no friends, and is prone to violent outbursts. Does not do any class work. Teachers are concerned about attitude, attendance, behavior

Overall classroom performance:
Very poor. Does not participate in class, either mainstream or ESL. Does not return homework.

Areas of strength in language acquisitions:	Areas needing improvement in language skills:
Teachers have had little chance to observe any language use.	

Areas of strength in content:	Areas needing improvement in content:
None	All.

Recommendations and goals:
Make this school year a profitable one for Abir. Modify goals & school agenda so that she can study her curriculum and still pass 8th grade.

Student will:	Teacher will:	Parent will:
Attend class every day. Turn in assignments.	Adapt lessons. Build in time for study of Egyptian curriculum at school. ↳ set up time in reading lab	make sure Abir is at school. Encourage English, Ensure homework completed. Send ↳ Egyptian curric. materials.

Comments:
Father seemed to be receptive to teachers' concerns. All parties agreed to meet again in one month.

Figure 9.7: Completed record of Abir's conference

point they were more concerned about Abir's absenteeism and behavior than anything else and wanted to talk about that.

Abir had been invited to the conference, but she did not come. The ESL teacher, Joan the counselor, and both team teachers were present. They stated their concerns politely, presented the father with Abir's absentee report, and showed him the curriculum and the areas they felt she needed to learn if she was going to pass the eighth grade. The father told them that they were returning to Egypt at the end of the school year; Abir was missing a year of school there and needed to pass some very difficult tests in her home language to progress through school and into a good college. Because both he and Abir's mother worked, Abir was needed at home to take care of the younger children. He didn't care if she passed eighth grade here or not. Her future in Egypt was far more important. Therefore, at home, they concentrated on her studies in Arabic.

Abir's conference resulted in a change of perception for the teachers. Since her father didn't have any goals for her as far as her English proficiency was concerned, the teachers set a few for themselves. They warned him about truancy, and their threats of reporting him to the authorities seemed to work because Abir's attendance improved. The teachers decided to try to make Abir's stay in the United States more pleasant. They arranged for her to have study time so she could bring her books to school. They set up additional times in the reading lab and the ESL room and drew up a plan for modifying grades so that the work she did turn in would count and the year wouldn't be lost.

AMOS

Five-year-old Amos arrived at the school at the end of January. He was tested NEP. He did not respond to any questions on the standardized oral test. He was placed in kindergarten. He was promoted to first grade, even though the ESL teacher felt his readiness skills were weak. On her report she wrote that he needed continued ESL support, and that he may need to repeat first grade.

At the conference, Amos showed his father proudly around the room. He sat quietly on his father's lap during the conference, where they reviewed Amos's portfolio (see figure 9.8). The teacher showed Mr. Vang the alphabet sheet given to Amos during his first month

NAME: *Amos Yang*   DATE: *Feb 13/91*

The alphabet letters your child can identify correctly are circled.

(E) (b) (C) (s) (K) (L)

(M) (h) (u) (B) (i)(j) (A)

(O) (T) (H) (i) (N) q

(F) (r) (c) (v) (m) (k)

(n) (V) (e) (P) (t) (a)

(Q) (W) (d) (J) (D) (Z)

(R) l (w) (g) (X) (U)

(S) (I) (Y) (G) (o) (x)

(z) f (P) y

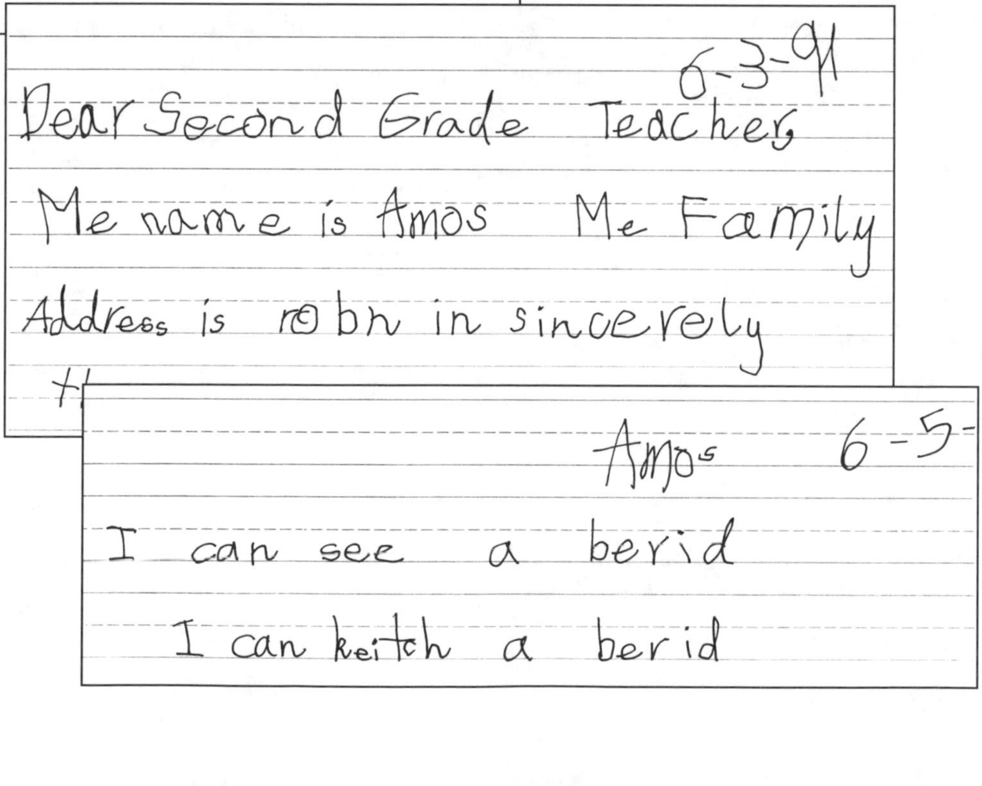

(figure 9.8a), as well as a more recent one that Amos had completed confidently, without error. They also looked at some writing samples. The letter to the second-grade teacher was particularly revealing (figure 9.8b). Most of it had been copied; Amos had been unable to fill in his address, could not tell the teacher anything about himself, and could not complete it. The final page showed much progress (figure 9.8c). Amos

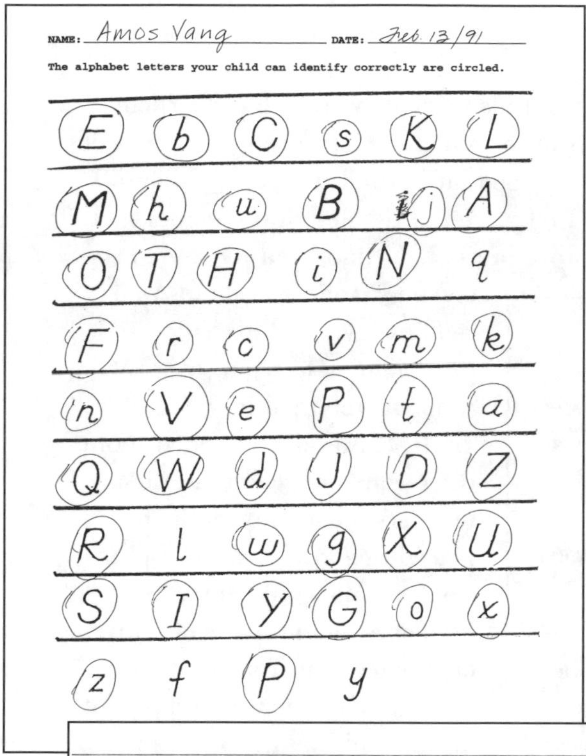

Figure 9.8: samples from Amos's portfolio, including (a) an alphabet identification sheet, (b) a letter to his teacher, (c) a later writing sample

6-3-91

Dear Second Grade Teacher,

Me name is Amos   Me Family

Address is robn in sincerely

H

Amos   6-5-

I can see   a   berid

I can keitch   a   berid

was moving along and demonstrating a good grasp of sound/letter correspondence in his spelling.

Amos had come a long way, but his teachers were still concerned he was not ready for the demands of second grade. His problems were not simply because of language; he lagged far beyond the skills and knowledge teachers can expect of a first grader at the end of the school year. After carefully reviewing the work presented, Amos's father shared the teachers' concerns about Amos's reading level and his English proficiency. He requested that Amos be retained in the first grade. However, concerned about the hazards of retention, the teachers recommended he be placed in a grade one-two split. That way, he could enter in grade one, and if he made sufficient gain, exit from grade two.

Together, teachers and parent decided this was the best solution.

READING LANGUAGE ARTS CHECKLIST
FIRST GRADE

Name Amos Vang School Elm Vale

Teacher Connie Greene

Key Beg. = the student is just beginning to develop behavior
Dev. = the student is developing the behavior
Secure = the behavior is characteristic of the student

Directions: Circle a descriptor on the continuum, or make a slash at the appropriate point.

Print Awareness & Conventions:	Date: X	Date: 5-91
1) Expects print to be meaningful	Not yet Dev. Secure	Not yet Dev. Secure
2) Recognizes letters of alphabet (upper and lower case)	Not yet Dev. Secure	Not yet Dev. Secure
3) Aware of letter-sound relationships	Not yet Dev. Secure	Not yet Dev. Secure
4) Understands directionality of lines of print and page sequences	Not yet Dev. Secure	Not yet Dev. Secure
Oral Reading:		
1) Joins in unison reading	Not yet Dev. Secure	Not yet Dev. Secure
2) Reads own dictated stories with fluency	Not yet Dev. Secure	Not yet Dev. Secure
3) Reads with expression	Not yet Dev. Secure	Not yet Dev. Secur-
4) Self-corrects miscues that do not make sense	Not yet Dev. Secure	Not yet Dev. Secure
5) Knows common sight words	Not yet Dev. Secure	Not yet Dev. Secure
Reading Strategies/Comprehension:		
1) Uses prior knowledge to make predictions	Not yet Dev. Secure	Not yet Dev. Secure
2) Uses clues (pictures, meaning, word order, phonics) when reading	Not yet Dev. Secure	Not yet Dev. Secure
3) Uses strategies to correct difficulties (e.g., rereading, reading ahead, pausing to reflect)	Not yet Dev. Secure	Not yet Dev. Secure
4) Retells stories (heard or read) in appropriate sequence	Not yet Dev. Secure	Not yet Dev. Secure

Listening:		
1) Listens to teacher-read stories	Not yet Dev. Secure	Not yet Dev. Secure
2) Listens to peers	Not yet Dev. Secure	Not yet Dev. Secure
3) Follows oral directions	Not yet Dev. Secure	Not yet Dev. Secure
Speaking:		
1) Dictates information	Not yet Dev. Secure	Not yet Dev. Secure
2) Participates in sharing time	Not yet Dev. Secure	Not yet Dev. Secure
3) Expresses ideas clearly	Not yet Dev. Secure	Not yet Dev. Secure
Writing:		
1) Uses some conventions of print -horizontal lines -spaces -capital letters -punctuation	Not yet Dev. Secure	Not yet Dev. Secure
2) Willing to use invented spellings	Not yet Dev. Secure	Not yet Dev. Secure
3) Able to read own writings	Not yet Dev. Secure	Not yet Dev. Secure
4) Begins to seek out conventional spellings in revision & editing processes	Not yet Dev. Secure	Not yet Dev. Secure
Attitudes & Habits:		
1) Appears to enjoy listening to stories	Not yet Dev. Secure	Not yet Dev. Secure
2) Maintains silent reading for a reasonable period of time	Not yet Dev. Secure	Not yet Dev. Secure
3) Self-initiates reading of books	Not yet Dev. Secure	Not yet Dev. Secure
4) Self-initiates writing activities	Not yet Dev. Secure	Not yet Dev. Secure

Figure 9.9: This detailed checklist of skills and strategies is another important component of Amos's portfolio

ESL Conference Record/Notes

Student _Amos_ _____ Date _____

Teacher _Mrs. Greene_ _____

Parents or Guardians _Mr. Vang_ _____

Others in attendance _ESL teacher_ _____

Reasons for conference: _Amos is working hard but teachers are concerned that he does not have the academic or language skills to succeed in 2nd grade. Conference called to explore possible options. He is at early emergent reading level. Has not begun to pay attention to words on page._

Overall classroom performance:
Amos is a sociable, friendly boy who works very hard to understand new skills.

Areas of strength in language acquisitions: _Amos knows vocabulary for: body parts, occupations, food, utensils, clothes, colors, numbers, home furnishings._	Areas needing improvement in language skills: _telling time sequencing_
Areas of strength in content: _Math – knows addition 0-12 subtraction 0-12 reading – short, long vowels Knows print is meaningful_	Areas needing improvement in content: _building repertoire of familiar books sight vocabulary reading strategies_

Recommendations and goals: _launch Amos to reading. Place Amos in a 1-2 split so next year he will be with his peers and have time to pull together reading and language skills._

Student will: _Go to library over summer; practice reading; learn to tell time; learn to use $_	Teacher will: . _Investigate reading recovery or Chapter 1. Recommend placement in 1-2 split_	Parent will: _read to Amos, enroll Amos in summer enrichment program_

Comments:

Figure 9.10:
Completed record of Amos's conference

Teachers

Teachers are critical stakeholders in the education of a student. Communication among ESL teachers, mainstream teachers, and other service providers is especially critical, and time must be allotted for conferring. Here again, when we discuss reporting to other stakeholders, the issue comes down to who is primarily responsible for the student. ESL teachers, because they assume responsibility for the student's English, tend to assume responsibility for the child. The "take-'em, fix-'em, don't-send-'em-back" syndrome is alive and well. However, if ESL teachers take responsibility for the student, they also need to take responsibility for establishing meetings, and assuring that information is exchanged. Adamson et al. (1990) report that many teachers schedule a block of time every day to meet with other teachers and arrange their schedules to have that contact on an ongoing basis.

There are several times during the year when teachers should meet:

- **At the first placement of student within the grade and the classroom.** It is only fair that a teacher be notified before entry that a new student is coming. Mainstream teachers justifiably resent having a new student presented at the door with no advance warning. A meeting with the teacher, to discuss the proficiency levels, the English, and reading skills the student has, as well as any other factors that may have an impact on the teacher and the class, is a wise course.

- **For intermittent reviews for parent/teacher conferences.** Each school must decide who is responsible for parent/teacher conferences. In many schools the ESL and mainstream teachers meet to plan what is going to be presented to the parent.

- **For progress reviews.** We have stressed throughout this book that ESL teachers should be teaching the curriculum, and classroom teachers should be teaching English. During this meeting teachers review the student's progress, coordinate instruction, and share ideas, impressions, concerns, and lesson plans.

- **When transferring students out of ESL into mainstream.** The definition of an ESL student comes into serious play here. We have deliberately avoided the whole question of entrance and exit criteria from programs. Unlike special education, which has had many years to establish eligibility requirements, and for which many states have established laws and procedures for exiting, these are nebulous issues in ESL. In most places these have not been resolved. Transfers are often determined by standardized test scores. However, if the district has done its homework, and has in place a sequence of courses or a plan for mainstreaming, then the transition will be easier.

When meeting at any of these times, teachers must prepare in the following ways:

◆ Have an agenda.
◆ Bring portfolios.
◆ Organize relevant information in preparation for conference.

Together, by discussing the following, the ESL teacher and mainstream teacher can define instruction that the child/children need:

◆ What are children achieving in the regular classroom? (ESL teacher reports on English proficiency.)

◆ What are children achieving in the ESL classroom? (Mainstream teacher reports on curriculum mastery)

◆ What does each teacher see?

◆ What does each teacher put into the student's portfolios and how do they share the portfolios?

CONCLUSION

Demonstrating what students have mastered, where their weak points are, and where they need to go next has always been a difficult hurdle. As districts and schools have struggled with the best approaches for change, important steps have emerged in the process. Before any reporting system can be successful, it must be clear who the data is for; the content must be organized with the audience in mind.

Fight to the Spinach!
MAKING THE CHANGE

In this chapter we discuss how to effect assessment changes in your school and district. We cover

- ◆ how and where to start the process
- ◆ how to involve your stakeholders
- ◆ how to collaborate with your colleagues

WORKING FOR CHANGE

Education is in a state of tremendous flux. We are frustrated and tired of the old ways. The new ways seem to offer great possibilities. Some advocates of alternative assessment envision a total overhaul of the old ways. Others are cautious, even fearful. There have already been backlash and real failure on the part of those who rushed in before they were ready. Change is going to be slow and will only become a reality if we work at it.

Norma Jean Schuldt (1993) writes, "Teachers need sufficient time to read, process, and practice alternatives to old grading methods. They need more than verbal support from the administration. Permission isn't enough. Time, tools, and training are essential for teachers to make this paradigm shift effectively." Schuldt reports that because the tradition in how we grade students is so strong, involving the stakeholders from the beginning is critical if we are to change from the traditional ways. She points out that the reality of the district must be taken into account, and if the position of the district is aligned with current research and learning, then the task of setting up alternative reporting methods is not the struggle that it will be if the district is reactionary, back-to-basics, or simply unmoved by research. If your school district is the latter, she notes, alternative assessment will probably be a defensive backup system, with an uphill battle to make it legitimate.

Whatever school district you live in, the benefits of alternative assessment *are* worth the effort. Braun (1992:76) writes, "Given intelligent use, patience and trust on the part of administrators and the public, portfolios can narrow the gap between assessment for accountability and assessment to inform learning and instruction." Broadfoot (1991) reports that instituting alternative assessment practices in Australia resulted in "improved students' learning, self-esteem, and personal maturity...that enabled students to outperform their more conventionally taught and assessed peers." It is not an easy change, more like a gradual evolution. One school, reports Lamme and Hysmith (1991), moved over time from no use of alternative methods and no systematic collection, through several stages, to total involvement and enthusiasm with an alternative assessment model.

FIVE STEPS TOWARD CHANGE

1. **Become an agent of change.** Even if we don't like to admit it, assessment and grading, like access and equal opportunity, are political issues. We need to fight on all fronts. Lobbying for ways to demonstrate the real capabilities of our students, instead of reducing them to numbers, grades, and statistics, is essential. According to Rhodes and Shanklin (1993), this means "identifying like-minded colleagues. Find people who think like you do, and get together." States and districts have already discovered the perils of mandating a change that teachers are not ready to implement. Broadfoot (1991) writes, "No amount of external coercion will make teachers change the affective relationships in their classrooms, or shoulder the heavy burden of a fundamental reconsideration of their teaching approach. Where teachers are so committed, however, the impact on the range and quality of pupils learning, and on teachers' morale, has been shown to be considerable." This means that change must come from the bottom up with support from the top. The battle must be fought on all fronts.

   Define the change you want to pursue. This is important. It's not enough to simply say you need change. It has to be clear and concrete:

"I want to change from grades to portfolio assessment. I am going to begin by...."; "I want to move away from skill-based assessment to developmental. I am going to...."

Establish a comfortable pace for change. As we have said before, change is a long process. It can't happen overnight. If you do try to change too fast, the odds are you will abandon the effort and return to the old ways. In addition, if you change overnight from report cards to narratives or portfolios, you risk negative reactions on the part of administrators or parents who are used to and comfortable with the old ways, and who may complain loudly enough so that your efforts have been for naught. Communication with the stakeholders is extremely important. This means educating all the stakeholders about the assessment process you are taking. They must understand what you are doing, why you are doing it, and that the assessment is accurate and valid and reflects the student information you are seeking.

Challenge yourself. Simply begin. Try something. Try something else. Add an item to your folder. Design a checklist. Modify one you've seen in this book or another. Give yourself the time and space you need to try and to learn. But don't try too much at first. Be reasonable and methodical.

2. **Approach the people involved.** This means, above all, do your homework. Collect articles and books (such as this one) that advocate alternative assessment. Present research and your intentions to the administration and other teachers (such as the mainstream teacher, or the ESL teacher) for both clearance and support.

3. **Involve parents from the outset with clear explanations and expectations.** With English-speaking, traditionally schooled parents, the task often involves selling them on the idea of alternative assessment. They are important stakeholders and want assurances that their children are succeeding at school. They need to understand why you are using alternative methods. In many cases, when parents can see their child's progress demonstrated through specific examples, they are very supportive of the new approach. With non-English-speaking parents, the task is more complex. Getting them to participate in the educational system is one big hurdle; communicating with them is another.

4. **Begin the process on the first day of school.** Discuss your assessment goals with your students. The students are also stakeholders, and communication with this group is critical. Acquaint the students with the idea of folders and portfolios. Schuldt advocates starting in with a literature log that goes in the folders at once.

5. **Introduce the process slowly.** Have clear objectives. Start small. Reams and reams of material with no criteria by which to make judgments, or no management systems, are worse than useless; they are a source of grief and frustration and an open invitation to abandon the idea altogether.

COLLABORATION IS CRITICAL

As ESL teachers, we know that the temptation is great to think of ESL students as ours, and ours alone. We often assume that the students are *our* responsibility and we must take charge of all aspects of their learning. In many cases, such as Barb's dreadful year in the self-contained classroom, total responsibility is a reality. However, that doesn't mean you have to accept it. All too many times we have seen (and been) teachers who load up their day with an overwhelming number of groups and levels, who run from building to building in an attempt to meet the needs of all the students. One study of a Midwestern school district found that the average teacher served as many as seventy-five students from as many as seventeen classrooms. Berman and Weiler (1992) comment: "The weakness of ESL pull-out lies in its structure—the inevitable discontinuity in student learning between the classroom teacher and the ESL pull-out teacher." We assert strongly that discontinuity is not inevitable. As we stated before, and will continue to state until doomsday, this is not the way it should or has to be.

Collaboration, especially in ESL, is critical. Collaboration means, essentially, coordinating the curriculum. This means that support people, such as the ESL teacher, complement the curriculum in the mainstream class by using the content learned in the regular classroom as the basis for their instruction.

Collaboration often doesn't happen, however, for the following reasons:

◆ There isn't time. Teachers feel there are too many other skills that need to be taught. Helen Catherine Flynn (1993) found that ESL teachers said that they were teaching oral skills, vocabulary, culture and customs, reading, writing, and grammar. What else could they teach in the half-hour to ninety minutes they were given?

◆ There isn't communication between teachers. Everybody's busy. You might catch a teacher in the hall before school starts, you might not. If you have three schools, or eight, or sixteen groups, coordinating instruction is a remote luxury.

◆ ESL teachers have too many levels at once to coordinate the instruction.

◆ Mainstream teachers don't feel competent to handle the issues and problems of ESL students. In our years as ESL teachers we have noted that many classroom teachers are reluctant to accept responsibility because they feel that they don't know enough.

Pugachi (1991) writes that the success of collaboration depends on "a mutual and reciprocal process between teachers and specialists.... Parity is an essential aspect of successful collaboration. Mutual respect cannot be taken for granted. Although the issue of parity is raised.... little direction is offered concerning the kinds of assistance classroom teachers can bring."

Resolving the problems

There are ways to overcome problems of negative attitudes, lack of time, and lack of resources.

Flynn (1993) makes these recommendations for building a collaborative service model:

◆ **Build in time to communicate.** Flynn writes, "The most important factor in establishing a collaborative relationship among teachers is communication." Time spent working with another teacher on what you can teach in common is probably as valuable or more so than one half-hour you might meet with the children. Set this time up *first*. Teachers and administrators who developed a collaborative model at Hale School in Minneapolis (1992) agree. They report that time for planning is essential:

> **Teachers need time to establish trust within their teams and share expertise. Instructional strategies need to be discussed and curricula aligned. Organization models must be established along with classroom expectations. Lessons need to be outlined and responsibilities designated. Assessments must be planned and student performances evaluated.**

Hale suggests building this time in

- at before- or after-school sessions
- through shared prep time
- by providing a substitute teacher once each month. (The sub can be shared so that four or five teams can provide planning time together.)
- by having a team member take over while others meet
- by scheduling planning time during staff development release days
- by a combination of methods

Hale teachers note that when time for planning was not built into the day or week, then implementing shared service became problematic. Thus, scheduling planning time is essential.

- **Classroom placement should be the criteria for forming ESL instructional groups.** When students are pulled by level from several different classrooms, the possibility of melding content with language becomes impossible.
- **The range of grade levels that an ESL teacher works with should be limited.** This, of course, is ideal. However, if there are several teachers in one school, it is appropriate to allocate several grades and several teachers to each.
- **Have ESL teachers use the mainstream curriculum as their guide for instruction.** We have advocated this from the beginning. Reading, writing, speaking, listening, grammar, can and should all be learned within the framework of the core curriculum. This is the strength that

mainstream classroom teachers have, and where they can bring their knowledge and skills to bear: by showing and aiding the ESL teacher in melding content and language.

◆ **Have a common schedule in place for all support services.** By doing this, you ensure that those students receiving support are not missing vital instruction in the mainstream classroom. Often students are pulled out from classes during science or math, the subjects they can most naturally succeed at.

◆ **Have ESL teachers maintain the role as advocate for their students.** One of the few good but altogether critical and worthwhile features of the self-contained classroom Barb taught in was that she was always there for the students. They had an expert who focused on their needs for the majority of the day. This should not be overlooked or slighted.

Collaboration in secondary schools

There are some specific issues that have to be addressed at the secondary-school level, especially in two situations: pull-out and sheltered classes.

At the secondary-school level, it is essential that students learn both English and academic skills as rapidly as possible. Collaboration between content-area teachers and ESL teachers is an important component of service delivery. The following are ways for the ESL teacher to meet this challenge:

◆ Obtain a copy of the textbook for each class.
◆ Ask the content-area teacher for copies of the syllabus and course objectives.
◆ Confer on what base-line competencies students need to succeed, and work on those in the ESL time you have.
◆ Establish a file of study guides.
◆ Amass lower-level, simpler texts of the same subject.
◆ Allocate time to meet with the content-area teachers regularly to talk about students in their classes.
◆ Use sheltered classes to follow through with the curriculum.

Berman and Weiler (1992) reported that the rigid structure of secondary schools has been a problem in implementing effective programming, and that departmentalization had major repercussions on programming. "By default, schools relied on department chairs to schedule courses for LEP students. This practice meant that faculty with no particular commitment to, or knowledge of, the academic needs of LEP students made crucial decisions about course availability." The result: access to content was limited and uneven, not necessarily by design but often by neglect.

However, in school districts in places like Green Bay, Wisconsin, North York, Ontario, and Winnipeg, Manitoba, leadership and collaboration have resulted in carefully thought-out programs. Courses are aligned with the curriculum. Each course has clearly stated goals and objectives. There is a master plan for each grade and level. Figure 10.1 is an excerpt from an ESL program document from the North York Board of Education in Toronto.

Figure 10.1: Reading guidelines reflect program objectives

ESL 1

The learning of a new language is enhanced by exposure to a wide variety of learning experiences that stimulate and encourage language use. Whenever possible, however, the teachers should strive for interaction among students so that they can draw upon one another's experiences, knowledge, and vocabulary. The ideas that follow are simply guidelines; individual schools should expand this information to accommodate their learners as they vary from school to school.

As entrants to ESL 1 may vary from those who have no English to those who have some knowledge of the alphabet and minimal vocabulary, exit criteria will also differ. The criteria listed are recommended as a guideline only. This course should be designed to meet the practical survival needs of the students.

Reading

Upon the completion of this course, students should be able to

- recognize the alphabet in both print and script

- begin to use reading comprehension strategies (e.g., predicting, guessing, finding the main idea)

- read and understand materials, including

  a) print materials in their environment, such as signs, labels, maps, and advertisements

  b) material written by the student or cooperatively composed by the class

  c) commercial ESL materials developed for beginners, such as texts, dictionaries, newspapers

  d) teacher-designed material

- complete cloze passages

- use school library facilities

North York Board of Education

ESL teachers are instrumental in the planning, designing, implementing, and scheduling of courses. Priority is given to teachers who are certified in both content subjects, such as science or history, and in ESL. In these cases, ESL teachers have taken an aggressive and active role in making the schools responsible for the education of their LEP population, rather than resigning themselves to the Boogie Room.

CONCLUSION

Bringing alternative forms of assessment to your school can be a positive experience and an opportunity to forge stronger ties among all the individuals involved in the educational process. Administrators, teachers, parents, and students need to believe in the process and make some investment in it. It cannot be achieved in a vacuum nor can it succeed when one group of the stakeholders doubts its validity. A successful assessment program comes with careful planning, training, communication, support, collaboration, and time. Alternative assessment offers all the stakeholders a better, more detailed profile of the learning process. The information we gather through this process allows us to develop better programs, improve teaching, foster communication, and help students invest in learning. These benefits beckon us to attempt the change and strive towards improved assessment goals.

CONCLUSION

"I don't know what to do with him," a frustrated Mrs. Myers told Mary one morning. "I know he understands the material, but then he hands in a paper like this one." She waved a test riddled with errors and bleeding with corrections. "I can't let him off easy just because his English isn't perfect yet. He should know this stuff by now, anyway. Being easy on him wouldn't be fair to the rest of the students. Besides, he goes to high school next year and I have to prepare him."

MAKE THE CHOICE

Mrs. Myers has legitimate concerns. One of the most difficult areas of working with ESL students is trying to assess what they can do. Teachers want to evaluate these students consistently, fairly, accurately, and within a framework that the other stakeholders will understand. Trying to discover this information using a traditional test-centered form of assessment is frustrating because, with ESL students, this approach falls too short of the mark. It shows more of what the student can't do rather than what he has accomplished and is capable of. Teachers must be willing to work towards a better, broader method of assessment.

One of the biggest hurdles in changing to alternative forms of assessment is *deciding* to change—deciding it is worth it to try a different approach. After all, changing demands more of us; we must find the time to learn more about assessment, how to implement it, how to communicate the assessment plan with our supervisors, colleagues, parents, and students. Change makes us more vulnerable; we put ourselves on the line. We risk making mistakes along the way. It comes down to wanting to change the way we've always done things—opening our minds to other options, other methods, and taking it one step at a time, adjusting to a new mind-set.

HAVE A PLAN

Know what you want to do when the ESL students arrive at your school. Scrambling to assess and place students at the last minute without a plan sets the stage for problems down the road. When the procedures are not clear, the staff can only guess at what needs to be done: Who is responsible for the intake? Where is it completed? Who places the student? And who determines whether or not the placement is appropriate? In many schools, this scenario is ripe for the staff to "pass the buck" to some other member. The students are often assessed improperly by someone untrained in ESL, in a rush, and then placed haphazardly "somewhere." This approach may get schools through in a pinch, but ultimately buys trouble as time goes on. In our experience, a lack of planning sows the seeds of everyone's discontent.

This scenario can be avoided if the school takes time out to plan before the students begin to arrive. Even if only one or two ESL students come to your school, there needs to be a plan in place. Each player needs to know what is expected of him. An assessment procedure needs to be established. The office staff should be clear on the procedure for working with non-English-speaking students. The teacher needs to be informed *before* the student walks in the door. The teachers need to have a game plan for what they can do to help their students settle in. Ongoing communication is the key.

All the parties need to communicate with one another to verify each student's assessment is appropriate and that the student is placed in the best class or program possible. Some students tests will not accurately reflect their abilities. Their placement needs to be reviewed to ensure that they are getting appropriate support. Mary once had a student who tested non-English-proficient (NEP). Tika was an extremely shy girl who was afraid of shaming her previous teachers; she left everything on the test that she was not absolutely certain about blank. As a result, she was placed in a pull-out ESL program. Tika really needed to be in some of the classes with her peers. She could speak well enough once she got over her shyness, and she could read and write on her own. Even though it was apparent to Mary, her ESL teacher, that Tika needed to be sent back to the classroom for part of the day, there was no opportunity to do this because the NEP label meant Tika was required to stay in the program she was placed in. Mary, as part-time ESL teacher at this particular school, had no power to get Tika retested. This could have been avoided had the school administration understood that the initial testing was just a starting point. To avoid this kind of scenario, schools need to have someone who oversees the placement and ongoing support of ESL students; someone who ensures that the support they are getting is in fact what they need.

CHANGE IN THE CLASSROOM

Once ESL students are placed in the classroom, the teacher needs to be able to assess what the students know in the content areas and in English. As content area is covered in class, the teacher needs to evaluate how the newcomers are progressing. The bottom line for teachers is knowing whether or not the lessons have succeeded. What did the students know coming into the lesson, and did they get what they needed to continue? How are their English skills coming along?

Alternative assessment gives you the tools to learn about your students so you can do your job. With ESL students there is nothing more frustrating than knowing they are not "getting it," but not knowing what you should do about it. When you use a wider range of assessment tools, you are liberated to observe a variety of contexts inside and outside the classroom. You begin to see a more detailed profile of your students. You see not only what they *can't* do but what they *can* succeed at and build on. Your primary basis of assessment is reduced in the decontextualized arena. This eliminates the whole nightmare so many teachers face: tests, work sheets, book reports, or essays, graded in a vacuum and handed back to students who glance at them, glower (or sigh with relief), and ultimately stuff the papers away never to look at the corrections the teacher dutifully put on the page.

While some worry that alternative methods will load the teacher with a more time-consuming system of assessment, teachers who use a broader approach have found that these methods simply formalize what they have been doing all along. They have found a way to see through the mist of language barriers. Teachers are finding that they can back up their instincts about their students with solid facts and observations. They have a way to present this data to their supervisors, the parents, next year's teachers, and the students themselves.

COMMUNICATE WITH THE STAKEHOLDERS

Using a variety of assessment approaches offers all the stakeholders more information, more understanding, and ultimately an investment in the learning process. Everyone knows what is expected of him. Students can take more responsibility for their own choices; parents know what kind of support to provide; teachers can make informed teaching choices; administrators can make decisions about programs and trends in the district, because instead of seeing a general outline of how things appear to be going, they are given specific answers to the questions they have about the learning process. Assessment that encourages involvement from the stakeholders also ensures a unified effort from everyone. Nobody shoulders sole responsibility for achieving success.

ESL students present some challenging hurdles. Because of their language deficiencies it is hard to know if they understand what you are saying, what you are teaching, and if they are making any progress in English. Traditional assessment for these students will always fall short. So much lies between the lines when your students are struggling to communicate. When we wrote *The More-Than-Just-Surviving Handbook*, we wanted to demonstrate how to teach students who were not able to speak English proficiently. During our research for that book, and as we talked to teachers about the issues they faced, we have found that assessing these students is a major struggle. We hope this book has provided more tools for you to work with as your students make their way down the "Yellow Big Road," and that you feel more confident in knowing how to assess the newcomers you teach.

Appendix A:
GRADING GUIDELINES
FOR WRITING

The following grading guidelines were developed by William Irmscher (From Irmscher, W., *Teaching Expository Writing*. New York: Holt, Rinehart, and Winston, 1979.) They can be adapted to content areas.

A — Demonstrates unusual competence [1]

1. An ability to avoid the obvious and thus gain insights that are personal and often illuminating
2. A capacity to develop ideas flexibly and fluently, yet with control and purpose
3. A special concern for the *bon mot*, even if it entails coining a word that the language does not provide
4. An ability to use punctuation rhetorically, using it for effect as well as clarity
5. A willingness to be inventive with words and structures to produce a clearly identifiable style, even though at times the efforts may be too deliberate or fall short of the writers intentions

B — Demonstrates competence

1. An ability to absorb ideas and experience and to interpret it meaningfully in a context of the writer's own conception
2. A capacity to develop an idea with a clear sense of order
3. A capacity to draw upon words adequate to express the writer's own thoughts and feelings

- - - - - - - - - - - - - -

1. An *A* does not necessarily mean perfection. It can have more mistakes according to Irmscher, than a traditional *B*. "There may be less control, less patience with detail, greater daring; and hence, upon occasion, greater bathos. The *A*-writer risks more and thus gains more or loses more depending upon the sense of the venture." The *A* presentation or the *A* portfolio may not be perfect, but show a depth and grasp of subject matter that other competent works do not demonstrate. Competence can be demonstrated or suggested in myriads of ways throughout the curriculum, whether the student has perfect command of the language or not.

4. An ability to use mechanics as integral part of the meaning and effect of the prose
5. A capacity to consider alternative ways of expression as a means of making stylistic choices possible

C — Suggests competence

1. A tendency to depend on the self-evident and the cliché for the writer to write uninformative discourse
2. A tendency either to make the organization obvious or to write aimlessly without a plan
3. A limitation in the range of words and thus a dependence on the clichés and colloquialisms most available
4. An ability to use mechanics correctly or incorrectly in proportion to the plainness or complexity of the style
5. A general unawareness of choices that affect style and thus an inability to control the effects a writer may seek

D or E — Suggests or demonstrates incompetence

1. A tendency to exploit the obvious either because of lack of understanding, inability to read, failure to grapple with a topic, or, in many cases, lack of interest. The substance of essays, therefore, ranges from superficial to barren.
2. A tendency to wander aimlessly because of a lack of overall conception or, in some instances, to have a semblance of form without the development that makes parts a whole
3. A tendency to play safe with words, using ones the writer ordinarily speaks or the ones the writer can spell. These tendencies place obvious limits upon the writer to vary the expression.
4. A frequent inability to make careful distinctions between periods, commas, semicolons, although some writers in these categories can write correct sentences if they keep structures simple. The incidence of error, however, is high.
5. Either a tendency to write highly convoluted sentences that are close to the rapid associations of our thoughts before we straighten them out or a tendency to play safe by avoiding the sentence elements that invite error

Appendix B:
REPRODUCIBLE MASTERS

Figures in this section may be reproduced for classroom use. To enlarge image to 8 1/2" x 11", set photocopier at 140%.

Home-Language Interview

Student's Name _____ **Date** _____ **Age** _____

1. Which language do you hear most at home? _____ .

2. Your father speaks to you in _____ .
   underline: 1. Always   2. Often   3. Sometimes   4. Never

3. Your mother speaks to you in _____ .
   underline: 1. Always   2. Often   3. Sometimes   4. Never

4. Your brothers and sisters speak to you in _____ .
   underline: 1. Always   2. Often   3. Sometimes   4. Never

5. Does your father ever speak English to you? _____
   How often? _____ When? _____

6. Does your mother ever speak English to you? _____
   How often? _____ When? _____

7. Do your brothers and sisters speak to you in English? _____
   When? _____

8. Which language does your parents consider most important for you
   to know? _____

9. If you have a TV at home, what channels does your family watch

   most often? _____

1

From: *Assessment and ESL: On the Yellow Big Road to the Withered of Oz*, Peguis Publishers. By Barbara Law and Mary Eckes © 1995. May be reproduced for classroom use.

Figure 3.2: Home-Language Interview

Primary-Language Literacy Questionnaire

Student's name _____   **Date** _____   **Age** _____

Primary Language _____

Interviewee's name _____   Relationship to student _____

1. How many years of formal education has the student completed

   in _____ ? Number of Years _____
   Country of origin

2. What language was used for instruction? _____

3. How long has it been since the student received instruction in the

   primary language? _____

4. Did your child attend school in another country while en route to the

   United States?   No _____   Yes _____

   If yes, which country? _____   How long?_____

   Language of instruction _____

5. Does your child read books in his own language at home?   No _____ Yes _____

6. How well does your child read compared to other children of his age?

   (a) very well   (b) the same as   (c) not as well

   (d) cannot read   (e) don't know

7. Does your child write to friends or relatives?   Yes _____   No _____

   In what language? _____

8. How well does your child write compared to other children his age?

   (a) very well   (b) the same as   (c) not as well

   (d) cannot write   (e) don't know

Figure 3.4: Primary-Language Literacy Questionnaire

LANGUAGE FUNCTION CHECKLIST

Student Name _____ Date _____

Age _____ Grade _____

F	S	N	BEHAVIOR/ABILITY	CONTEXT/COMMENTS
			Demonstrates comprehension nonverbally	
			Uses physical motion to communicate (pushing, pulling, etc.)	
			Listens and attends to the work at hand	
			One-word response	
			Uses English in an informal conversation	
			Makes a request "I want" or "I need…"	
			Talks about himself/herself	
			Participates in formal classroom discussion within small group	
			Understands and answers questions about material presented through discussion	
			Volunteers additional information in the class discussion	
			Asks for additional information privately	
			Asks for additional information within the group	
			Presents a dissenting point of view	
			Uses language to communicate sadness	
			Uses imaginative language, i.e., "If I were a bird, I would fly home to my country."	
			Uses language to be funny	
			Uses language sarcastically	
			Uses language to show anger	
			Uses authoritative language, i.e., "You must…"	
			Uses language to anticipate a future event	
			Communicates using indirect coding, i.e., "You must be tired of correcting all our papers," meaning, "Don't give us so much homework."	
			Other:	

N – Never   S – Seldom   F – Frequently

Figure 6.1: Language Function Checklist

From: *Assessment and ESL: On the Yellow Big Road to the Withered of Oz.* Peguis Publishers. By Barbara Law and Mary Eckes © 1995. May be reproduced for classroom use.

STUDENT VOCABULARY CHECKLIST

Teacher_____ Student _____ Grade _____

Have student identify using English vocabulary. Use check marks to note those words the student knows. Leave others blank.

1. Colors
   - ❏ red
   - ❏ blue
   - ❏ green
   - ❏ yellow
   - ❏ orange
   - ❏ black
   - ❏ purple
   - ❏ brown
   - ❏ white

2. Numbers—Kindergarten
   - ❏ 1
   - ❏ 4
   - ❏ 7
   - ❏ 9
   - ❏ 2
   - ❏ 5
   - ❏ 8
   - ❏ 10
   - ❏ 3
   - ❏ 6

   Grades 1–3, as above plus
   - ❏ 11
   - ❏ 14
   - ❏ 17
   - ❏ 19
   - ❏ 12
   - ❏ 15
   - ❏ 18
   - ❏ 20
   - ❏ 13
   - ❏ 16

3. Shapes
   - ❏ circle
   - ❏ square
   - ❏ triangle
   - ❏ rectangle

4. Alphabet (present in random order)
   - ❏ A
   - ❏ H
   - ❏ O
   - ❏ U
   - ❏ B
   - ❏ I
   - ❏ P
   - ❏ V
   - ❏ C
   - ❏ J
   - ❏ Q
   - ❏ W
   - ❏ D
   - ❏ K
   - ❏ R
   - ❏ X
   - ❏ E
   - ❏ L
   - ❏ S
   - ❏ Y
   - ❏ F
   - ❏ M
   - ❏ T
   - ❏ Z
   - ❏ G
   - ❏ N

5. Holiday names
   - ❏ Easter
   - ❏ Halloween
   - ❏ Valentine's Day
   - ❏ Christmas
   - ❏ Thanksgiving
   - ❏ New Year's Day

6. Personal information
   - ❏ name
   - ❏ age
   - ❏ address
   - ❏ phone number

7. Body parts
   - ❏ eye
   - ❏ nose
   - ❏ cheek
   - ❏ mouth
   - ❏ neck
   - ❏ chest
   - ❏ shoulder
   - ❏ arm
   - ❏ hand
   - ❏ stomach
   - ❏ leg
   - ❏ knee
   - ❏ foot
   - ❏ finger

8. Spatial orientation
   - ❏ left
   - ❏ right
   - ❏ in front of
   - ❏ out
   - ❏ over
   - ❏ above
   - ❏ beside
   - ❏ behind
   - ❏ in
   - ❏ near
   - ❏ far

1

Figure 6.2: English Vocabulary Checklist, page 1

9. School vocabulary
   - ❏ recess
   - ❏ playground
   - ❏ teacher
   - ❏ tardy slip
   - ❏ math
   - ❏ drinking fountain
   - ❏ hall
   - ❏ locker
   - ❏ lunch room
   - ❏ school
   - ❏ school bus
   - ❏ washroom
   - ❏ office
   - ❏ principal
   - ❏ science
   - ❏ language arts
   - ❏ auditorium
   - ❏ lunch
   - ❏ secretary
   - ❏ phys. ed.

10. Classroom words
    - ❏ desk
    - ❏ crayons
    - ❏ chalk
    - ❏ rug
    - ❏ table
    - ❏ books
    - ❏ notebook
    - ❏ clock
    - ❏ scissors
    - ❏ window
    - ❏ paper
    - ❏ pencil
    - ❏ eraser
    - ❏ seat
    - ❏ wastebasket
    - ❏ blackboard
    - ❏ glue
    - ❏ page
    - ❏ chair

11. Clothing
    - ❏ coat
    - ❏ gym shoes
    - ❏ shoes
    - ❏ dress
    - ❏ mittens
    - ❏ skirt
    - ❏ jacket
    - ❏ pants
    - ❏ socks
    - ❏ hat
    - ❏ shirt
    - ❏ sweater

12. Safety terms
    - ❏ stop
    - ❏ go
    - ❏ walk
    - ❏ don't walk

13. Time
    - ❏ morning
    - ❏ tomorrow
    - ❏ next week
    - ❏ noon
    - ❏ yesterday
    - ❏ night
    - ❏ year
    - ❏ afternoon
    - ❏ month

14. Other vocabulary
    - ❏ first
    - ❏ small
    - ❏ last
    - ❏ smaller
    - ❏ big
    - ❏ little

15. Money
    - ❏ penny
    - ❏ cent
    - ❏ nickel
    - ❏ cost
    - ❏ dime
    - ❏ dollar
    - ❏ quarter

16. Transportation
    - ❏ bus
    - ❏ car
    - ❏ truck
    - ❏ plane

17. Everyday directions
    - ❏ wait
    - ❏ come here
    - ❏ touch
    - ❏ wash your hands
    - ❏ sit down
    - ❏ line up
    - ❏ cut out
    - ❏ stand up
    - ❏ pick up
    - ❏ wait
    - ❏ raise your hand
    - ❏ sit on floor
    - ❏ open book
    - ❏ copy

18. Home words
    - ❏ address
    - ❏ mother
    - ❏ table
    - ❏ brother
    - ❏ home
    - ❏ bed
    - ❏ sister
    - ❏ sofa
    - ❏ father
    - ❏ chair

2

From: *Assessment and ESL: On the Yellow Big Road to the Withered of Oz*, Peguis Publishers. By Barbara Law and Mary Eckes © 1995. May be reproduced for classroom use.

Figure 6.2: English Vocabulary Checklist, page 2

Student Name _____ Date _____

Age _____ Grade _____

CHECKLIST FOR ASSESSING EMERGING READERS			
	Not yet	Emerg-ing	Yes
Listens to story but is not looking at pages			
Tries to read environmental print			
Demonstrates book-handling knowledge (right side up)			
Watches pictures as story is read aloud.			
Makes up words for picture			
Demonstrates directionality of written language (left to right, page order)			
Pretends to read			
Recognizes some words from a dictated story			
Participates in reading by supplying rhyming words and some predictable text			
Memorizes text and pretends to read story			
Looks at words and tracks words when reading or is being read to from a familiar story			
Recognizes words in a new context			
Reads word-for-word			
Reads familiar stories fluently			
Reads unfamiliar stories haltingly			
Uses context clues, phonic analysis, sentence structure, to read new words and passages			
Reads easy books fluently			
Chooses to read independently			
Reads fluently			

Figure 6.3: Checklist for Assessing Emerging Readers

WRITING SAMPLE CHECKLIST

SKILL AREAS	DESCRIPTION	LEVEL
Content	❏ theme developed ❏ related ideas and examples supplied	**Fluent**
	❏ thought development adequate ❏ some unrelated ideas used	**Intermediate**
	❏ uneven (or no) theme development ❏ many unrelated ideas included ❏ few (or no) examples given ❏ insufficient writing for evaluation	**Beginner**
Organization	❏ good topic development ❏ opening sentence/or introductory paragraph included ❏ concluding sentence/paragraph included ❏ ideas well organized, clearly stated, and backed-up ❏ transitions included	**Fluent**
	❏ topic or opening sentence included, but no closing sentence provided ❏ weak organization ❏ inadequate back-up information provided ❏ few transitions included	**Intermediate**
	❏ no topic sentence development ❏ no opening or closing sentence included ❏ little or no organization ❏ no back-up information provided ❏ no transitions included ❏ ideas confused or unrelated ❏ insufficient writing for evaluation	**Beginner**
Vocabulary	❏ correct use of word forms (prefixes, suffixes, etc.) and idioms ❏ sophisticated word choice ❏ meaning clear	**Fluent**
	❏ generally correct use of word forms and idioms ❏ word choice correct ❏ meaning clear	**Intermediate**
	❏ many errors in word forms and idioms ❏ ineffective word choice ❏ words selected through direct translation ❏ meaning confused or obscured ❏ insufficient writing for evaluation	**Beginner**
Language skills	❏ correct use of verb tense ❏ good sentence variety and complex construction ❏ good control of agreement, number, word order, parts of speech	**Fluent**
	❏ most verb tenses correct ❏ simple sentence construction ❏ errors in agreement, number, word order, parts of speech	**Intermediate**
	❏ frequent errors in tense ❏ forced sentence constructions ❏ many errors in agreement, number, word order, parts of speech ❏ insufficient writing for evaluation	**Beginner**
Mechanics	❏ few errors made in spelling, punctuation, capitalization	**Fluent**
	❏ occasional errors in spelling, punctuation, capitalization	**Intermediate**
	❏ many errors in spelling, punctuation, capitalization ❏ handwriting unclear or illegible ❏ insufficient writing for evaluation	**Beginner**

From: *Assessment and ESL: On the Yellow Big Road to the Withered of Oz.* Peguis Publishers. By Barbara Law and Mary Eckes © 1995. May be reproduced for classroom use.

Figure 6.4: Writing Checklist

Portfolio Self-Evaluation

Name _____

1. What does your portfolio reveal about you as a reader?

    _____

2. What does your portfolio reveal about you as a writer?

    _____

3. What does your portfolio suggest your strengths are?

    _____

4. What does your portfolio suggest about how you have changed?

    _____

5. What do you think people will learn about you from your portfolio?

    _____

6. Select what you think is your best piece of writing from your portfolio.

    a. How does this piece compare with other items you've written this semester?

    _____

    b. How does this piece reflect your strengths in writing?

    _____

    c. How does this piece reflect any difficulties you are having in writing?

    _____

    d. Why did you choose this selection as best? What were your criteria?

    _____

    e. In reflecting on this piece of writing, what do you think you would do differently if you were writing it again?

    _____

7. How has your English improved over the past semester?

    _____

8. How can you document that improvement in your portfolio?

    _____

Figure 9.2: Portfolio Self-Evaluation Form

ESL Conference Record/Notes

Student _____ Date _____

Teacher _____

Parents or Guardians _____

Others in attendance _____

Reasons for conference:

Overall classroom performance:

Areas of strength in language acquisitions:	Areas needing improvement in language skills:
Areas of strength in content:	Areas needing improvement in content:

Recommendations and goals:

Student will:	Teacher will:	Parent will:

Comments:

Figure 9.6: ESL Conference Record Form

GLOSSARY OF TERMS

Assessment. Evaluation based on a collection of information about what a student knows and can do. The data is collected at different times, in different contexts, in a variety of ways, using a variety of methods.

BICS—Basic Interpersonal Communication Skills. The skills involved in everyday communication—listening, speaking, carrying on basic conversation, understanding speakers—and in getting one's basic needs met.

Chapter One. A federally funded program in the United States that seeks to provide direct reading instruction to identified students.

Evaluation. The actual process of making inferences about the student data collected.

FEP—Fully English Proficient. This characterizes students able to participate fully in regular classroom activities. ESL students are usually designated FEP after scoring beyond a designated percentile on a standardized proficiency test. Educators need to keep in mind that the FEP designation does not necessarily mean the student will be able to perform successfully in the content area. Many FEP students struggle with the cognitive academic language in the content areas and may continue to need some support.

LEA—Language Experience Approach. A method of promoting reading in which the teacher begins with the experiences the students bring to the class (or experience together as a class), and then develops oral and written activities around these experiences. The teacher uses the students' own words to write stories, which are then used in a variety of ways.

LEP—Limited English Proficient. Understands some English, but is not fluent enough to compete academically with English-speaking peers.

Miscues. A deviation from the text. Such errors are natural to the process of reading, and it is through monitoring for meaning that the reader makes corrections. These errors are made while the reader is attending to the four-language cuing system (semantics, syntax, graphophonics, and pragmatics).

The most crucial aspect is whether the miscue results in a loss of meaning, or whether it simply reveals that the reader is imposing meaning. (For example, where text reads, "He ran through the forest," the student reads, "He ran through the trees.")

Native speakers. Students whose primary language is English.

Nonnative speakers. Students who do not speak English in the home and who have had to learn to speak English as an additional language.

NEP—Non-English proficient. Speaks little or no English

NES—Non-English speaking. Speaks no English.

Open entry. A program that allows students to enter or leave at any point in the instruction year.

Portfolio. The meaningful collection of student work that presents the student's efforts, progress, and achievement to the stakeholders. The student plays an active role in creating, evaluating, and maintaining his or her portfolio.

Proficiency. Having a thorough level of competency or skill in comprehension, speaking, reading, and writing.

Pull-out. LEP students are "pulled out" of the classroom for the purpose of becoming proficient in English, but otherwise take content classes in English, with English-speaking students.

Push-in. ESL teachers are "pushed into" the content classroom to teach the content lesson to the LEP students as well as to the English-speaking students.

Reporting. Communicating student achievement and progress to the stakeholders. There are two steps to reporting: putting the information into usable form, and conveying the information effectively to the stakeholders.

Sheltered English. Content is presented to a class of LEP students. The teacher uses English appropriate for the students and modifies the teaching techniques to make the instruction comprehensible to the LEP students.

Standardized test. Commercially designed and produced tests given on single occasions. The tests are frequently timed, are one-dimensional, and often consist of multiple-choice and short-answer questions. The results compare the student's knowledge against a set core of knowledge and skills that have been determined as essential for students to know.

Title Seven. Federally funded program in the United States, that, through the Elementary and Secondary Education Act of 1965, was designed to provide monies for bilingual or ESL services for identified students.

BIBLIOGRAPHY

Adamson, D., P. Matthews, and J. Schuller. "Five Ways to Bridge the Resource-Room-to-Regular-Classroom Gap." *Teaching Exceptional Children* (Winter 1990): 74–77.

Alvarez, M. "Psychoeducational Assessment of Language Minority Children: Current Perspectives and Future Trends." In *Bilingual Education and English as a Second Language: A Research Handbook, 1988–1990,* edited by A. Ambert. New York: Garland, 1991.

Anthony, R. et al. *Evaluating Literacy: A Perspective for Change.* Portsmouth, N.H.: Heinemann, 1991.

Atwell, N. *In the Middle: Writing, Reading, and Learning with Adolescents.* Portsmouth, N.H.: Boynton/Cook-Heinemann, 1987.

Au, K. *Literacy Instruction in Multicultural Settings.* Fort Worth, Tex.: Harcourt Brace College Publishers, 1993.

Baker, K. "Bilingual Education's 20-year Failure to Provide Civil Rights Protection for Language-Minority Students." In *Children at Risk: Poverty, Minority Status, and Other Issues in Educational Equity.* Edited by A. Barona and E. Garcia. Washington, D.C.: National Association of School Psychologists (1991): 29–49.

Barrs, M. et al. *The Primary Language Record: A Handbook for Teachers.* [Center for Language in Primary Education] Portsmouth N.H.: Heinemann, 1989.

Belanoff, P., and M. Dickson. *Portfolio Grading: Process and Product.* Portsmouth, N.H. Heinemann, 1991.

Berman and Weiler Associates. *Meeting the Challenge of Language Diversity: An Evaluation of Programs for Pupils with Limited English Proficiency.* Sacramento, Calif.: California State Department of Education, Program Evaluation and Research Division, 1992.

Bloom, B., G. Madaus, and J. Hastings. *Evaluation to Improve Learning.* New York: McGraw Hill, 1981.

Bouffler, C. *Literacy Evaluation: Issues and Practicalities.* Portsmouth, N.H.: Heinemann, 1992.

Braun, C. *Looking, Listening, and Learning: Observing and Assessing Young Readers.* Winnipeg: Peguis, 1993.

Broadfoot, P. *Toward Profiles of Achievement: Developments in Europe.* Washington, D.C.: Taylor and Francis, 1990.

Clay, M. *Stones: The Concepts About Print Test.* Auckland, New Zealand: Heinemann, 1979.

——. *What Did I Write?* Auckland, New Zealand: Heinemann, 1975.

——. *Becoming Literate: The Construction of Inner Control.* Auckland, New Zealand: Heinemann, 1991.

——. *An Observation Survey of Literacy Achievement.* Portsmouth, N.H.: Heinemann, 1993.

Coballes-Vega, C., and B. Salend. "Guidelines for Assessing Migrant Handicapped Students." *Diagnostique* 13 (1988).

Covey, S. *The Seven Habits of Highly Effective People.* New York: Simon and Schuster, 1989.

Cummins, J. *Empowering Minority Students.* Sacramento, Calif.: California Association for Bilingual Education, 1989.

——. "The Role of Primary Language Development in Promoting Educational Success for Language Minority Students." In *Schooling and Language Minority Students: A Theoretical Framework.* Los Angeles: California State University, 1981.

Davies, A., C. Cameron, C. Politano, and K. Gregory. *Together Is Better: Collaborative Assessment, Evaluation and Reporting.* Winnipeg: Peguis, 1992.

Doake, D. "Reading-like Behavior: Its Role in Learning to Read," In *Observing the Language Learner,* edited by A. Jaggar and M. T. Smith-Burke. Newark, Del.: International Reading Association, 1985.

Donaldson, R., and J. Christiansen. "Consultation and Collaboration: A Decision-Making Model." *Teaching Exceptional Children* (Winter 1990): 22–25.

Erickson, J., and D. Omark, eds. *Communication Assessment of the Bilingual, Bicultural Child.* Baltimore: University Park Press, 1981.

Ferreiro, E., and A. Teberosky. *Literacy before Schooling.* Portsmouth, N.H.: Heinemann, 1982.

Fillmore, L. Wong. "A Question for Early-Childhood Programs: English First or Families First?" *Education Week* (June 19, 1991).

Fitzgerald, J. "Literacy and Students Who Are Learning English as a Second Language. *The Reading Teacher* 46, no.8 (May 1993): 638–645.

Flynn, H. C. "A Collaborative Model of Service for LEP Students." Master's thesis, Hamline University, 1992.

Fradd, S., and W. Tikunoff, eds. *Bilingual Education and Bilingual Special Education: A Guide for Administrators.* Boston: Little Brown, 1987.

Fradd, S., and J. Weismantal, eds. *Meeting the Needs of Culturally and Linguistically Different Students: A Handbook for Educators.* Boston: Little, Brown, 1989.

Forester, A., and M. Reinhard. *The Learners' Way.* Winnipeg: Peguis, 1989.

Galda, L., B. Cullinan, and D. Strickland. *Language, Literacy and the Child.* Fort Worth, Tex.: Harcourt Brace Jovanovich, 1993.

Genesee, F. *Learning Through Two Languages: Studies of Immersion and Bilingual Education.* Cambridge, Mass.: Newbury House, 1987.

Genishi, C., and A. Dyson. *Language Assessment in the Early Years.* Norwood, N.J.: Ablex, 1984.

Gibbons, P. *Learning to Learn in a Second Language.* Portsmouth, N.H.: Heinemann, 1993.

Gomez, M. et al. "Reassessing Portfolio Assessment: Rhetoric and Reality." *Language Arts* 68 (December 1991): 620–628.

Goodman, D. "Evaluation, Reporting, and Grading." In *The Whole Language Catalog.* See K. Goodman et al., 1992.

Goodman, K. et al. *The Whole Language Catalog: Supplement on Authentic Assessment.* Chicago: SRA Macmillan/McGraw Hill, 1992.

Goodman, K., Y. Goodman, and W. J. Hood. *The Whole Language Evaluation Book.* Portsmouth, N.H.: Heinemann, 1988.

Goodman, Y., and C. Burke. *The Reading Miscue Inventory.* New York: Macmillan, 1972.

Graves, D. H., and B. S. Sunstein, eds. *Portfolio Portraits.* Portsmouth, N.H.: Heinemann, 1992.

Hamayan, E. et al. *Assessment of Language Minority Students: A Handbook for Educators.* Arlington Heights, Ill.: Illinois Resource Center, 1985.

Hamayan, E., and J. Damico, eds. *Limiting Bias in the Assessment of Bilingual Students.* Austin, Tex.: Pro-Ed, 1991.

Hayes-Brown, Z. "Linguistic and Communicative Assessment of Bilingual Children." In *Placement Procedures in Bilingual Education.* Washington, D.C.: Taylor and Francis, 1984.

Hills, J. "Apathy Concerning Grading and Testing." *Phi Delta Kappan* (March 1991): 540–545.

Hymes, D. "The Ethnography of Speaking." In *Anthropology and Human Behavior*, edited by T. Gladwin and W. Sturtevant. Washington, D.C.: Anthropology Society of Washington, 1962.

Imhoff, G., ed. *Learning in Two Languages: From Conflict to Consensus in the Reorganization of Schools.* New Brunswick, N.J.: Transaction Publishers, 1990.

Irmscher, W. *Teaching Expository Writing.* New York: Holt, Rinehart and Winston, 1979.

Johnston, P. *The Constructive Evaluation of Literate Activity.* White Plains, N.Y.: Longman, 1992.

Jongsma, K. "Questions and Answers: Portfolio Assessment." *The Reading Teacher* (December 1989): 264–265.

Kalantzis, M. et al. *Cultures of Schooling: Pedagogies for Cultural Difference and Social Access.* London: Falmer Press, 1990.

Krashen, S., and T. Terrell. *The Natural Approach: Language Acquisition in the Classroom.* San Francisco: Alemany Press, 1983.

Lamme, L. L., and C. Hysmith. "One School's Adventure into Portfolio Assessment." *Language Arts* 68 (1991): 629–640.

Landerholm, E. "The Transdisciplinary Team Approach in Infant Intervention Programs." *Teaching Exceptional Children* (Winter 1990): 66–70.

Law, B., and M. Eckes. *The More-Than-Just-Surviving Handbook: ESL for Every Classroom Teacher.* Winnipeg: Peguis, 1990.

Leeman, E. "Evaluating Language Assessment Tests: Some Practical Considerations." In *Communication Assessment of the Bilingual Bicultural Child*. See Erickson and Omark, 1981.

Loacker, G., L. Cromwell, and K. O'Brien. "Assessment in Higher Education: To Serve the Learner." In *Assessment in American Higher Education*, edited by Clifford Adelman. Washington, D.C.: Office of Educational Research and Improvement, U.S. Department of Education, 1986.

Los Angeles County Office of Education, Division of Curriculum Programs and Instructional Technologies. "Bilingual Education: What Does the Research Really Say?" Los Angeles, 1992.

Maeroff, G. "Assessing Alternative Assessment." *Phi Delta Kappan* (December 1991): 272–281.

Malherbe, E. *The Bilingual School*. Johannesberg, S. Africa: Rostra, 1943.

Manning, M., and G. Manning. "How to Assess the Spelling Levels of Young Children." In *The Whole Language Catalog*. See K. Goodman et al., 1992.

Mathews, J. "Assessment: From Computer Management to Portfolio Assessment." *The Reading Teacher* (February 1990): 420–421.

Merino, A. "When Bad Things Happen to Good Ideas." *NEA Today* (October 1993).

Meyer, C. "What's the Difference between Authentic and Performance Assessment?" *Educational Leadership* (May 1992).

Mitchell, R. *Testing for Learning: How New Approaches to Evaluation Can Improve American Schools*. New York: Free Press, 1992.

Murphy, S. "Writing Portfolios: Implications for Linguistically Diverse Students." Plenary Address, CaTESOL State Conference, April 5, 1992.

Navarette, C., J. Wilde et al. "Informal Assessment in Educational Evaluation: Implications for Bilingual Education Programs." Fairfax, Va.: National Clearinghouse for Bilingual Education, 1990.

Neill, D. M., and N. Medina. "Standardized Testing: Harmful to Educational Health." *Phi Delta Kappan* (May 1989).

Nuttall, E. "A Critical Look at Testing and Evaluation from a Cross-Cultural Perspective." In *Education of Cultural and Linguistically Different Exceptional Children*, Chin. 1984.

Olsen, L. *Crossing the Schoolhouse Border: Immigrant Youth In California Public Schools*. San Francisco: California Tomorrow, 1988.

Omark, D. "Pragmatic and Ethological Techniques for the Observational Assessment of Children's Communicative Abilities." In *Communication Assessment of the Bilingual, Bicultural Child*. See Erickson and Omark, 1981.

Paulson, F. et al. "What Makes a Portfolio a Portfolio?" *Educational Leadership* (February 1991): 60–63.

Pena, Sylvia. "Identifying and Placing the Limited English Proficient Student." In *Assessment and Placement of Minority Students*, See Samuda, R. et al., 1989.

Pikulski, J. "The Assessment of Reading: A Time For Change?" *The Reading Teacher* 43 (1989): 686–688.

Pugachi et al. "The Challenge of Implementing Collaboration between General and Special Educators." *Exceptional Children* (1990).

Ramirez, A. G. "Perspectives on Language Proficiency Assessment." In *Children at Risk: Poverty, Minority Status and Other Issues in Educational Equity*. See Baker.

North York Board of Education, Curriculum and Instructional Services. *Reception, Assessment, Placement and Monitoring of ESL/ESD Students in Secondary Schools*. Toronto, 1994.

Reid, J. *Teaching ESL Writing*. Englewood Cliffs: Regents/Prentice Hall, 1993.

Rhodes, L. K., and N. Shanklin. *Windows Into Literacy*. Portsmouth, N.H.: Heinemann, 1992.

Rivers and Associates. *Settlement Services for Immigrant Children: A Needs Assessment*. Report prepared for British Columbia Ministry of Education, Victoria, British Columbia, 1991.

Routman, Regie. *Invitations: Changing as Teachers and Learners*. Portsmouth, N.H.: Heinemann, 1991.

Samuda, R., S. Kong, J. Cummins, et al. *Assessment and Placement of Minority Students*. Toronto: C. J. Hogrefe, 1989.

Smith, F. *Joining the Literacy Club: Further Essays into Education*. Portsmouth, N.H.: Heinemann, 1988.

Stayter, F. and P. Johnston. In *Reading and Writing Together: New Perspectives for the Classroom*, edited by T. Shanahan. Norwood, Mass.: Christopher-Gordon, 1990.

Stiggins, R. "Assessment Literacy." *Phi Delta Kappan* (March 1991): 534–539.

Strickland, B., and A. Turnbull. *Developing and Implementing Individualized Education Programs.* Columbus, Ohio: Merrill Publishing, 1990.

Teale, W. H. "Emergent Literacy: Reading and Writing Development in Early Childhood." In *Research in Literacy: Merging Perspectives. Thirty Sixth Yearbook of the National Reading Conference,* edited by J. E. Readence and R. S. Baldwin. Rochester, N.Y.: National Reading Conference, 1987.

Tierney, R. J. et al. *Portfolio Assessment in the Reading-Writing Classroom.* Norwood, Mass.: Christopher-Gordon, 1991.

Ulibarri, D. "Use of Achievement Tests with Non-Native-English-Speaking Language Minority Students." In *Children at Risk: Poverty, Minority Status and Other Issues in Educational Equity.* See Baker.

Underhill, N. *Testing Spoken Language: A Handbook of Oral Testing Techniques.* Cambridge, U.K.: Cambridge University Press, 1987.

Valencia, S. "A Portfolio Approach to Classroom Reading Assessment: The Whys, Whats and Hows." *The Reading Teacher* 43 (January 1990): 338–340.

———. "Assessment: Portfolio Assessment for Young Readers." *The Reading Teacher* 44, no.9 (May 1991): 680–681.

Valentin, T. "English as a Second Language: Get Ready for the Onslaught." *NASSP Bulletin* 76 (January 1993): 30–38.

Weaver, C. *Reading Process and Practice: From Socio-Psycholinguistics to Whole Language.* Portsmouth N.H.: Heinemann, 1994.

Wiggins, G. "A True Test: Toward Authentic and Equitable Forms of Assessment." *Phi Delta Kappan* (1989): 703–713.

Winograd, P., S. Paris, and C. Bridge, "Improving the Assessment of Literacy." *The Reading Teacher* 45, no.2 (October 1991).

Wisconsin State Reading Association. *Position Statement.* Madison, Wis.: 1990.

Wolf, D. et al. "To Use Their Minds Well: Investigating New Forms of Student Assessment." In *Review of Research in Education,* edited by G. Grant. Washington, D.C.: American Educational Research Association, 1991.

Worthen, B. "Critical Issues That Will Determine the Future of Alternative Assessment." *Phi Delta Kappan* (February 1993): 444–454.

———. "Is Your School Ready for Alternative Assessment?" *Phi Delta Kappan* (February 1993).

Zanger, V. "Social and Cultural Dimensions of the Education of Language Minority Students." In *Bilingual Education and English as a Second Language: A Research Handbook*, edited by A. Ambert. New York: Garland, 1991.

Zirkel, P. "A Method for Determining and Depicting Language Dominance." Paper presented at TESOL '73, ERIC #234845.

INDEX

Also from Barbara Law and Mary Eckes,

The More-Than-Just-Surviving Handbook: ESL for Every Learner

"This book is definitely a winner! Every teacher should have the opportunity to read and use this book."
  Darlene Brackenreed
  ESL Resource Teacher

"Chapter 1 alone makes the book worthwhile for mainstream teachers who are anxious and concerned about having new ESL students in their classrooms."
  Pat Robinson
  Washington Area TESOL News

"...[the book] offers many good suggestions for dealing with ESL students in an integrated classroom".
  Teaching K–8

For teachers with even one non-English-speaking student, this book is invaluable. Written for regular classroom teachers—as well as ESL specialists—it provides the vital support needed to help integrate ESL students into the classroom and get them learning. Practical activities and strategies show how to:

- help ESL students get acquainted with school and classmates
- measure skills and place new students in the appropriate grades
- integrate whole language methods to teach reading, writing, speaking, and listening
- modify lessons in content area classes to promote success
- tap into school and community resources and use them effectively

Barbara Law and Mary Eckes refer to teaching ESL learners as "a challenge and a delight—a passion, not just a job." The reader will find their enthusiasm contagious.

209 pages, appendix, glossary, bibliography
ISBN 0-920541-98-4

ORDER FORM
Photocopy this form to order

PLEASE SEND:

The More-Than-Just-Surviving Handbook

_____ copy/ies @ 19.00 ea. _____

Subtotal _____

Shipping and handling _____
$3.00 or 8%, whichever is greater

Subtotal _____

Canadian residents add 7% GST _____

TOTAL _____

☐ Purchase order attached
☐ Check enclosed
☐ Please charge my ☐ VISA ☐ MasterCard

Card Number _____ Expiry Date _____

Signature _____

DELIVER TO:

Name _____

Address _____

City _____

State/Province _____ Zip Code/Postal Code _____

ORDER BY MAIL:
Peguis Publishers
100–318 McDermot Ave.
Winnipeg, Manitoba
Canada R3A 0A2
Tel.: (204) 987-3500

CALL TOLL FREE:
1-800-667-9673

ORDER BY FAX:
1-204-947-0080

BF-1